The Roll 'em & Stuff 'em COOKBOOK

The Roll 'em & Stuff 'em COOKBOOK

The Art of Filling & Saucing Gourmet Food

by

Carol Reuter & Susan Freelund

SEA CLIFF PRESS, Ltd.
New York

Published in the United States by Sea Cliff Press, Ltd.

Library of Congress Catalogue Card Number: 74-83013

ISBN: 0-913604-01-1

Printed in the United States of America

For the next generation –

Susan, Elizabeth and David

CONTENTS

The Roll'em & Stuff'em Cookbook

I. INTRODUCTION

Why Roll 'em and Stuff 'em?

Quite simply, rolled and stuffed creations, prepared with love and imagination, can add romance, glamour and fascination to your menus—for gala occasions or otherwise. Artful filling and saucing can embellish your cuisine with an aura of excitement and luxury, dress up and dramatize any honest components, and transform even the ordinary into something rich, elegant and rare.

Who doesn't relish a surprise, a soupçon of the exotic, a dash of culinary intrigue? A perfectly prepared roast of beef is succulent and tempting indeed, but is surely lacking in mystery. There it sits in all its pink and juicy glory, revealing everything at a glance. But when a clever hostess presents an enticing tray of interesting-looking, pastry-wrapped hors d'oeuvres from Greece, Spain or the Far East, one can't help wondering about the delectable morsels they enclose. It is delicious fun to sample them, and they can be depended upon to lend instant spice and sparkle to any conversation. If an exquisite crepe is served, haven't you ever caught yourself musing about the way the sauce, redolent with wine and mushrooms, complements its companion ingredients?

It is not hard to guess that we are firm believers in the notion that if foods are good separately, they can often be more delightful together, when flavors, textures and aromas blend to bring out the best in each other. Thus, this book is a treasury of favorites in the art of great pairings.

Roll 'ems and Stuff 'ems have the added advantage of being extremely cosmopolitan. Nearly every country in the world has its own roster of piquant variations, and we have tried to include mouth-watering winners from many climes and times. For exciting examples of what we mean, you will find a robust stuffed pork roast from Central America, a cream-smothered Austrian crepe, a zesty bacon-spiked German beef roulade, a luscious chocolate Christmas log from France and a meltingly delicious Greek dessert pastry rolled in honey and nuts.

More broadly speaking, we have considered a wide range of treatments for the ordinary—a veal or chicken cutlet, a fish fillet. How can you stuff and sauce a duck, a roast, or a plump purple eggplant to make it a little different this time? We have the answer. We have tried to take the mystery out of quiches and crepes, hors d'oeuvres, and desserts around the world so that you can put it back again for the enchantment of your family and friends. In many cases we've commented on the fascinating origins of various dishes and added notes on sauces and accompaniments for a most glamorous presentation.

It is pertinent to add that we have not garnered our collection as the glamorous wives of diplomatic spies—but through travel, from friends of many lands, and especially from years of pleasurable adventuring in our own kitchens. And we've gathered from the lore and literature of world-wide cookery—from Apicius to Escoffier, and even Alice B. Toklas.

Perhaps most important of all, Roll 'ems and Stuff 'ems are endlessly versatile. They can be used for hors d'oeuvres, appetizers, splendiferous main dishes, memorable desserts, and for brunches, lunches, dinners, late suppers and snacks. Ingredients and components can be mixed and matched endlessly for ever-delightful results. And many are simple to prepare, for we are not above adapting the classic repertoire to today's harried schedules, to using prepared and convenience foods as short cuts, and lots of appliances. Hints are included on how to prepare ahead and on freezer usage, so that you can be on hand in the living room, looking cool and collected, to receive the wild raves of your delighted guests. Behind the scenes, economy is also vitally important, and so we have been careful to include some down-to-earth hints on delectable concoctions that can be whipped up with left-overs.

Now it is time to let good food speak for itself, to let your own good taste, curiosity and imagination roam and wander around the intriguing world of rolled and stuffed cookery. We hope you will enjoy our gems and also be inspired to create your own fresh new combinations; artistic and dramatic productions that will soon become specialties of the house—your house!

II. STATE SECRETS REVEALED

The Secret Techniques of Rolling and Stuffing

"THE DOUGH"

Because many rolled hors d'oeuvres call for pastry and because we do not care for the rubbery quality of most commercial pie-crust mixes, now is as good a time as any to reveal one of our state secrets. Here, then, is the basic, foolproof dough, which can be used with the same dependably fantastic results for quiches, pastry-wrapped main courses, pies, dessert tarts—what you will. There is absolutely no magic about making it, it is even ridiculously easy, but the scrumptious end product is worth the tiny amount of extra time and effort because of its magically uniform excellence.

What equipment do you need? The simplest: a good-size wooden board for working, rolling and cutting the pastry. A hand pastry cutter or blender is needed for blending the ingredients—but two sharp knives will do. A rolling pin is a must. For cutting the pastry into shapes, cookie cutters are ideal—but the rims of drinking glasses will do.

We advise using margarine because it is cheaper and provides a better consistency. If you prefer the flavor of butter, by all means use it. However, it is harder to work.

It is also more difficult to work dough on a humid day, and often at such times you will need more flour. On hot, humid days, if the dough becomes too sticky, return it to the refrigerator until it is workable.

"The Dough"

¼ lb. margarine
1 C. flour
3 tbsp. ice water

1. Let the margarine soften. With your pastry blender, cut it well into the flour until it is all absorbed. Chill well for 1 hour. **Note:** this mixture can be kept for months in a sealed plastic container in the refrigerator.
2. When ready to use the dough, add 2 to 3 tbsp. ice water and mix it well with a fork until dough is uniformly lumpy.
3. Using your hands, work the mixture into a ball. Place it on a lightly-floured board and roll it out with a lightly-floured rolling pin to the desired size—of your pie tin, or large enough to cut out the smaller pastry shapes described in the various recipes.

One recipe of "The Dough" is enough for a 9" bottom pie crust. If you want to cover the pie, make 1½ times the basic recipe. It is also enough for 10 2½" to 3" square hors d'oeuvres or miniature dessert pastries.

The 3" squares can either be folded triangularly with the edges pinched together, or fashioned by drawing the ends together handkerchief-basket style. Make sure all edges are sealed so the filling does not escape.

A 2" cookie cutter will make 14 rounds. If these are used sandwich style, place 1 rounded tbsp. of filling in the center of one and place a second round on top. Seal the edges carefully by crimping with your fingers which have been dipped in water, or egg white and water mixed. Or you can crimp with a fork.

Brush the tops of the pastries with beaten egg white to brown them while they bake. Bake at 350 F. until golden.

Note: Almost any filling can be used with this dough–vegetables, meats, rice with various spices, fruits and leftovers galore. Most baked hors d'oeuvres can be frozen and then heated through just before serving time.

Variations with "The Dough"

1. Add ½ C. sugar to obtain a sweet dough for pies and pastries.
2. Normally margarine is used, but in some cases the flakiness and shortness of butter is desired, and then we specify it.
3. Cream cheese can be added to obtain a more richly-textured pastry for selected recipes. We have specifically indicated where Cream Cheese Pastry is especially desirable.
4. Sour cream or yoghurt may also be added, but there are no other exotic additions. The basic dough is composed of ingredients generally expected in any kitchen larder.

Alternatives to "The Dough"

Filo, or phyllo, is simply Greek pastry leaves or strudel leaves. It is an alternate basic dough which we cover in detail in the next chapter. However, we do not recommend making this yourself as it can be purchased at reasonable cost in any good gourmet store or Greek-Armenian grocery. Filo can be used for Greek hors d'oeuvres (various cheese, meat and vegetable-filled triangles), for some main courses and for numerous desserts. When using filo the leaves must be kept moist with brushed-on melted butter, or they tend to harden and stick together.

Top quality frozen pie shells may also be used for quiches, or pies, when time is short. Also available in good food markets are ready-baked patty shells and mini-patty shells of a respectable grade. The use of canned, prepared dough–biscuit or crescent rolls–is also a good short cut, and we have made suggestions for using it in some recipes. All of these products, in fact, make good short cuts for rolled and stuffed foods, and can be adapted to a host of dishes–from appetizers and hors d'oeuvres to main courses and desserts.

THE BECHAMEL SAUCE

The Béchamel Sauce is used ubiquitously throughout this book and can be dressed up in many ways by adding cheeses, spices, wines or what have you. We highly recommend using instant blending flour because it dissolves quickly, never lumps, does not have to be smoothed or beaten very much, and thickens rapidly.

The Basic Béchamel Sauce

3 tbsp. butter
3 tbsp. instant blending flour
1 C. hot milk
salt and pepper to taste

1. Melt butter and stir in flour until well-blended.
2. Add hot milk slowly, stirring over low heat until mixture is thick and creamy. Makes 1 C. of sauce.

For meat dishes, hot chicken broth or beef stock will often be substituted for the milk. The various recipes will specify this.

When eggs are to be added to the sauce, cool the basic mixture and add the eggs gradually, or the sauce may curdle.

FLASH FREEZING

Because so many of our recipes recommend the use of fresh parsley or chives, you can always have them on hand by our handy method of flash freezing. Buy them very fresh, chop them up and spread them on a cookie sheet. Then sprinkle with water and place the cookie sheet in the freezer. When they are frozen, scrape them off the cookie sheet and freeze them in plastic bags.

III. FANFARE

Hors d'Oeuvres and Appetizers

The French phrase hors d'oeuvres means, in short, something unusual, out of the ordinary pattern, and that's what this chapter is all about. If your prelude is exciting enough, the success of any occasion is assured. Whatever else follows can be relatively straightforward—which is as it should be so that you can relax, not only to savor the applause, but also the drama and conversation kindled by your interesting beginnings.

But how to achieve that special sense of expectation, the notion that something delectable is in the offing? Part of the secret—if it may be so termed—is in artfully setting a mood, planning your dinner as a kind of mini-production with all the fun and theatrics one can bring to it. By all means, use lowered lights and soft music, and flavorful touches such as festive cocktail napkins, distinctive picks, and lace paper underliners for trays and dishes. You can embellish your coffee table, as well as the buffet or dining table, with one or two small, warmly glowing candles and an undersized bowl of brilliant flowers. And you can embellish your culinary creations by learning one or two facts about each dish so that you can offer a note of background to your guests.

For serving, why not make your own centerpiece by grouping together some attractive small dishes in an interesting arrangement—on one level or in a tiered or layered affair? A cake stand need not be prosaically confined to cake, nor a bread basket to bread. Appetizers lend themselves perfectly to imaginative serving, so let your imagination roam by unusual improvising. The art of great pairings can be practiced in the presentation as well as in the preparation.

And do not forget some special aids and appliances. Just as a bubbling fondue pot lends fun and flare, a diminutive cocktail table hibachi will dramatize the toasting of many treats, such as exotic rumaki. An electric warming tray is an absolute must for maintaining the tempting goodness of your creations. It will also help you keep your cool by giving you time to tend to other last minute details and to mix drinks.

Cocktails should be simple so as not to overpower the food. Often a chilled apéritif wine—vermouth or sherry on the rocks with a twist of lemon or orange peel—makes a delightful variation on the classic scotch and vodka openers. An interesting May Wine Punch can be achieved by mixing a bottle of May Wine, three ounces of cognac, and crushed strawberries.

Garnish lovingly with a liberal hand, as an artist would apply decoration to his canvas. Keeping in mind the flavors and colors of what you are serving, you can introduce a tomato or radish rose, fresh green sprigs of parsley, a sprinkling of chopped chives or golden hard-cooked egg, slices of olive, pimiento, or cups of hollowed-out whole canned beets filled with a mixture of cheese, mayonnaise and capers. Garnishes often add so much in attractiveness and require only a tiny investment in time and effort. They should, of course, be applied to other courses as well.

But presentation is only half the picture. The rest is in the fabulous food itself—exotic, delectable, and looking for all the world as if you simply spent hours making it. But don't be put off! That is all only window dressing or sheer good showmanship. Actually, most of these recipes are scandalously easy, quick, and quite within the grasp of the beginner and experienced cook alike. The fare may well be glamorous, but it is all offered here with an eye to uncomplicated preparation, to planning and freezing ahead. We are definitely for short cuts—for using processed and prepared foods of good quality, and for using leftovers to vary the basic fillings. For the most part, the ingredients are easily obtainable, and the majority of them can be found in the average kitchen larder.

A word about dough—your worries are absolutely at an end. The flaky, delicious, foolproof, and very basic one we have given—"The Dough"—can be used for most of the concoctions that call for pastry. And, what's more, we tell you exactly how to dress it up or down—with delectable variations.

Variety, in fact, is the keynote, for we hope to inspire you to dabble in the fun of concocting endless permutations and combinations on basic themes, to devise memorable creations of your own. And, as a footnote to the keynote, it is important to keep in mind that the food in this chapter is interchangeable—for use as hors d'oeuvres or appetizers.

FASCINATING FILO

The food and hospitality of Greece are legendary. Filo, the special flaky Greek pastry, is one of the foundations of Greek cookery, especially of Greek hors d'oeuvres called mezedakia. In Greece, mezedakia are generally served with drinks, often with retsina, the characteristic resinated wine of the land. They are served in homes and in the atmospheric taverns found in many Greek cities, especially Athens, where the taverns are located in the historic old section.

Mezedakia can consist of a simple fare of olives and slices of pungent white feta cheese, or more elaborate stuffed grape leaves, and the many varieties of hot, filled pastries we have offered here.

Greek filo is one of the most versatile of doughs. In addition to hors d'oeuvres, it can readily be fashioned into appetizers, delectable main courses and luscious desserts. It is usually sold in one-pound packages, frozen or refrigerated, and is ready to use. Actually, filo is almost interchangeable with German strudel dough.

But filo tends to dry out very quickly. It should always be kept moist with melted butter while working with it. Try to use the entire pound at once. If any should be left over, keep it frozen wrapped in plastic or aluminum foil to prevent its drying out.

The Basic Filo Triangle

1. Remove 1 leaf of filo and place it on a flat surface. Brush well with melted butter. Cover remaining leaves with a dampened towel.
2. Cut filo leaf into 3" strips. Place 1 tsp. of filling at the bottom of each strip. Fold corners to form a triangle, crimping edges to seal in the filling. Continue this process until all of the strip is used. Use remaining leaves in same fashion.
3. Brush each triangle with melted butter and place it on a buttered cookie sheet.
4. Bake triangles at 375 F. for 15 to 20 minutes. Serve hot. Makes about 100 triangles.
5. Triangles can be prepared ahead of time and frozen. Just reheat until golden and puffy when ready to serve.

Greek Cheese Triangles (Bourekakia)

1 lb. filo leaves
3 egg yolks, beaten
1 lb. feta cheese, crumbled
1 3-oz. package cream cheese
½ C. grated cheddar or Swiss cheese
dash of nutmeg
2 tbsp. chopped fresh parsley
3 tbsp. melted butter
1 C. melted butter (for brushing filo leaves)

1. Combine eggs and cheeses in a blender. Add nutmeg and whip until creamy.
2. Add parsley and 3 tbsp. melted butter. Stir gently.
3. Follow directions for Basic Filo Triangle and baking. Makes 85 to 100 triangles.

Meat Triangles

1 lb. filo leaves
1½ C. chopped beef, or lamb
1 medium onion, chopped
1 hard-cooked egg, chopped
2 tbsp. grated Parmesan cheese
salt, pepper and garlic powder to taste
1 C. melted butter (for brushing filo leaves)

1. Sauté meat with onion until browned. Add egg, cheese and seasonings.
2. Follow directions for Basic Filo Triangle and baking. Makes 85 to 100 triangles.

Fish Triangles

1 lb. filo leaves
1½ C. finely chopped cooked shrimp, or crab meat
½ C. Béchamel sauce, or ½ can cream of celery soup
1 tbsp. minced fresh parsley
dash of lemon juice
1 C. melted butter (for brushing filo leaves)

1. Mix all ingredients together.
2. Follow directions for Basic Filo Triangle and baking. Makes 85 to 100 triangles.

Zesty Seafood Triangles

1 lb. filo leaves
2 C. finely chopped cooked crab meat, or lobster
2 3-oz. packages cream cheese
1 egg, beaten
½ tsp. minced fresh parsley
¼ tsp. Tabasco sauce
1 tsp. Worcestershire sauce
½ tsp. salt
freshly ground pepper to taste
1 C. melted butter (for brushing filo leaves)

1. Pick over crab meat to remove all cartilage. Mix all ingredients together.
2. Follow directions for Basic Filo Triangle and baking. Makes 85 to 100 triangles.

Mushroom Triangles

1 lb. filo leaves
¼ C. butter
1½ lb. fresh mushrooms, finely chopped
3 shallots, chopped, or 2 scallions or 2 medium onions, chopped
2 3-oz packages cream cheese
1 egg, beaten
1 tsp. salt
freshly gound pepper to taste
1 C. melted butter (for brushing filo leaves)

1. Sauté mushrooms and shallots in butter until soft and beginning to brown.
2. Mix with cream cheese, egg, salt and pepper. Stir well.
3. Follow directions for Basic Filo Triangle and baking. Makes 85 to 100 triangles.

Spinach Triangles

1 lb. filo leaves
1½ lb. fresh spinach, washed, dried and chopped
½ C. olive oil
5 scallions, finely chopped
1½ tbsp. minced fresh parsley
3/4 tbsp. chopped fresh dill
3 eggs, beaten
½ lb. feta cheese, crumbled
salt and pepper to taste
1 C. melted butter (for brushing filo leaves)

1. Brown scallions in olive oil until tender. Combine with spinach, parsley, dill, eggs and cheese. Add salt and pepper and mix well.

2. Follow directions for Basic Filo Triangle and baking. Makes 85 to 100 triangles.

Frankfurter Triangles

½ lb. filo leaves
3 tbsp. butter
4 tbsp. instant blending flour
½ C. hot milk
4 frankfurters, skinned and chopped
¼ C. grated cheese
1 egg yolk
salt and pepper to taste
½ C. melted butter (for brushing filo leaves)

1. Melt 3 tbsp. butter in a saucepan and add flour. Blend well and add hot milk. Cook until thick and creamy. Add frankfurters.
2. Combine with cheese, egg yolk, salt and pepper and mix well.
3. Follow directions for Basic Filo Triangle. Bake at 350 F. for 15 to 20 minutes. Makes about 35 triangles.

Ham Triangles

½ lb. filo leaves
3 tbsp. butter
4 tbsp. instant blending flour
½ C. hot milk
3 tbsp. grated cheese
2 egg yolks
6 oz. cooked ham, chopped
salt and pepper to taste
½ C. melted butter (for brushing filo leaves)

1. Melt 3 tbsp. butter in a saucepan and add flour. Blend well and add hot milk. Cook until thick and creamy. Add remaining ingredients and mix well.
2. Follow directions for Basic Filo Triangle. Bake at 350 F. for 15 to 20 minutes. Makes about 35 triangles.

Crab Meat Triangles

1 lb. filo leaves
butter for sautéing onions
1 small onion, chopped
2 tbsp. instant blending flour
2 C. hot milk
1½ lb. flaked crab meat
½ tsp. dried dill
½ lb. mushrooms, chopped
½ C. chopped celery
1 tbsp. dry sherry
½ C. bread crumbs
salt and pepper to taste
1 C. melted butter (for brushing filo leaves)

1. Sauté onions in butter. Add flour and blend well. Add hot milk and stir until mixture is thick and creamy.
2. Remove from heat and add remaining ingredients.
3. Follow directions for Basic Filo Triangle. Bake at 350 F. for 15 to 20 minutes. Makes 85 to 100 triangles.

Meat Roll in Filo

4 filo leaves
6 tbsp. butter
½ lb. ground beef
1 medium onion, chopped
2 tbsp. dry red wine
1 tsp. tomato paste
2 tbsp. water
1 tsp. chopped fresh parsley
salt and pepper to taste
3 tbsp. instant blending flour
1 C. hot milk
2 tbsp. grated Parmesan cheese
1 egg yolk

1. Sauté meat and onion in 2 tbsp. of the butter. Add wine and tomato paste, dissolved in water, with parsley, salt and pepper. Simmer until there

is no liquid left.
2. Melt 2 tbsp. butter in a saucepan. Add flour and blend well. Add hot milk and stir until sauce is thick and creamy.
3. Remove from heat and cool slightly. Add cheese and egg yolk.
4. Combine 2 mixtures.
5. Melt remaining 2 tbsp. butter and brush each leaf of filo. Place 1 on top of another. Spread filling on top leaf and roll. Brush butter over the top.
6. Bake at 350 F. for 30 to 35 minutes. Serves 4.

Note: Remember that with all filo triangle recipes, the appetizers can be completely prepared and baked ahead of time, then frozen. When you wish to serve them, simply remove from freezer, let thaw and reheat them until they are crisp. If you have leftover filo, this of course can be frozen for use at another time.

SAMOSAS

Here is a selection of tasty Indian tid-bits that are often served at afternoon teas, much as we offer cakes in the West. These savory, somewhat spicy curried snacks are typical of Indian hospitality, for the Indians love variety and the surprises that are concealed within these pastry-wrapped treats. Samosas are made in India with ghee, or clarified butter, and are generally cooked by dropping into hot fat, as Indians do not as a rule use ovens. However, we have adapted the recipe for baking in the United States. Usually, Indians serve their samosas, really assorted turnovers, on brass or silver—either small bowls or trays. Samosas are nice warmed and are definitely a finger-food.

The Basic Pastry

2 C. sifted flour
1 tsp. salt
1/8 C. margarine
5 to 7 tbsp. yoghurt

1. Sift the flour with the salt. Melt the margarine and add to the flour.

Mix well. Stir in the yoghurt gradually, working it with your hands for about 5 minutes. Knead until smooth. **Note:** If desired, you can use double the recipe of "The Dough" instead of the yoghurt pastry.

The Filling

1 garlic clove, minced
½ C. minced onions, or 2 tbsp. instant minced onion
2 tbsp. margarine
3/4 lb. ground beef
1 tomato, chopped
1 tsp. salt
1 tsp. curry powder
1/8 tsp. dried chili peppers
1 tsp. finely chopped fresh parsley
1 egg white, slightly beaten (for brushing pastry edges)

1. Sauté garlic and onions in margarine. Add meat and cook over high heat until browned. Mix frequently. Add remaining ingredients. Cook over medium heat for 5 minutes, drain off liquid. Cool.
2. Roll out pastry very thinly on a lightly-floured board. Cut into circles with 2¼" cookie cutter or glass rim. Brush edges lightly with egg white.
3. Place rounded teaspoon of the filling in the center of each circle. Fold over and crimp edges with a fork. Make sure turnovers are well sealed.
4. Bake until golden brown at 400 F. for 12 to 15 minutes. Makes about 40 turnovers.

Variations

Instead of using beef you can substitute 3/4 lb. of leftover chicken, chopped shrimp or ground lamb for the filling.

CAPPELLETTI ALLA ROMANA

Heading back toward Europe now, we come to Italy which has

produced its famous cappelletti, among other dishes, in the way of rolled and stuffed cookery. Cappelletti can be used as soup dumplings or as a first course pasta served with tomato sauce. They can also be a delicious luncheon dish when put into a casserole and served with sauce, and cheese, and baked. Cappelletti are to be found in all parts of Italy and are extremely versatile. For example, if they are made in squares with their edges sealed, instead of in circles, one can have a kind of ravioli.

The Cappelletti Dough

2 C. sifted flour
2 eggs
¼ C. water
½ tsp. salt
chicken broth (for boiling cappelletti)

1. Place flour on a board. Make a depression in the center. Place all other ingredients in the depression. With a fork, gradually beat eggs and water with the flour until half the flour is used up. Add the remaining flour by hand and knead to form a smooth paste. If the dough is too soft, add a little more flour. Knead about 5 minutes.
2. Cut the dough in half and roll out on a floured board into two thin, round sheets. Cut rounds with a 2½" cookie cutter.
3. Place ¼ tsp. filling in the center of each round and fold in half. Seal edges with fingers that have been dipped in water. Then fold corners together again, using water to make them stick.
4. Boil in chicken broth for 15 to 20 minutes. Makes 24 pieces.

Suggested Fillings

chopped ham
chopped chicken
grated mozzarella cheese
chicken and mozzarella cheese
ham and ricotta cheese
chicken and ricotta cheese

1. Fillings can certainly be leftovers. However, when using meat make sure it is cooked before filling the cappelletti.

SPANISH EMPANADILLAS

Empanadillas are little cocktail pastries with a variety of fillings—meat, fish, vegetables, or any combination—that are very popular all over Spain and in the Spanish-speaking countries of the Americas. Often they are sold and eaten on the street. There are fillings to suit many tastes and with the basic recipes given here you can invent your own creations with ease. You can also adapt the size of the pastries to the needs of the moment and the leftovers you have on hand.

Small empanadillas served with soup make a lovely light supper or lunch. Tinier ones can be delicious cocktail tidbits. The serving of appetizers, or "tapas," is one of the very gracious customs of Spain and Spanish America. Toasted almonds, olives, and slices of chorizo sausage may be served along with the empanadillas. A glass of chilled sherry is a fine accompaniment.

Fresh dough for the empanadillas is easy to prepare and can be made in advance. Actually, the pastries themselves can also be baked ahead and frozen so that you need only thaw them and heat to the desired crispness at serving time.

The Empanadilla Dough

1½ C. flour
1 egg
2 tbsp. milk
2 tbsp. olive oil
1 tsp. baking powder
1 tsp. salt

1. Place flour on a board. Make a hole in the center and add all the ingredients. Mix well with fingers.
2. Roll into a ball and cover with a damp cloth. Rest the dough for 15 minutes. (The dough can be kept in a cool place for 24 hours before baking.) Makes about 40 bite-sized pastries or 30 little tarts.

The Filling

1 pepperoni sausage, thinly sliced
1 egg white, lightly beaten (for brushing rounds)

1. Divide the dough into 2 parts. Roll out on a lightly-floured board.
2. Cut 1½" circles with a cookie cutter. Place 1 slice of sausage on each round and top with another round. Crimp edges. Brush with egg white. Prick with a fork.
3. Bake at 400 F. for 15 to 20 minutes, or until browned. Makes about 40 bite-sized pastries.

Variations

You can also stuff the rounds with bits of leftover roasts, ham, chicken, hash, pizza sauce, cheddar cheese, ricotta cheese, or any other filling to suit your fancy.

TARTALETAS

Spain has also given us open-face tartlets which can be made from the same dough as the empanadillas. The tartlet shells can be baked well in advance and frozen. However, we recommend that the fillings be added shortly before serving.

Tartaletas a la Castillana

1 recipe Empanadilla Dough
pebbles or dried beans (for baking tartlets)
2 small cans pimientos
1 hard-cooked egg yolk, mashed
2 cans rolled anchovies
salt and pepper to taste

1. Roll out the dough on a lightly-floured board. Cut and mold into shells to fit 1½" tartlet pans. (You can use mini-muffin tins.) Place in tartlet pans, prick bottoms with a fork and line with aluminum foil. Then fill shells with pebbles or dried beans so they will hold their shape during baking.

2. Bake in a pre-heated oven at 375 F. for about 10 minutes, or until firm. Remove the pebbles, or beans, and aluminum foil.
3. Just before serving, dice the pimiento and season it with salt and pepper. Fill the shells with the pimiento, sprinkle with bits of mashed egg yolk and top with a rolled anchovy. Makes about 30 tartlets.

Variations

Among other filling suggestions: caviar, anchovy with chopped, hard-cooked egg, chicken salad, tuna salad with capers, fish salads spiced with chopped scallions and celery, vegetable salads and ham salads. The tartlets can also take a number of shapes–such as boats, oblongs, squares or rounds.

VEGETABLE APPETIZER MEDLEY

Here is an interesting array of crunchy, cold stuffed vegetables that have style, dash and something appealingly different. Any of the fillings can be used to stuff beautiful raw mushroom caps, celery stalks, cherry tomatoes, olives black or green–or what you will.

Spinach Filling

2 C. sour cream
1½ C. chopped raw spinach
1/3 C. chopped chives
1/3 C. chopped fresh parsley
salt and freshly ground pepper to taste

1. Wash spinach leaves, dry on paper towel and chop.
2. Mix other ingredients together with the spinach and heap into your favorite raw vegetable. Mushroom caps and celery stalks are particularly good.

Ham Filling

2 C. finely chopped boiled ham
1 tbsp. grated onion
pinch of dry mustard
sour cream sufficient to bind mixture

1. Mix ingredients together and heap into raw vegetables. Scooped out boats of raw cucumbers or hollowed out caulifloweretted are nice variations.

Roquefort Filling

1. Cream together in a bowl equal amounts of Roquefort cheese and soft, sweet butter. Moisten the mixture with cognac.
2. Spoon into fresh mushroom caps, cherry tomatoes or even melon balls.
3. Garnish with slivered almonds.

Liptauer

This is Vienna's favorite appetizer spread that you can heap into crunchy vegetables for delightful and unforgettable effects.

2 8-oz. packages cream cheese
1/8 lb. butter (¼ cup)
2 anchovies, chopped
1 tsp. anchovy paste
2 tsp. mild, prepared mustard
½ tsp. chopped capers
1 tsp. caraway seeds, crushed
2 tbsp. chopped chives
2 tbsp. sweet paprika
½ tsp. salt
dash of freshly ground pepper

1. Mix all ingredients together and stuff into a variety of vegetables or melon balls.

Caponata

This delicious Italian vegetable concoction is zesty and memorable and can be taken right out of a can. It can be purchased in nearly any supermarket (Italian section) and is a quick, convenient vegetable stuffer.

Eggplant "Caviar"

A Russian favorite, this stuffing can be nicely adapted as a sensational vegetable stuffer.

2 medium eggplants
½ medium green pepper
olive oil
1 medium onion, grated
1 tomato, peeled, seeded and chopped
salt, pepper and garlic powder to taste

1. Bake eggplants whole at 350 F. about 45 minutes, or until tender. When done, peel and chop.
2. Remove pith and seeds from pepper, then chop.
3. Heat a small quantity of olive oil in a frying pan. Add onion and fry until light brown. Add tomato, green pepper, salt, pepper and garlic powder. Cook gently until the mixture is soft.
4. Put mixture through a sieve. Mash the eggplant until smooth and mix.
5. When completely blended, put the mixture into a dish and chill. Stuff later into any vegetables you like.

Variations

You can add vinegar, dill, lemon juice or more olive oil until the flavor and consistency please you.

Cheese-Stuffed Mushrooms

20 medium-sized mushrooms, washed, dried and stems removed
1 3-oz. package cream cheese
¼ C. grated Parmesan cheese
2 tbsp. milk
flavored bread crumbs

1. Cream the cheeses with milk until smooth. Fill mushroom caps. Top with bread crumbs.
2. Bake in a greased pan at 350 F. for 15 minutes.

Tuna-Stuffed Mushrooms

1 lb. large mushrooms, washed, dried and stems removed
2 tbsp. lemon juice
1½ tsp. finely chopped onion
3 tbsp. mayonnaise
freshly ground pepper to taste
1 tbsp. capers
1 7-oz. can tuna, flaked
3 tbsp. grated Parmesan cheese

1. Combine lemon juice, onion, mayonnaise and pepper. Add capers and tuna. Fill mushroom caps. Sprinkle with cheese.
2. Bake in a greased pan at 350 F. for 20 minutes.

RUMAKI

A famous oriental favorite that originated in China–yet bear a Japanese name–Rumaki are enjoyed throughout the Orient and Pacific, as well as in the United States and Europe.

12 chicken livers
1 small can water chestnuts
12 strips of bacon, halved
salt and pepper to taste

1. Cut chicken livers in half. Wrap ½ a liver and 1 water chestnut in ½ a strip of bacon. Salt and pepper to taste.
2. Skewer and broil until crisp. Makes about 24 pieces.

INTRIGUE WITH ROLL-UPS

Chicken Liver Bacon Rolls

½ lb. chicken livers
3 tbsp. soy sauce

1 tbsp. dry sherry
¼ tsp. garlic powder
1 tbsp. white horseradish
1 can button mushrooms
7 strips of bacon

1. Cut livers into 2 or 3 pieces.
2. Mix soy sauce, sherry, garlic powder and horseradish. Pour over livers and marinate for 3 hours in the refrigerator.
3. Cut bacon strips into thirds. Wrap each piece around livers and mushrooms.
4. Fasten with skewers and broil until crisp. Makes about 20 rolls.

Curried Banana and Bacon Rolls

bananas
curry powder
lemon juice
bacon
chopped chutney

1. Cut each banana into 5 or 6 pieces. Dip into a mixture of curry powder and lemon juice. (Adjust mixture to taste.)
2. Wrap 1/3 a strip of bacon around each banana piece.
3. Skewer and bake at 375 F. until bacon is almost cooked.
4. Dip rolls into chutney and return to oven for 5 to 10 minutes. Serve immediately.

Shrimp and Bacon Rolls

1 lb. cleaned and deveined partially cooked shrimp
½ C. soy sauce
1 bunch scallions
bacon

1. Marinate the shrimp in soy sauce for 1 hour.
2. Cut scallions into 2" pieces and wrap with shrimp in ½ a strip of bacon.
3. Skewer and broil until bacon is done. Turn over if needed.
4. Serve with a Chinese sweet and sour sauce.

Bleu Cheese and Walnut Ham Rolls

½ lb. bleu cheese
½ lb. sweet butter
¼ C. chopped walnuts
2 tbsp. kirschwasser
2 lb. boiled ham, thinly sliced

1. Beat cheese and butter together until creamy. Add walnuts and kirschwasser. Mix well and chill.
2. Spread mixture on ham slices. Roll and cut into 3" lengths.
3. Skewer and serve. Makes about 50 pieces.

Puffy Cheese Rolls

3/4 lb. sharp cheddar cheese, grated
4¼ tsp. flour
½ tsp. salt
½ tsp. pepper
5 egg whites
unflavored bread crumbs
oil for deep frying

1. Mix cheese, flour, salt and pepper.
2. Beat egg whites until stiff and fold into cheese mixture.
3. Shape mixture into small rolls about 1½" long. Roll in bread crumbs.
4. Deep fry the rolls in oil until golden brown and nicely puffed. Makes about 48 rolls. (These rolls can be made up to 24 hours before they are needed and fried just before serving.)

Mushroom Bread Rolls

12 to 14 thin slices white bread
sweet butter (for spreading on bread)
½ lb. fresh mushrooms, finely chopped
2 tbsp. butter (for sautéing mushrooms)
½ tbsp. curry powder
1 tbsp. lemon juice
pinch of cayenne pepper
½ tbsp. salt
ground black pepper to taste
melted butter (for brushing bread rolls)

1. Roll bread thinly with a rolling pin. Remove crusts and spread slices with sweet butter.

2. Sauté mushrooms in butter. Add curry powder, lemon juice, cayenne pepper and salt and pepper.
3. Spread 1 tbsp. of the filling mix on each slice of bread. Roll and fasten with toothpicks. Brush with melted butter.
4. Bake at 425 F. for 15 minutes, or until golden brown.

Ham Rolls en Papillote

12 thin slices cooked ham
¼ lb. fresh mushrooms, chopped
1 garlic clove, minced
1 tbsp. butter (for sautéing mushrooms)
1 C. cooked long grain and wild rice mix
¼ tbsp. curry powder

1. Sauté mushrooms and garlic in butter. Add to the rice. Add curry powder.
2. Divide mixture and place on ham slices. Roll and skewer.
3. Place ham rolls in a well-sealed aluminum foil package.
4. Bake at 350 F. for 15 to 20 minutes. Serves 6.

GARNISHED CHEESE LOGS

Roquefort Log

1 lb. Roquefort cheese
1 8-oz. package cream cheese
¼ lb. butter
1 oz. cognac
2 tbsp. minced chives
½ C. chopped toasted almonds

1. Mix Roquefort, cream cheese and butter. Add cognac and chives. Blend well and chill until firm.
2. Shape mixture into a roll about 2" in diameter. Roll in toasted almonds. Serve with crackers.

Cheddar Cheese Log

½ lb. sharp cheddar cheese, grated
1/3 C. crumbled Roquefort cheese
1 small garlic clove, finely minced
¼ C. sour cream
1/3 tsp. Tabasco sauce
¼ C. finely chopped olives
½ C. minced fresh parsley

1. Combine cheeses, garlic and enough sour cream to bind. Add Tabasco and chopped olives. Blend well and chill until firm.
2. Shape mixture into a roll about 2" in diameter. Roll in fresh parsley. Serve with crackers.

Coconut Cheese Log

1 8-oz. package cream cheese
1 4-oz. package bleu cheese
2 tbsp. whiskey
3/4 tsp. dry mustard
1-1/3 C. toasted coconut

1. Combine cheeses and blend until soft. Add whiskey and mustard. Blend well and chill until firm.
2. Form into a roll about 2" in diameter. Roll in toasted coconut. (This mixture can also be formed into small balls. Makes about 40.) Serve with crackers.

CREAM PUFFERY

Many believe there is a special mystique about making puff shells. But here are all the basic secrets you need know about what is in reality a surprisingly easy endeavor. Once they are baked, puff shells can be frozen and reheated later when you need them. They should be frozen filled when used as hors d'oeuvres so that the fillings will have been cooked. When the puffs are used as a dessert, they can be filled just before serving. The dessert fillings can include whipped cream flavored with instant coffee, vanilla or brandy; or custard and fruits, or puddings.

The Basic Puff Shell

1 C. water
6 tbsp. butter
1 tsp. salt
pepper to taste (omit if using for dessert)
1 C. sifted flour
4 eggs
1 egg, beaten well with 1 tbsp. water (for brushing puffs)

1. Combine water, butter, salt and pepper in a saucepan and simmer until all the butter is melted. Add the flour and mix well. Simmer over low heat until dough pulls away from the sides of the pan. This should take about 2 minutes.
2. Remove from heat and add the eggs, one at a time, making certain that each egg is well-absorbed before adding the next one.
3. Make the puffs with a pastry bag which has a large, plain nozzle. The puffs should be at least 1" in diameter and 3/4" high. If you do not have a bag, simply drop puffs from a spoon onto a well-greased cookie sheet.
4. Brush puffs with the beaten egg. Do not permit the egg to drip on the cookie sheet or the puffs will not rise.
5. Bake at 425 F. for 20 minutes. Remove from the oven and slit the side of each puff. Return to the oven for 2 more minutes.
6. Fill and serve. Or, fill and freeze for later use. Makes about 50 puffs.

Fish Puffs

1 recipe Puff Shell Pastry
1 7-oz. can tuna, salmon or crab meat, drained
¼ C. cream cheese
1 tbsp. sour cream
2 tbsp. capers, well-drained
½ C. finely chopped celery
½ tsp. dried parsley
dash of cayenne pepper
1 egg, beaten well with 1 tbsp. water (for brushing puffs)

1. Mix ingredients well and use for Puff Shell filling. Makes about 1 cup, or enough for 50 puffs.

Chicken and Cashew Puffs

1 recipe Puff Shell Pastry
1 C. minced cooked chicken
3/4 C. well-chopped unsalted cashews
2 tbsp. sour cream
2 tbsp. mayonnaise
1 tbsp. minced chives (frozen)
½ tsp. paprika
salt and pepper to taste
1 egg, beaten well with 1 tbsp. water (for brushing puffs)

1. Mix ingredients well and use for Puff Shell filling. Makes about 1¼ cups, or enough for about 50 puffs.

CREAM CHEESE PASTRY

Cream cheese pastry is extraordinarily versatile. The stuffings that can be used for it are limited solely by your imagination and personal tastes.

The Basic Cream Cheese Pastry

1 8-oz. package cream cheese
½ lb. butter
2¼ C. flour
1 tsp. salt
1 egg white, beaten (for brushing pastry)

1. Beat cheese and butter together with an electric beater until smooth and creamy. Gradually add flour and salt and blend at a low speed.
2. Knead the dough in a bowl until it clings together. Wrap in waxed paper and refrigerate for 4 hours. (If chilled overnight, allow to stand for ½ hour before rolling.)
3. Roll dough out on a lightly-floured board or between 2 sheets of waxed paper.

4. Spread filling evenly. Roll and brush lightly with beaten egg white.
5. Bake seam side down at 325 F. for 25 to 30 minutes, or until golden.
6. Cool for 1 hour and slice slantwise. Makes 48 slices.

The Fillings

And here follows an exciting medley of fillings for the basic Cream Cheese Pastry guaranteed to elicit compliments from all quarters. The fillings are different, exotic, and inspired by the cuisines of many nations.

Potato

1 recipe Cream Cheese Pastry
3 medium to large potatoes, peeled
3 oz. Roquefort or cheddar cheese, grated
2 tbsp. butter
4 to 6 scallions, finely chopped
¼ C. chopped fresh parsley
salt and pepper to taste
1 egg white, beaten (for brushing pastry)

1. Cook potatoes until just tender. Rinse well and add cheese and butter. Beat together until smooth.
2. Add remaining ingredients and mix well.
3. Follow directions for filling and baking Cream Cheese Pastry. Makes about 2 cups of filling, or about 48 slices.

Chicken

1 recipe Cream Cheese Pastry
2 C. finely chopped cooked chicken
1 small onion, finely chopped
2 tbsp. butter
1 egg, lightly beaten
2 tbsp. finely minced celery
½ tsp. salt
pepper to taste
1 egg white, beaten (for brushing pastry)

1. Sauté onion in butter. Add remaining ingredients and mix well. Cool.
2. Follow directions for filling and baking Cream Cheese Pastry. Makes about 2 cups of filling, or about 48 slices.

Spinach

1 recipe Cream Cheese Pastry
4 strips of bacon, diced
2 tbsp. butter
2 tbsp. diced onion
2 garlic cloves, chopped
1 10-oz. package frozen spinach, partially thawed
1 C. pot, ricotta or feta cheese
2 tbsp. chopped celery
1/8 tsp. nutmeg
salt and ground pepper to taste
1 egg white, beaten (for brushing pastry)

1. Sauté bacon until crisp and reserve.
2. Melt butter and sauté onion and garlic until tender. Add spinach and cook well. Drain off all remaining liquid.
3. Add bacon, cheese, celery and seasonings and mix well. Cool.
4. Follow directions for filling and baking Cream Cheese Pastry. Makes about 2 cups, or about 48 slices.

Beef

1 recipe Cream Cheese Pastry
3 tbsp. butter
1 large onion, chopped
2 C. ground beef
2 tsp. chopped chives
2 eggs, lightly beaten
½ C. chopped fresh parsley
salt and pepper to taste
1 egg white, beaten (for brushing pastry)

1. Sauté onion in butter. Add meat and chives. Stir in beaten eggs

and remaining ingredients. If mixture is too dry, add another lightly-beaten egg. Cool.
2. Follow directions for filling and baking Cream Cheese Pastry. Makes about 2 cups, or about 48 slices.

Shrimp and Water Chestnut

1 recipe Cream Cheese Pastry
2 tbsp. butter
1½ C. minced cooked shrimp
salt and pepper to taste
2 tsp. instant blending flour
½ C. light cream
3 tbsp. dry white wine
1 tsp. tomato paste
1 small can water chestnuts, chopped
1 tbsp. chopped chives
1 tbsp. chopped fresh parsley
1 egg white, beaten (for brushing pastry)

1. Heat butter and sauté shrimp lightly. Add salt and pepper. Add flour and mix well.
2. Combine cream, wine and tomato paste to make a smooth sauce. Add this sauce to the shrimp. The mixture should bind well. Add remaining ingredients. Cool.
3. Follow directions for filling and baking Cream Cheese Pastry. Makes about 2 cups, or about 48 slices.

Deviled Ham and Cheese

1 recipe Cream Cheese Pastry
2 4-oz. cans deviled ham
3/4 C. grated cheddar cheese
1 4-oz. can mushrooms, drained and finely chopped
¼ C. mayonnaise
1 egg white, beaten (for brushing pastry)

1. Combine all ingredients. Add more mayonnaise if mixture seems too dry.

2. Follow directions for filling and baking Cream Cheese Pastry. Makes about 2 cups, or about 48 slices.

Crab

1 recipe Cream Cheese Pastry
2 tbsp. butter
½ C. chopped onion
1 garlic clove, minced
¼ C. chopped celery
½ tsp. salt
2 6½-oz. cans crab meat, flaked
1 tbsp. lemon juice
1 tbsp. dry sherry
2 tsp. Worcestershire sauce
1 egg white, beaten (for brushing pastry)

1. Sauté onion, garlic and celery in butter. Add salt. Add crab meat, lemon juice, sherry and Worcestershire. Cool.
2. Follow directions for filling and baking Cream Cheese Pastry. Makes about 2 cups, or about 48 slices.

Note: This filling can also be used for turnovers. Cut 3" circles from the rolled-out pastry. Place 1 tsp. of filling in the center of each circle. Fold over and seal. Place turnovers on a greased cookie sheet. Brush with beaten egg white. Bake at 350 F. for 25 to 30 minutes. Makes about 48 turnovers.

CHINESE STEAMED DUMPLINGS-DEEM SUM

Steamed dumplings are popular all over China. They are served both as hors d'oeuvres and as luncheon dishes. A favorite New York City restaurant features an entire luncheon composed of these savory dumplings. They can be filled with any leftover cooked meat, fish or variety of vegetables. The seasonings can run the gamut of bland to the fiery chili pepper and sesame oil style of Szechuan. Deem Sum can be made well in advance and frozen. They should be steamed just before serving. When you serve them, offer duck sauce, Chinese mustard and soy sauce for dipping.

The Deem Sum Dough–Fermented

3/4 tsp. dry yeast
3/4 C. lukewarm water
2 C. flour
1½ tsp. sugar
cheesecloth

1. Dissolve yeast in 2 tbsp. lukewarm water. Add the flour and sugar. Add remaining water gradually and mix until well-blended.
2. Knead dough on a lightly-floured board for 7 to 8 minutes.
3. Place dough in a bowl. Cover and let stand in a warm, draft-free place for 3 hours.
4. Knead dough again for 2 to 3 minutes. Shape into a roll about 2 ft. long and 1" thick. Slice into 1" pieces and stretch each piece slightly.
5. Place 1 tbsp. of filling on each piece. Draw the sides together and pinch top closed. The result should resemble a fat teardrop.
6. Place in a steamer whose rack has been covered with cheesecloth, and steam for 25 minutes. Makes about 24 "teardrops."

Note: If you do not own a steamer, place a cake rack at the bottom of a large skillet. Fill with water to just under the rack, or about 1". Place the cheesecloth over the rack and the "teardrops" on the cheesecloth. Cover skillet tightly and steam as directed.

The Deem Sum Dough–Nonfermented

2 C. water
1 C. flour

1. Combine the flour and water and mix well.
2. Knead for 3 minutes and cover. Allow to stand 30 minutes before shaping into a roll.
3. Cut, fill and steam as directed for Fermented Dough.
4. Makes about 24 "teardrops."

The Meat Filling

1 recipe Deem Sum Dough
½ lb. ground pork, or minced chicken
2 leeks, chopped
2 scallions, chopped
1 tbsp. soy sauce
2 tsp. sugar
1 tsp. salt
few drops of sesame oil (optional),
or ¼ tsp. ground ginger

1. Combine all filling ingredients.
2. Follow directions for shaping, filling and steaming "teardrops" in Fermented Dough recipe.
3. Makes about 24 pastries.

The Shrimp Filling

1 recipe Deem Sum Dough
½ lb. cleaned and deveined cooked shrimp, chopped
1 tsp. diced pork or bacon fat
1 tsp. dry sherry
¼ tsp. ground ginger
1 tsp. salt

1. Combine all filling ingredients.
2. Follow directions for shaping, filling and steaming "teardrops" in Fermented Dough recipe.
3. Makes about 24 pastries.

Flower-Wrapped Deem Sum

1 recipe Deem Sum Dough
¼ C. boiled chopped ham
¼ C. cooked chopped spinach
3 hard-cooked egg yolks, crumbled

1. Combine all filling ingredients.

2. Follow directions for preparation of the Deem Sum Dough. When the slices are cut and stretched, however, place a pinch of the filling on each slice and draw up the sides slightly to form a cup.
3. Pleat the edges around the filling, leaving the center exposed. This style of wrapping is more pleasing visually when you have a tri-colored filling.
4. Makes about 24 Flower-Wrapped Deem Sum.

DOLMADAKIA-STUFFED GRAPE LEAVES

Dolmadakia are another type of famous Greek and Middle Eastern mezedakia or hors d'oeuvres. In these lands where hospitality is lavish and legendary, they are served everywhere—in private homes and in the taverns—before dinner with the customary ouzo, retsina, or raki. But perhaps it would be more in keeping with *our* tastes to serve this unusual appetizer with some chilled rosé wine.

1 12-oz. jar grape leaves
1 lb. onions, chopped
1 C. olive oil
1 C. rice soaked in 1 C. water for ½ hour
salt and pepper to taste
1 tbsp. chopped fresh parsley
2 tbsp. pine nuts
juice of 1 lemon
1 tsp. dried mint leaves
½ tsp. dried dill
1 tbsp. currants
1 C. boiling water

1. Rinse grape leaves well and drain.
2. Sauté onions in ½ the oil. Drain the rice and add to the oil and onions. Add salt and pepper and cook mixture slowly for 20 minutes.
3. Add parsley, pine nuts, lemon juice, mint, dill and currants. Pour boiling water over the mixture and cook until all water is absorbed. Cool.

4. Place 1 tsp. of the mixture on each leaf. Tuck in the ends and roll.
5. Place extra leaves in the bottom of the skillet and place rolls on top. Pour over remaining oil and enough water to cover. Place a plate on top to hold down rolls.
6. Cook over low heat for 1 hour. Serves 6 to 8. Can be frozen for later use.

BOREK

From Turkey to Lebanon, to Kurdistan, to Egypt, these tasty turnovers are popular in all the countries of the Middle East. Because of the lack of refrigeration in these areas, borek are commonly made and consumed quickly. They are made by commercial bakers as well as at home. Often they are sold on the street by vendors and are a favorite snack or quick lunch. For the convenience of the harried hostess, however, they can be produced in quantity and frozen in advance.

They are excellent served with a chilled rosé wine and sliced fresh cucumbers dipped in a mixture of yoghurt and mashed garlic clove.

Borek with Cheese

1 recipe "The Dough" made with butter
2 mushrooms, chopped
1 tbsp. butter
½ lb. pot or farmer cheese
1 egg yolk, beaten
3 tbsp. chopped fresh parsley
salt and pepper to taste
1 egg, beaten (for brushing pastry)

1. Sauté the mushrooms in butter until tender. Cool. Combine with cheese, egg yolk and parsley. Add salt and pepper.
2. Roll out "The Dough" on a lightly-floured board and cut into 4" circles. Divide the filling and place on circles. Fold over and seal with fingers that have been dipped in water. Brush the borek with beaten egg.
3. Bake on a greased cookie sheet at 350 F. for 30 minutes. Serves 4.

Borek with Chicken

1 recipe "The Dough" made with butter
3 tbsp. butter
3 tbsp. instant blending flour
1 C. half-and-half milk
3/4 C. chopped boiled chicken
1 egg yolk, beaten
2 tsp. shredded coconut
¼ tsp. rosemary
1 tsp. paprika
salt and pepper to taste
1 egg, beaten (for brushing pastry)

1. Melt the butter in a saucepan, add flour and blend. Add the half-and-half milk and cook until the mixture is thick and creamy.
2. Add chicken, egg yolk, coconut, rosemary and seasonings. Blend well and remove from heat.
3. Roll out "The Dough" on a lightly-floured board and cut into 4" circles. Divide the filling and place on circles. Fold over and seal with fingers that have been dipped in water. Brush the borek with beaten egg.
4. Bake on a greased cookie sheet at 350 F. for 30 minutes. Serves 4.

Borek with Lamb

1 recipe "The Dough" made with butter
½ lb. ground lamb
2 large onions, finely chopped
¼ tsp. mace
¼ tsp. thyme
½ tsp. black pepper
salt to taste
1 egg, beaten (for brushing pastry)

1. Place lamb and onions in a pan and cook for 7 minutes, without water or fat. Stir to prevent sticking.
2. Add remaining ingredients and cook until all liquid is absorbed.
3. Roll out "The Dough" on a lightly-floured board and cut into 4" circles. Divide the filling and place on circles. Fold over and seal with fingers that have been dipped in water. Brush the borek with beaten egg.
4. Bake on a greased cookie sheet at 350 F. for 30 minutes. Serves 4.

Borek with Lamb and Wine

2 recipes "The Dough" made with butter
2 tbsp. butter
1 lb. ground lamb
4 scallions, chopped
½ tbsp. ketchup
½ C. dry white wine
¼ tsp. thyme
½ tsp. white pepper
½ tsp. garlic salt
1 egg, beaten (for brushing pastry)

1. Melt the butter and add the lamb and scallions. Cook slowly for 30 minutes.
2. Add the ketchup, wine and seasonings and cook for 1 hour longer.
3. Roll out "The Dough" on a lightly-floured board and cut into 4" circles. Divide the filling and place on circles. Fold over and seal edges with fingers that have been dipped in water. Brush borek with beaten egg.
4. Bake on greased cookie sheet at 350 F. for 30 minutes. Serves 8 to 10.

STUFFED PEPPER APPETIZERS

Italian Stuffed Peppers

1 C. bread crumbs
1/3 C. milk
3 tbsp. minced olives
3 tbsp. minced pickled vegetables
3 tbsp. minced fresh parsley
1 tbsp. minced anchovy
1 garlic clove, crushed
salt and pepper to taste
3 green peppers
olive oil

1. Soak bread crumbs in milk.
2. Combine with olives, pickled vegetables, parsley, anchovy, garlic, salt and pepper. Chop until a smooth paste is formed with the soaked bread crumbs.
3. Stem and seed the peppers. Fill with mixture.
4. Arrange peppers in an oiled baking dish, which is just large enough to

hold them. Sprinkle the peppers with a little olive oil.
5. Cover with aluminum foil and bake at 350 F. for 45 minutes. Remove cover and bake for 10 minutes longer. Serves 6.

Stuffed Peppers with Anchovies

1½ C. peeled, seeded and cubed tomatoes
½ C. minced anchovies
3 tbsp. dry bread crumbs
3 tbsp. olive oil
3 garlic cloves, thinly sliced
3 green or red peppers
butter

1. Combine all ingredients except for the peppers and butter.
2. Stem and seed the peppers. Fill with mixture.
3. Dot with butter. Bake at 375 F. for 30 minutes. Chill. Serves 6.

FILLETS A LA RUSSE

This is a rich and elegant concoction from the kitchens of old St. Petersburg. Both versions make truly fine appetizers. (Serve either with a knife and fork.)

8 fillets of beef bracciole
1 medium onion, grated
1 tsp. horseradish
1 tsp. chopped fresh dill, or ¼ tsp. dried dill
1 tbsp. chopped fresh parsley
½ C. sour cream
1 small jar caviar (This can be a can of lumpfish, the least expensive type of caviar, drained.)
salt and pepper to taste
rye bread rounds

1. Pound fillets until very thin. Spread each with grated onion, a little horseradish, dill, parsley, sour cream, caviar and salt and pepper. Roll.
2. Serve each rolled fillet on a fresh rye bread round. Serves 8.

The Warm Version

1. Sauté the fillets. Douse them with any kind of brandy and ignite.
2. Add onion, horseradish, dill, parsley, sour cream, and salt and pepper. Cook until fillets are done.
3. Place fillets in a serving dish. Spread with caviar and roll. Secure with picks.
4. Pour the warm, brandied sour cream sauce over cooked rolls and serve on rye bread rounds. Serves 8.

STUFFED CABBAGE APPETIZER

1 head of white cabbage
1 lb. ground pork, beef or lamb
2 onions, chopped
¼ C. raw rice
¼ tsp. dried dill
3 tbsp. butter
chicken bouillon
Egg and Lemon Sauce

1. Core cabbage and separate the leaves. Parboil leaves in salted water for 5 minutes.
2. Combine pork, onion, rice and dill. Divide and place on 8 cabbage leaves. Fold 2 sides inward and roll.
3. Place a few of the other leaves in the bottom of a heavy pan. Put the cabbage rolls on top and dot them with butter.
4. Simmer in chicken bouillon (enough to barely cover) for 1 hour. Remove from heat and add The Egg and Lemon Sauce. Serves 6 to 8.

The Egg and Lemon Sauce

2 egg yolks
2 tbsp. lemon juice
4 tbsp. hot bouillon

1. Beat egg yolks and lemon juice together. Slowly add the hot bouillon, making certain that the sauce does not curdle. Use immediately.

STUFFED SHELLFISH APPETIZERS

Stuffed Mussels

This is an interesting Italian appetizer that can complement any hearty main dish. Serve with any chilled dry white or rosé wine.

1 lb. mussels
½ C. olive oil
2 large onions, chopped
½ C. rice soaked in ½ C. cold water for ½ hour
½ C. chicken bouillon
1 tbsp. chopped fresh parsley
½ tsp. dried dill
¼ C. pine nuts
¼ C. white raisins
salt and pepper to taste
1 tsp. lemon juice

1. Scrub the mussels well under running water. Open the shells, being careful to keep them joined at the pointed end. Remove the small, black "tail" and rinse again carefully.
2. Sauté onion in a small portion of the oil until tender. Add the remaining oil and the drained rice. Fry for 15 minutes.
3. Gradually add the bouillon and simmer the mixture until all liquid is absorbed. Add remaining ingredients, except lemon juice, and mix well.
4. Stuff shells, placing mixture on top of mussel meat, and close. Be careful not to overstuff, as the mixture will expand while cooking.

5. Place stuffed mussels in a skillet and cover with water mixed with lemon juice. Simmer covered until all liquid is gone–about 30 to 35 minutes. Serves 6 to 8.

Deviled Clams

2 dozen clams, in shells
½ C. flavored bread crumbs
¼ C. chopped fresh parsley
2 tbsp. chopped celery
2 tbsp. Worcestershire sauce
2 tbsp. lemon juice
2 tbsp. dry white wine
salt to taste
2 tbsp. melted butter

1. Brush clams well under running water to remove all sand. Open and remove inedible parts. Chop clam meat.
2. Combine remaining ingredients, except butter, with the clam meat.
3. Stuff shells with the mixture. Brush tops with butter.
4. Bake at 350 F. for 20 minutes. Serves 4 to 6.

Stuffed Clams Oregano

12 to 16 clams, in shells
¼ C. flavored bread crumbs
1 garlic clove, minced
2 tbsp. minced fresh parsley
1 tsp. oregano
olive oil

1. Brush clams well under running water to remove all sand. Open and remove inedible parts. Chop clam meat.
2. Combine bread crumbs, garlic, parsley and oregano with clam meat.
3. Stuff shells with the mixture. Drizzle olive oil over the tops.
4. Broil until golden. Serves 4.

TORTILLAS

Popular in Mexico and Central America, a tortilla is a dry, cornmeal pancake. In Spain, curiously, it is an omelette. The Mexican version is the one we have given here, and it makes an excellent appetizer.

1 can tortillas
1 can chili con carne
grated cheddar cheese to taste
shredded lettuce to taste
chopped onions to taste
corn oil

1. Deep fry tortillas in corn oil until they are golden on both sides.
2. Drain tortillas and fold in half.
3. Fill each tortilla with chili and top with cheese, lettuce and onion. Serves 6.

SAUSAGE EN CROUTE

1 medium onion, chopped
butter
½ lb. ground beef
½ lb. chopped Italian sausage, casing removed
2 tbsp. prepared mustard
pinch of marjoram
2 C. biscuit mix
½ C. milk
garlic powder

1. Sauté onion in butter. Add beef and sausage and brown. Add mustard and marjoram and mix well.
2. Mix biscuit mix and milk according to package directions and roll into 2 large rectangles on a lightly-floured board.
3. Place ½ the filling on each rectangle. Roll and place seam side down in a greased baking dish. Brush with butter and sprinkle with garlic powder.
4. Bake at 400 F. for 30 minutes. Serves 8 to 10.

TARTS AND TARTLETS

Salmon Tarts

1 recipe "The Dough"
pebbles or dried beans (for baking shells)
butter (for sautéing mushrooms)
¼ lb. chopped mushrooms
¼ C. dry sherry
¼ C. chopped green pepper
¼ C. chopped pimiento olives
1 tbsp. Worcestershire sauce
1 tbsp. dry mustard
2 C. flaked canned salmon
pinch of cayenne pepper
½ tsp. salt
pepper to taste
1 recipe Basic Béchamel Sauce

1. Roll out "The Dough" on a lightly-floured board. Fill a 9" pie tin or 6 5½" tart pans. (Use the type with loose bottoms.) Prick the shells with a fork and line bottoms with aluminum foil. Cover bottoms with pebbles so they will hold their hollow shape during baking.
2. Bake at 400 F. for 10 minutes. Remove pebbles and aluminum foil and bake 8 to 10 minutes longer.
3. Sauté mushrooms in butter. Combine with remaining ingredients and fill shells with the mixture.
4. Bake at 350 F. for 5 to 10 minutes, or until a knife inserted in the center comes out clean. Serves 6.

Mushroom Cheese Tarts

1 recipe "The Dough"
pebbles or dried beans (for baking shells)
3/4 C. shredded Swiss cheese
1 small can mushrooms, chopped
1 egg
1 egg yolk

salt to taste
2 tsp. dry mustard
dash of cayenne pepper
½ C. scalded light cream

1. Roll out "The Dough" on a lightly-floured board. Cut into circles for 10 3½" tart pans. Form into shells. Prick bottoms with a fork and line with aluminum foil. Cover bottoms with pebbles so they will hold their hollow shape during baking.
2. Bake in a pre-heated oven at 375 F. for about 10 minutes, or until firm. Remove pebbles and aluminum foil.
3. Divide the cheese and mushrooms among the shells.
4. Beat the egg, egg yolk, salt, mustard and cayenne in a bowl. Add the scalded cream. Spoon this mixture over the mushrooms and cheese in the shells.
5. Bake at 350 F. for 25 to 30 minutes. Serve hot. Serves 10.

Shrimp Tartlets with Mushroom Purée

1 recipe "The Dough"
pebbles or dried beans (for baking shells)
1 lb. fresh mushrooms, finely chopped
½ tsp. chopped fresh dill
salt and pepper to taste
1 C. heavy cream
½ tsp. grated lemon peel
1 can baby shrimp, well-drained

1. Roll out "The Dough" on a lightly-floured board. Cut into circles for 1¼" tartlet pans. Form into shells. Prick bottoms with a fork and line with aluminum foil. Cover bottoms with pebbles so they will hold their hollow shape during baking.
2. Bake in a pre-heated oven at 375 F. for about 10 minutes, or until firm. Remove pebbles and aluminum foil.
3. Place mushrooms in a blender with the dill, salt and pepper. Blend, scraping down the sides until the mixture is puréed.
4. Transfer mixture to a saucepan and cook until all liquid is absorbed.
5. Remove from heat and cool slightly. Add the cream and lemon peel.
6. Return to the heat and simmer 3 minutes. (This mixture will keep at

least 1 week, covered, in the refrigerator.)
7. Add shrimp, mix well, and fill tartlet shells. Makes about 18 tartlets.

CHEESE TURNOVERS

1 recipe "The Dough"
½ C. chopped ham, or cooked sweet sausage
1 C. ricotta cheese
1 C. mozzarella cheese, grated
2 tbsp. Parmesan cheese
1 egg yolk, beaten
salt to taste
olive oil (for frying turnovers)

1. Roll out "The Dough" on a lightly-floured board. Cut into 4" circles.
2. Combine all ingredients. Divide mixture and place on circles. Fold over and seal edges carefully.
3. Fry turnovers in olive oil and serve. Serves 8.

MOZZARELLA TURNOVERS

biscuit dough, prepared
mozzarella cheese, grated
fresh parsley, chopped
oregano to taste
salt and pepper to taste

1. Roll out biscuit dough on a lightly-floured board. Cut into 3" circles.
2. Place cheese, parsley, oregano and salt and pepper on the circles. Fold over and seal edges carefully.
3. Bake at 375 F. until golden. This recipe makes as many or as few as you wish.

STUFFED CRESCENT DELIGHTS

1 package prepared crescent rolls
1 egg
¼ C. Caesar salad dressing
1 C. herb-flavored prepared stuffing
¼ C. flaked tuna or salmon
¼ C. grated Parmesan cheese
1 egg, beaten (for brushing crescents)

1. Mix egg and salad dressing. Add stuffing, tuna and cheese. Mix well. Add more dressing if mixture is too dry to bind.
2. Open each crescent and slice to form two triangles. Divide filling and place on each triangle. Re-roll in crescent fashion.
3. Place on a greased cookie sheet and brush with beaten egg. Bake at 375 F. until golden brown. Makes about 16 small crescents.

CHICKEN THIGHS WITH MOZZARELLA

8 fryer thighs, boned
1 tbsp. dried parsley
1 tbsp. chopped onion
salt to taste
¼ lb. mozzarella cheese
1 16-oz. jar marinara sauce

1. Bone chicken thighs by slitting along bone from end to end. Carefully cut meat away so that it comes off in 1 piece. Remove any cartilage that may adhere. Remove skin and place thighs flat in a baking dish. Sprinkle with parsley, onion and salt.
2. Cut cheese into 8 pieces. Place 1 piece of cheese on each thigh and secure with skewers.
3. Bake at 400 F. for 35 to 40 minutes.
4. Heat marinara sauce and pour over thighs just before serving. Serves 4.

IV. RUFFLES AND FLOURISHES

Omelettes, Quiches, Crepes and Blini

The world of omelettes, quiches, crepes and blini, and related dishes, is indeed one of ruffles and flourishes. Certainly, they lend an aura of finesse, expertise and high art to any meal. Many are minor masterpieces of gastronomy which will bring drama to any occasion.

Although these dishes may seem difficult, they are not. We clearly outline all the steps that will take the mystery out of crepes and quiches, and the others, and will make an expert of you in very little time.

THE OMELETTE

Omelettes have a long history. The ancient Romans made an omelette preparation called "Ova Mellita" which was simply eggs beaten with honey and cooked in an earthenware dish. Later the French cooked an egg dish, naming it "omelette" from the word "alemette," which merely means slice. The original French omelette pan was flat.

Omelettes are extremely adaptable–they can be served for breakfast, luncheon, a first course, dessert (when they are interchangeable with crepes), and they can be filled and garnished in myriad ways. The "omelette garnie" is served with vegetables around it, the "omelette fourrée" is made with fillings and the "omelette sucrée" is the dessert omelette, made with sugar, fruits or jams. The dessert omelette can be particularly exotic when accompanied by a host of seemingly unlikely ingredients–from pineapple and kirschwasser, to rum, apples and calvados, and even filberts with chocolate sauce.

The point is, one should stop thinking of omelettes as a prosaic breakfast dish. Their variety is boundless–limited only by the kaleidoscope of sauces and fillings you prepare for them. When the omelette is cooked, you can pour the sauce on top, or fold it into the omelette as you roll it onto a plate. The flavorings and fillings are often cooked with the omelette and mixed in. Just to illustrate the variety of embellishments, here are some you might try: mushrooms; hot curry sauce with tuna, crab, lobster or chicken; cheeses in combination; spiced tomatoes and sauces; creamed meats and fish; vegetables; herbs; bacon and sausage; chicken livers; ham; foie gras; nuts; croutons–or any permutations that appeal to you.

The Basic Omelette

Ideally, omelettes should be cooked individually in a 6" to 8" heavy cast iron or aluminum skillet. Preferably, the skillet should be only used for cooking omelettes. In any case, it should be absolutely clean.

For an absolutely plain omelette, the eggs should be beaten with salt, and a little milk or water if a soft mixture is desired. The eggs should be whipped lightly and immediately before cooking. Only a moderate amount of butter should be used for the cooking. Simply melt it in the skillet until it is bubbly hot–but not smoking or brown–and pour in the eggs. Use a high heat.

Then start loosening the edges of the omelette with a spatula, lifting the eggs where they have set, to let the uncooked top part run underneath. When the omelette is almost cooked, and still a bit creamy on top, slip the spatula under one edge and roll it over, folding it as you put it on a hot plate to be served at once.

Although, as we have said, a 6" skillet is ideal for individual servings, we have given recipes designed for 6-egg omelettes, which will serve 2 or 3 persons, depending upon appetites. A large skillet, of 10" or 12" is best for the 6-egg omelette because it will give you the maximum cooking surface and will also produce a thinner omelette. (If you wish to make individual omelettes, which generally turn out neater and better, use 2 eggs per omelette and divide the filling ingredients accordingly.)

There are two chief methods of preparation for omelettes. The first is simply beating the eggs and adding a little liquid and seasoning, then frying and filling. The other method is extremely rewarding and is not commonly known in this country. The results, however, make it well worth trying. Separate the eggs, then beat the yolks with a little liquid. Whip the whites separately until they hold stiff peaks. The yolks should be folded into the whites as if you were preparing cake batter. Pour the mixture into a lightly-buttered pan and fry on one side. Flip over and cook briefly on the other side. Then fold the omelette quickly and fill it in the same manner as you would the other version. The result is something like a soufléed pancake—a fascinating and memorable substitution for the regular omelette.

Here then is the basic recipe:

6 eggs
2 tbsp. water, milk or stock, depending on your own taste
salt and pepper to taste
1½ tbsp. butter for frying

Note: Dessert omelettes require cream for the liquid portion.

The Fillings

Fillings can be prepared separately or cooked at the bottom of the pan before the eggs are poured in. Many of the fillings can be made in advance and frozen so that all you have to do when you want an interesting omelette is to thaw the filling and get your eggs and pan ready.

Cheese

4 tbsp. of any grated cheese

Tomato

5 thin slices tomato, browned first, and seasoned with ¼ tsp. oregano

Potato

2 medium potatoes, cooked and cubed
¼ tsp. chervil

Onion

2 medium onions, sautéed

Garlic

4 garlic cloves, sliced thinly and sautéed

Chive

5 tbsp. chopped fresh chives

Herb

3 tbsp. chopped fresh parsley
2 tsp. chopped fresh chives
½ tsp. chervil
¼ tsp. tarragon

Mushroom

8 medium mushrooms, sliced and sautéed

Eggplant

5 slices peeled eggplant, browned on both sides

Spinach

3/4 C. cooked spinach, squeezed free of liquid
garlic powder to taste

Ham

3/4 C. chopped cooked ham

Sausage

3 well-cooked sausages, sliced

Chicken Liver

3/4 C. cooked chicken livers, chopped

The following fillings are a little more elaborate and offer you an international selection:

Chinese

½ C. cooked shrimp
¼ C. diced water chestnuts
¼ C. bean sprouts
2 tsp. soy sauce

Alsatian

Fry the omelette in animal or bacon fat
½ C. sauerkraut
½ C. chopped cooked ham

Hungarian

3/4 C. diced cooked ham
1 small onion, sautéed
½ tsp. paprika

Creole

1 small onion, chopped and sautéed and added to the egg mixture
1 pimiento, chopped and sautéed and added to the egg mixture
1 sliced okra, sautéed with garlic
1 tomato, peeled, seeded, chopped and sautéed with garlic
tomato sauce

1. Fill omelette with okra and tomato. Pour tomato sauce over omelette before serving.

Italian

¼ C. chopped fresh parsley, added to the egg mixture
¼ lb. diced mozzarella cheese, for filling omelette

1. This omelette should be folded and filled in the pan and cooked slowly until the cheese melts.

Spanish

1 onion, chopped and sautéed
tomato sauce for saucing the omelette before serving

Western

1 small onion, chopped
¼ C. diced green pepper
½ tomato, peeled, chopped and sautéed
½ C. chopped cooked ham, sautéed with the tomato

Tomato Vegetable

5 thin slices tomato, browned and seasoned with ¼ tsp. oregano
¼ C. chopped green peppers
¼ C. sliced zucchini
¼ C. diced peeled eggplant
¼ C. chopped mushrooms, sautéed in butter
1 small cooked potato, diced
6 tbsp. cooked rice

Garden

¼ C. chopped cooked string beans
2 cooked carrots, sliced
½ C. cooked peas

Tuna

1 small can tuna, drained and flaked
3/4 C. cooked peas
1 pimiento, chopped
1 tbsp. butter
½ tbsp. instant blending flour
½ C. hot milk
salt and pepper to taste

1. Melt butter in a saucepan. Add flour and mix well. Add hot milk and stir until thick and creamy. Add salt and pepper to taste.
2. Combine with other ingredients. Fill omelette and serve.

Crab

½ C. flaked crab meat; or shrimp, cooked lobster or cooked bay scallops
3/4 C. cooked peas
1 tbsp. butter

½ tbsp. instant blending flour
½ C. hot milk
salt and pepper to taste

1. Melt butter in a saucepan. Add flour and mix well. Add hot milk and stir until thick and creamy. Add salt and pepper to taste.
2. Combine with other ingredients. Fill omelette and serve.

Fish

2 tbsp. beer
3/4 C. of any cooked, flaked fish

ZUCCHINI OMELETTE CASSEROLE

Here is a fine dish for luncheon or for a first course. It goes very well with a light, dry white wine.

1 lb. zucchini squash
2 tsp. salt
cheesecloth
4 eggs, separated
1 medium onion, grated
1 C. grated Parmesan cheese
1 large potato, boiled, peeled and mashed
1 garlic clove, finely chopped
1 tbsp. olive oil
¼ tsp. basil
¼ tsp. oregano

1. Peel zucchini and coarsely grate it into a bowl. Sprinkle with 2 tsp. salt and allow to stand 10 minutes. Place small amounts of zucchini in cheesecloth and squeeze until all the moisture is extruded.
2. Combine zucchini, egg yolks, onion, ½ C. cheese, potato, garlic, olive oil and seasonings.
3. Beat egg whites until they form stiff peaks. Fold gently into mixture.
4. Pour into a greased 9" pie tin. Sprinkle with ½ C. cheese. Bake at 350 F. for 30 minutes, or until well-browned. Serves 6 to 8.

MACARONI OMELETTE

1 C. macaroni
4 eggs
¼ C. diced mozzarella cheese
¼ C. chopped Genoa salami
¼ C. chopped prosciutto ham
salt and pepper to taste
1½ tbsp. olive oil

1. Cook macaroni al dente (just slightly chewy).
2. Beat eggs and add cheese, meats and salt and pepper.
3. Mix ½ the cooked macaroni with egg mixture.

4. Heat olive oil in an 11" frying pan. Spread mixture into pan and cover with remaining macaroni. Press down firmly.
5. Cook over high heat until the underside is brown. Invert on a dish and slide back into frying pan. Cook until the underside is lightly browned. Then transfer to a serving dish. Serve hot or cold. Serves 6 to 8.

STEAMED OMELETTE ROLLS

A delicacy from Peking, this dish offers a marvelous way to dress up leftovers.

½ C. chopped cooked chicken, duck or turkey
1 small onion, finely chopped
2 garlic cloves, minced
½ tsp. ground ginger
salt to taste
3 eggs
1/3 C. chicken stock
2 tbsp. dry sherry
1 tsp. monosodium glutamate (MSG), optional

1. Mix well-chopped chicken with onion, garlic and ginger. Season with salt.
2. Beat eggs, add salt to taste.
3. Grease an 8" omelette pan and heat over low heat. Remove from heat and pour in 1/3 the eggs. Cook until set but not too dry, and invert on a platter. Cook the remaining eggs in the same fashion.
4. Spread the omelettes with the meat mixture. Roll tightly and skewer. Place in an oven-proof dish.
5. Place dish on the rack of a large roasting pot or double boiler. Add a little water to the bottom of the pot. Cover.
6. Bring water to a boil. Reduce to a simmer. Steam rolls for 15 minutes. Place in a serving dish.
7. Heat chicken stock. Add sherry and MSG. Pour over the rolls. Cut each roll into 1" slices to serve. Serves 3 to 6.

AMAZING EGG ROLL

What are normally served in Chinese restaurants as egg rolls are, in fact, spring rolls, which can be found under crepes where they actually belong. Egg rolls are simply omelettes that have been filled and deep fried.

3 eggs, beaten
salt to taste
oil
½ lb. ground beef, pork, chicken or cooked and diced shrimp
2 tsp. dry sherry
2 tsp. soy sauce
½ tsp. ground ginger
¼ tsp. cornstarch

1. Beat the eggs well and add salt to taste. Using a 10" skillet, fry 5 or 6 very thin omelettes. The skillet should be well-oiled so that the omelette will slide out easily, retaining a circular shape.
2. Combine remaining ingredients and divide among the omelettes. Pat the mixture evenly over the surface of each one. Roll each omelette like a jellyroll. Seal the edges with a mixture of flour and water in equal parts.
3. Slice each omelette, and deep fry slices separately in oil until golden.
4. Serve with duck sauce and prepared mustard. Serves 8 to 10.

DESSERT OMELETTES

These omelettes make unusual desserts and are excellent when complemented with a dessert wine, or coffee and liqueur.

All of the 6-egg dessert omelettes require 2 tbsp. of cream as the liquid and 1 tbsp. of sugar. Salt and pepper should be omitted. Follow the general directions for making omelettes.

The Fillings

The following recipes are suggested embellishments for the basic dessert omelette.

Jam

Fill three 2-egg omelettes with a jam of your choice. Place them side by side on a platter and sprinkle with confectioners' sugar.

Rum

Sprinkle one 6-egg omelette with sugar and douse with warmed rum. Ignite and serve immediately. You can substitute brandy, cognac, whiskey or kirschwasser for the rum.

Apple

2 large apples, cored, peeled and sliced
butter
sugar
vanilla extract
brandy
sweetened whipped cream

1. Cook apples in butter with sugar, vanilla and a little brandy until tender. Fill one 6-egg omelette.
2. Serve the omelette topped with sweetened whipped cream.

Pineapple

pineapple ice cream
canned crushed pineapple
cornstarch
rum

1. Fill one 6-egg omelette with pineapple ice cream. Fold over and cover with crushed pineapple thickened with cornstarch and flavored with rum. Serve immediately.

QUICHES PAR EXCELLENCE

Quiches are another delightful masterwork of gastronomy. They are, quite simply, custard pies. Served with a crisp green salad, hot French bread, and chilled white wine, quiches make a perfect light meal. They also make good first courses, late suppers and snacks. And they are delightful either hot or cold.

The original notion of the quiche seems to have come from the French province of Lorraine, although there is also a claim that this creamy custard creation hailed first from Germany. In Germany, the quiche is known by the name "kuchen," or cake, from which the German word "kiche" may have come. In France, quiches are particularly popular in the provinces of Alsace and Lorraine, but many varieties are served throughout the country.

The diversity of elegant quiches we offer here has been inspired by culinary ideas from around the world. Here are pies with meat, cheese, vegetables, or fish and seafood fillings—to suit your fancy for appetizers, first courses, luncheons or late suppers. We give a fine, basic pie crust. But, if you are pressed for time, acceptable frozen pie crusts can be purchased for 9" pie tins that will serve quite well.

The Quiche Dough

1 C. flour
¼ C. butter or margarine
1 tsp. salt
1 egg
3 tbsp. ice water
pebbles or dried beans (for baking pie shell)

1. Place flour, butter and salt in a bowl and mix well with a pastry blender. Add egg and water and work into a rolling consistency. Refrigerate for 1 hour.
2. Roll out dough on a lightly-floured board and place it in a 9" pie tin. Crimp edges with a fork. Cover bottom with pebbles so it will remain flat during baking.
3. Pre-bake pie shell at 400 F. for 10 minutes, or until pastry begins to set. Remove pebbles and pour in the filling of your choice. This will make 6 good-sized servings. **Note:** If you use a frozen pie shell, it should also be pre-baked for 10 minutes in the same manner.

Quiche Lorraine

This is the best known of all quiches—the classic one of France. Once you have made and tasted this you will want to try many others.

8 strips of bacon
2 small onions, sliced
1 C. cubed Gruyère or Swiss cheese
¼ C. grated Parmesan cheese
4 eggs
¼ tsp. nutmeg
salt and pepper to taste
2 C. heavy cream

1. Sauté the bacon until it is crisp. Remove bacon from the pan, let drain and then crumble it. Cook the onion in the bacon fat.
2. Place the bacon and onion on the bottom of a 9" pre-baked pie shell. Sprinkle over with the cheeses.
3. Beat eggs well with the seasonings. Add cream and beat again until well-blended.
4. Pour egg mixture into the pie shell, covering the layer of bacon, onion and cheese.
5. Bake at 350 F. for 40 minutes, or until a knife inserted in the center comes out clean. Serves 6 to 8.

Ham and Cheese Quiche

1 onion, diced
1½ C. diced boiled ham
2 C. grated cheddar cheese
4 eggs
salt and pepper to taste
2 C. heavy cream

1. Sauté onion. Combine with ham and cheese and spread on the bottom of a 9" pre-baked pie shell.
2. Beat the eggs well with salt and pepper. Add cream and beat again until well-blended.
3. Pour egg mixture into the pie shell, covering onion, ham and cheese.
4. Bake at 350 F. for 40 minutes, or until a knife inserted in the center comes out clean. Serves 6 to 8.

Frankfurter Quiche

4 frankfurters, skinned and thinly sliced
1 onion, diced and sautéed
½ lb. Swiss cheese, grated
1/8 C. instant blending flour
salt and pepper to taste
4 eggs
¼ tsp. nutmeg
1½ C. light cream

1. Spread the frankfurters, onion and cheese on the bottom of a 9" pre-baked pie shell.
2. Sprinkle with flour and season with salt and pepper.
3. Beat the eggs with the nutmeg. Add cream and beat again until well-blended.
4. Pour egg mixture into the pie shell, covering the layer of frankfurters, onion and cheese.
5. Bake at 350 F. for 40 minutes, or until a knife inserted in the center comes out clean. Serves 6 to 8.

Quiche of Seafood Newburg

This is a variation on a Newburg theme which is fresh, different and truly memorable.

1 C. crab meat, flaked
1 tsp. paprika
1 tbsp. butter
2 tbsp. dry sherry
2 eggs
1 C. heavy cream
dash of Tabasco sauce
salt and pepper to taste

1. Sauté crab meat and paprika in the butter. Add the sherry.
2. Beat the eggs. Add cream and blend well. Mix with the crab meat. Season to taste with Tabasco, salt and pepper.
3. Pour mixture into a 9" pre-baked pie shell.

4. Bake at 350 F. for 30 to 40 minutes, or until a knife inserted in the center comes out clean. Serves 6 to 8.

Shrimp Quiche

3 tbsp. chopped shallots
3 tbsp. butter
3/4 lb. cleaned and deveined cooked shrimp
½ C. grated Swiss cheese
4 eggs
¼ tsp. nutmeg
salt and pepper to taste
1½ C. heavy cream

1. Sauté the shallots in butter and place on the bottom of a 9" pre-baked pie shell. Place the shrimp and cheese on top.
2. Beat the eggs and seasonings well. Add cream and blend well again. Pour over the shallots, shrimp and cheese.
3. Bake at 350 F. for 40 minutes, or until a knife inserted in the center comes out clean. Serves 6 to 8.

Shrimp and Cod Quiche

1 onion, diced
¼ lb. cleaned and deveined cooked shrimp
1½ lb. cooked cod, flaked
¼ lb. mushrooms, sliced
4 eggs
salt and pepper to taste
1 C. light cream

1. Sauté onion.
2. Arrange the shrimp on the bottom of a 9" pre-baked pie shell. Add the flaked cod, onion and mushrooms.
3. Beat the eggs with the salt and pepper. Add cream and blend well. Pour over the contents of the pie shell.
4. Bake at 350 F. for 40 minutes, or until a knife inserted in the center comes out clean. Serves 6 to 8.

Scallop Quiche

1 lb. bay scallops
¼ C. finely chopped celery
2 tbsp. chopped fresh parsley
¼ C. dry white wine
salt and pepper to taste
4 eggs
¼ tsp. nutmeg
1½ C. heavy cream
3 tbsp. Parmesan cheese

1. Combine scallops, celery, parsley, wine, salt and pepper. Spread on the bottom of a 9" pre-baked pie shell.
2. Beat the eggs and nutmeg. Add cream and cheese and blend well. Pour over the contents of the pie shell.
3. Bake at 350 F. for 40 minutes, or until a knife inserted in the center comes out clean. Serves 6 to 8.

Shellfish Quiche Florentine

Florentine always means the addition of spinach in a dish and here is a delightfully different quiche–one of the most original we have used–that combines spinach with shellfish for fascinating results.

2 packages frozen chopped spinach, cooked
½ lb. shellfish, cleaned
4 eggs
¼ tsp. nutmeg
salt and pepper to taste
1½ C. heavy cream

1. Drain the spinach and squeeze out all of the liquid. Place spinach and shellfish on the bottom of a 9" pre-baked pie shell.
2. Beat the eggs and seasonings. Add cream and blend well. Pour over the contents of the pie shell.
3. Bake at 350 F. for 40 minutes, or until a knife inserted in the center comes out clean. Serves 6 to 8.

Flounder Quiche

1 small onion, minced
½ tbsp. minced garlic
¼ C. butter

3/4 lb. flounder fillets
½ tsp. nutmeg
salt and pepper to taste
4 eggs
¼ C. Parmesan cheese
¼ lb. Swiss cheese, grated
1½ C. heavy cream

1. Sauté onion and garlic in butter. Add fish fillets and cook on both sides until done. Flake. Add nutmeg and salt. Spread on the bottom of a 9" pre-baked pie shell.
2. Beat the eggs. Add cheeses and cream, salt and pepper. Blend well. Pour over the contents of the pie shell.
3. Bake at 350 F. for 40 minutes, or until a knife inserted in the center comes out clean. Serves 6 to 8.

Tuna Quiche

1 7-oz. can tuna, drained and flaked
¼ C. grated Swiss cheese
¼ C. grated Parmesan cheese
1 tbsp. instant blending flour
4 eggs
dash of cayenne pepper
salt to taste
1½ C. heavy cream

1. Place the tuna on the bottom of a 9" pre-baked pie shell. Sprinkle with the cheeses and flour.
2. Beat the eggs with the cayenne and salt. Add cream and blend well. Pour over the contents of the pie shell.
3. Bake at 350 F. for 40 minutes, or until a knife inserted in the center comes out clean. Serves 6 to 8.

Sardine and Tuna Quiche

This quiche, and the following one, are Mediterranean inspired. With a tossed green salad and a dry white wine they make excellent meals.

1 7-oz. can tuna, drained and flaked
1 4-oz. can sardines, drained and boned
2 hard-cooked eggs, chopped
3 eggs, beaten
2 tbsp. chopped fresh parsley
2 tbsp. grated onion
1 tsp. capers
1/8 tsp. dried red chili peppers
1/8 tsp. cumin
1/8 tsp. thyme
¼ C. olive oil
salt to taste

1. Mash the sardines with the tuna and combine with remaining ingredients. Place in a 9″ pre-baked pie shell.
2. Bake at 350 F. for 40 minutes, or until a knife inserted in the center comes out clean. Serves 6 to 8.

Tomato Anchovy Quiche

½ 1-lb. can tomatoes, drained and seeded
1 can anchovies
1 large onion, sliced
½ C. grated Swiss cheese
4 eggs
¼ tsp. dried dill
salt and pepper to taste
1½ C. heavy cream

1. Combine tomatoes and anchovies and place on the bottom of a 9″ pre-baked pie shell. Top with onion and cheese.
2. Beat the eggs and seasonings well. Add the cream and blend well. Pour over the contents of the pie shell.
3. Bake at 350 F. for 40 minutes, or until a knife inserted in the center comes out clean. Serves 6 to 8.

Cheese and Potato Quiche

3 boiled potatoes, diced
½ C. grated Parmesan cheese
½ C. grated cheddar cheese
3 eggs
salt and pepper to taste
1½ C. heavy cream

1. Spread the potatoes on the bottom of a 9" pre-baked pie shell and top with the cheeses.
2. Beat the eggs, salt and pepper. Add the cream and blend well. Pour over the contents of the pie shell.
3. Bake at 350 F. for 40 minutes, or until a knife inserted in the center comes out clean. Serves 6 to 8.

Vegetable Quiche

This is another unusual Mediterranean quiche. It is an adaptation of ratatouille, the eggplant and vegetable mixture so popular in the south of France, particularly in Provence.

1 small eggplant, peeled and sliced
2 tomatoes, thickly sliced
flour
olive oil
1 onion, thinly sliced
2 tbsp. chopped fresh parsley
½ tsp. thyme
½ lb. Swiss cheese, diced
4 eggs
¼ tsp. nutmeg
salt and pepper to taste
2 C. heavy cream

1. Dredge eggplant and tomatoes in flour and fry in olive oil until they are tender. Sauté the onion and parsley until wilted. Place these vegetables on the bottom of a 10" pre-baked pie shell. Sprinkle with thyme and cheese.
2. Beat the eggs and seasonings. Add the cream and blend well. Pour over the contents of the pie shell.
3. Bake at 350 F. for 40 minutes, or until a knife inserted in the center comes out clean. Serves 6 to 8.

Quiche Provençal

1 small onion, sliced
1 small green pepper, diced
1 1-lb. can tomatoes, drained and seeded
1 garlic clove, crushed
2 tbsp. olive oil
1 pimiento, diced
4 slices boiled ham, diced
3 eggs
salt and pepper to taste
1½ C. heavy cream

1. Sauté onion, green pepper, tomatoes and garlic in olive oil until tender. Combine with pimiento and ham and spread on the bottom of a 10" pre-baked pie shell.
2. Beat the eggs, salt and pepper. Add the cream and blend well. Pour over the contents of the pie shell.
3. Bake at 350 F. for 40 minutes, or until a knife inserted in the center comes out clean. Serves 6 to 8.

Onion Quiche

1½ C. diced onion
oil
tangy prepared mustard
1 C. grated Swiss cheese
4 eggs
¼ tsp. nutmeg
salt and pepper to taste
1½ C. heavy cream

1. Sauté onion in oil until tender and browned.
2. Brush the bottom of a 9" pre-baked pie shell with mustard. Spread onion on the bottom and sprinkle with cheese.
3. Beat the eggs and seasonings. Add the cream and blend well. Pour over the contents of the pie shell.
4. Bake at 350 F. for 40 minutes, or until a knife inserted in the center comes out clean. Serves 6 to 8.

Spinach Quiche

2 packages frozen spinach, cooked
tangy prepared mustard
1 C. grated Swiss cheese
4 eggs
¼ tsp. nutmeg
salt and pepper to taste
1½ C. heavy cream

1. Squeeze all of the liquid out of the cooked spinach.

2. Brush the bottom of a 9" pre-baked pie shell with mustard. Spread spinach on the bottom and sprinkle with cheese.
3. Beat the eggs and seasonings. Add the cream and blend well. Pour over the contents of the pie shell.
4. Bake at 350 F. for 40 minutes, or until a knife inserted in the center comes out clean. Serves 6 to 8.

THE DELICATE ART OF CREPERY

As with quiches, crepes can be considered another tour de force of gourmet cooking. Actually, they are simply thin pancakes filled with myriad succulent stuffings and sauced in a variety of ways. Crepes are not only festive desserts, but are an attractive way to turn leftovers or simple ingredients into unusual and nourishing meals.

For crepes you will need a 6" frying pan and about a teaspoon of butter for each crepe. Use only enough batter to make a thin coating on the bottom of the pan—usually about 2 tablespoons is ample.

The batter should be smooth and creamy and the cooking process requires a deft hand and some authority, which comes with practice. The pan should be rotated quickly to spread the batter evenly, and the cooking is best done over brisk heat. Crepes need only a minute or two to brown on each side. Each crepe should of course be made individually.

Our filling and saucing suggestions have been largely inspired by European and American cuisine. The basic crepe is an excellent one and there are fillings galore to please all moods and palates. In estimating portions, we suggest you allow 2 crepes per person as a general rule.

The Basic Crepe

1 C. flour
½ tsp. salt
1 tsp. sugar
2 eggs, beaten
1¾ C. milk
melted butter

1. Sift flour, salt and sugar together. Place in a blender with eggs and milk.
2. Blend at high speed for 30 seconds. If bits of flour adhere to jar,

dislodge with a rubber spatula and blend for 2 to 3 seconds more. The batter should be smooth and have the consistency of heavy cream. If it gets any heavier, add more milk, a spoonful at a time. If made without a blender, strain the batter through a sieve. Either method requires refrigeration for at least 2 hours before using. If instant flour is used, however, the chilling can be omitted.
3. Brush a 6" skillet with about 1 tsp. melted butter. Heat the skillet. Pour about 1½ tbsp. batter into the skillet and rotate it quickly to spread the batter over the bottom. Cook over brisk heat until bubbly and lightly browned on one side. Turn and brown the other side lightly. Slide crepe onto a plate. Butter skillet again and proceed until all the batter is used. Makes about 30 crepes.

Note: Batter will keep in the refrigerator at least 3 days. The crepes may be refrigerated or frozen after cooking. When freezing, place a sheet of waxed paper between each crepe and wrap the package carefully to prevent drying out. Bring to room temperature in order to separate.

Filled crepes can be frozen in a freeze-bake-and-serve dish, all ready to pop into the oven for baking.

Crepes Denise

12 to 15 crepes
6 shallots, finely chopped
5 tbsp. sweet butter
½ lb. crab meat, canned or cooked fresh
2 tbsp. instant blending flour
1 C. light cream
2 egg yolks, beaten
1 tbsp. madeira wine
salt and pepper
1 tbsp. chopped chives
3 tbsp. heavy cream, whipped

1. Sauté shallots in 3 tbsp. butter. Add crab meat and mix well. Remove from heat.
2. Melt remaining 2 tbsp. butter in a heavy saucepan. Add flour and blend well. Slowly add light cream, stirring constantly with a whisk.
3. When sauce thickens, remove from heat and add egg yolks and madeira.

Season to taste.
4. Reserve ¼ C. of the sauce. Add remaining sauce and the chives to the crab meat mixture.
5. Spread the crepes with the filling. Roll and place in a greased baking dish, seam side down.
6. Fold whipped cream into remaining ¼ C. sauce and pour over the crepes, covering them completely.
7. Glaze under broiler until brown. Serve hot.

Crepes Venetian

20 to 24 crepes
½ lb. mozzarella cheese
¼ lb. prosciutto ham
2 egg yolks
1 C. heavy cream
5 tbsp. butter
5 tbsp. instant blending flour
1½ C. hot milk
½ tsp. salt
¼ tsp. pepper
½ tsp. nutmeg
1 C. tomato purée
1 garlic clove, crushed

1. Cut 3 slices of mozzarella cheese and reserve. Finely dice remaining cheese and prosciutto.
2. Beat egg yolks and heavy cream together. Reserve.
3. Melt butter in a saucepan and blend in the flour. Slowly add hot milk and cook until mixture thickens. Stir constantly. Season with salt, pepper and nutmeg.
4. Stir in yolk-cream mixture and cook until heated through, but not boiling. Remove from heat.
5. Add prosciutto and major portion of diced cheese, stirring until cheese is melted. Cool slightly.
6. Mix tomato purée, salt to taste and garlic. Spread a thin coating on each crepe. Cover with a generous layer of cheese sauce. Roll crepes.
7. Place crepes in a lightly-buttered, shallow baking dish, seam side down.

Cover with remaining diced cheese and refrigerate for several hours—or place in freezer for ½ hour.
8. When ready to bake, spoon a bit of remaining tomato purée mixture over each crepe and top with slices of mozzarella. Bake at 350 F. for about 20 minutes, or until top is lightly browned.

Crepes à la Suisse

20 crepes
½ C. dry white wine
2 C. grated Swiss cheese
2 tsp. cornstarch
1 tbsp. kirschwasser
pepper to taste
dash of nutmeg
freshly-grated Parmesan cheese
butter

1. Heat wine in a saucepan. Add grated Swiss cheese and stir until smooth and creamy.
2. Add cornstarch dissolved in kirschwasser, and stir until it simmers. Season with pepper and nutmeg and keep warm over hot water.
3. Spread each crepe with Swiss cheese mixture. Roll and arrange, seam side down, in a buttered baking dish. Bake at 450 F. for 5 minutes.
4. Remove from oven and dust generously with Parmesan. Dot with butter and place under broiler until cheese is melted and top is browned.

Danish Crepes with Ham-Apple Filling

30 crepes
2 medium apples, cored, peeled and diced
½ C. diced onion
½ C. diced green pepper
½ C. diced celery
½ C. butter
1 C. flour
2 10½-oz. cans chicken broth
2 tsp. curry powder
2 C. light cream
4 C. diced cooked ham

1. Sauté diced vegetables and apple in ½ C. butter until tender. Sprinkle

with flour and stir until smooth.
2. Stir in broth, curry powder and cream until mixture thickens. Fold in ham.
3. Divide filling among crepes. Roll and place seam side down in a heavily-buttered casserole.
4. Bake at 400 F. for 15 to 20 minutes.

Spinach-Filled Crepes with Mozzarella

12 crepes
2/3 C. chopped cooked spinach
½ C. ricotta cheese
2 tbsp. grated Parmesan cheese
2 eggs, lightly beaten
salt and pepper to taste
½ lb. mozzarella cheese, thinly sliced
1 recipe Basic Béchamel Sauce

1. Squeeze all liquid from the spinach. Combine spinach with ricotta, Parmesan, eggs, salt and pepper. Mix well.
2. Divide filling among crepes. Roll and place seam side down in a lightly-buttered, oven-proof dish. Top with Béchamel Sauce.
3. Cover rolls with mozzarella slices and bake at 375 F. for 10 to 15 minutes.
4. Place under broiler until the cheese is browned.

Ham and Mushroom Crepes

8 crepes
¼ C. chopped celery
¼ lb. mushrooms, thinly sliced
½ an onion, diced
2 tbsp. butter
salt and pepper to taste
8 slices boiled ham
1 can cream of mushroom soup
1/3 C. light cream
½ C. sour cream

1. Sauté the celery, mushrooms and onion in butter until tender. Season with salt and pepper.
2. Place 1 slice of ham on each crepe. Divide sautéed vegetables among the

crepes and roll. Place seam side down in a lightly-buttered baking dish.
3. Combine soup, cream and sour cream. Pour over the crepes.
4. Bake at 350 F. for 15 minutes.

Crepes with Ricotta and Prosciutto

12 crepes
1 lb. ricotta cheese
1/8 lb. prosciutto ham, chopped
2 tbsp. milk
dash of salt
Parmesan cheese, grated
butter

1. Combine ricotta, prosciutto, milk and salt.
2. Fill crepes and fold. Place in a buttered baking dish. Sprinkle with Parmesan and dot with butter.
3. Bake at 350 F. for 15 minutes.

Crab Meat Crepes

12 crepes
¼ C. thinly sliced small mushrooms
1 small onion, finely chopped
1 tbsp. butter
2 C. flaked crab meat
dash of Worcestershire sauce
dash of Tabasco sauce
2 tbsp. dry sherry
1 tbsp. chopped fresh parsley
salt and pepper to taste
3/4 recipe Basic Bèchamel Sauce
1 can condensed cheddar cheese soup
1½ C. milk
¼ tsp. dry mustard
Parmesan cheese, grated

1. Sauté mushrooms and onion in butter until tender.

2. Combine with flaked crab meat, Worcestershire, Tabasco, sherry and parsley. Season with salt and pepper. Combine with Béchamel Sauce.
3. Divide the filling among the crepes. Fold and place in a lightly-buttered baking dish.
4. Combine cheddar cheese soup with the milk. Add mustard and bring to a boil. Pour over crepes and sprinkle with Parmesan.
5. Bake at 350 F. for 15 minutes, or until bubbling. Place under broiler until top is browned.

Seafood Crepes with Herbs

Make ½ the Basic Crepe recipe, and add ½ tsp. tarragon, 1 tbsp. chopped fresh parsley and 1 tbsp. chopped chives to the batter.

16 crepes
8 small mushrooms, sliced
2 tbsp. finely chopped onion
3 tbsp. butter
½ tsp. tarragon
1 tbsp. chopped fresh parsley
1 tbsp. chopped chives
1/3 C. dry white wine
1 C. flaked crab meat
1 C. diced cooked shrimp
1 C. diced cooked lobster
salt and pepper to taste
1 can condensed cream of mushroom soup
1 C. milk
½ tsp. curry powder (optional)

1. Sauté mushrooms and onion in butter for about 3 minutes. Add the tarragon, parsley and chives. Mix well. Add the wine and simmer until the liquid is reduced to about half.
2. Add shellfish to the mixture and season with salt and pepper.
3. Divide the filling among the crepes. Fold and place in a lightly-buttered baking dish.
4. Combine mushroom soup with the milk. Bring to a boil and add curry powder. Pour over crepes.
5. Bake at 350 F. for 15 minutes.

A French Variation

If you wish to make French seafood crepes, proceed as in the previous recipe, but substitute the following sauce for the mushroom soup, milk and curry powder combination.

2 tbsp. butter
3/4 C. grated Swiss cheese
2 tbsp. instant blending flour
1½ C. heavy cream
salt and pepper to taste
1/3 C. dry white vermouth

1. Place the crepes in a lightly-buttered baking dish. Dot with butter and sprinkle with ¼ C. Swiss cheese.
2. Combine flour, cream, remaining cheese and salt and pepper. Mix well.
3. Heat vermouth in a saucepan and boil until it is reduced to about half. Add the sauce mixture and heat slowly until it thickens. Pour over the crepes.
4. Bake at 350 F. for 20 minutes. Then place under broiler to brown top.

Chicken Crepes

16 crepes
¼ C. diced mushrooms
½ an onion, diced
3 tbsp. butter
3 C. diced cooked chicken
1 C. diced boiled ham
½ tsp. oregano
½ C. dry white wine
salt and pepper to taste

1. Sauté mushrooms and onion in butter until tender. Add chicken, ham and oregano and heat for 2 minutes. Add the wine and cook over a fairly high heat until all of the liquid has been absorbed. Season to taste with salt and pepper. Add The Binding Sauce.

The Binding Sauce

3 tbsp. butter
3 tbsp. instant blending flour
1 C. heavy cream
½ C. chicken bouillon
salt and pepper to taste

1. Melt butter in a saucepan. Add the flour and blend well. Add the cream and chicken bouillon and cook until the sauce thickens. Season with salt and pepper.
2. Combine enough of this sauce with the filling mixture to bind well.
3. Divide among the crepes. Roll and place seam side down in a lightly-buttered baking dish.

The Topping Sauce

Make the French sauce in the previous recipe, adding ¼ C. Swiss cheese.

1. Pour over crepes. Bake at 350 for 20 minutes, or until bubbling. Place under broiler to brown top.

Crepes Filled with Cheese and Spinach

12 crepes
1½ C. chopped cooked spinach
1 C. sliced small mushrooms
1 C. ricotta cheese
1 egg, beaten

1. Squeeze all liquid from the spinach.
2. Sauté mushrooms. Combine with spinach, ricotta and egg.
3. Make The Cheese Sauce.

The Cheese Sauce

4 tbsp. butter
4 tbsp. instant blending flour
2½ C. hot half-and-half milk
1 C. grated Swiss cheese
¼ tsp. nutmeg
salt and pepper to taste

1. Melt the butter in a saucepan. Add the flour and blend well. Add the hot half-and-half milk and cheese and stir until sauce thickens. Add seasonings.

2. Add 3 tbsp. of The Cheese Sauce to the spinach mixture. Divide among the crepes. Roll and place in a lightly-buttered baking dish, seam side down. Pour remaining sauce over rolls.
3. Bake at 350 F. for 20 minutes, or until bubbling. Place under broiler until top is browned.

Chinese Spring Rolls

Here is a Chinese version of crepes that originated in Canton. As mentioned before, spring rolls are actually what we commonly call "egg rolls" in this country.

The Spring Roll

1 C. flour
3/4 C. water
½ tsp. salt
peanut oil

1. Combine flour, water and salt. Mix well and let stand for ½ hour.
2. Grease a heated skillet with peanut oil. Pour a small amount of batter into the skillet and quickly tip in all directions to spread it. Cook over brisk heat until lightly browned on 1 side. Turn and brown the other side lightly. Slide crepe onto a plate. Repeat until all batter is used. Makes about 12 spring rolls.

The Filling

½ lb. cooked chicken or pork, diced
1 C. diced shrimp, crab or lobster
cornstarch
2 tsp. dry sherry
peanut oil
1 can bamboo shoots, drained and sliced
3/4 C. shredded Chinese mushrooms
3 tbsp. water
1 tbsp. soy sauce

1. Combine 2 tsp. cornstarch with the sherry. Add meat and fish.

2. Heat 4 tbsp. peanut oil in a skillet and sauté the mixture over high heat for 3 minutes. Remove from heat.
3. Heat 2 tbsp. peanut oil and sauté bamboo shoots and mushrooms over high heat for 2 minutes, stirring constantly.
4. Combine 1 tbsp. cornstarch with 3 tbsp. water. Combine with meat and vegetable mixtures and add soy sauce. Stir until liquid thickens.
5. Divide filling among the crepes. Fold bottom edge up and sides inward. Roll and seal with a mixture of flour and water in equal parts.
6. Deep fry rolls in peanut oil until golden. Serve with duck sauce and prepared mustard. Serves 12.

DESSERT CREPES

Dessert crepes make an elegant, finishing flourish for any meal. Here is a medley of distinguished crepe desserts from several parts of the world. You will find the famed crepes of France–Crepes Suzette–and zesty crepes from Normandy redolent with the mixed accents of apples and brandy. There is a variety of flamboyant flaming crepes, interesting recipes from Germany and Austria, and unusual crepes with nuts, chocolate and exotic berry sauces. With a diminutive cup of dark demi-tasse or espresso coffee, and a thin glass of brandy or liqueur, any of these will make a memorable dessert.

The Basic Dessert Crepe

1-1/8 C. flour
4 tbsp. sugar
3 eggs, beaten
1½ C. milk
pinch of salt
1 tbsp. melted sweet butter
1 tbsp. cognac, or brandy

1. Blend flour, sugar, eggs, milk, salt. Add butter and cognac. Mix well.

2. Refrigerate for at least 2 hours. If you use instant blending flour, however, chilling can be omitted.
3. Refer to directions for frying The Basic Crepe on page 83. Makes about 30 crepes.

Palacsinta (Austro-Hungarian dessert crepes)

15 dessert crepes
1 12-oz. jar apricot preserve
1½ C. sliced almonds
2 C. sour cream
confectioners' sugar

1. Spread crepes with preserve. Sprinkle with almonds and roll.
2. Place in a buttered baking dish, seam side down. Spoon the sour cream over the rolls and sprinkle with almonds.
3. Bake at 325 F. for 10 to 15 minutes. Serve hot, sprinkled with confectioners' sugar.

Crepes Flambées (Flaming Crepes)

1. Place strawberries, raspberries or sliced bananas in a bowl with a sprinkling of sugar and kirschwasser. (Orange liqueur or cognac can substitute for the kirschwasser.) Let stand for 1 hour. Fill crepes with the mixture and fold.
2. Flame by pouring warmed cognac over the crepes and setting alight. Serve immediately.

Crepes à la Normande

12 dessert crepes
2 lbs. crisp apples, peeled, cored and roughly chopped
sugar to taste
2 tbsp. heavy cream
¼ tsp. almond extract
2 tbsp. rum, cognac or apple brandy

½ C. ground almonds
2 tbsp. melted butter
2 tbsp. sugar
2 tbsp. slivered blanched almonds
½ C. cognac, rum or apple brandy, warmed

1. Cook apples, in a little water, in a covered pan over low heat for 20 minutes. Stir occasionally until apples are tender.
2. Add sugar and raise heat. Boil until mixture is fairly thickened–about 4 to 5 minutes. Add more sugar if necessary while cooking.
3. Stir in cream, almond extract and rum. Mix well.
4. Divide mixture among crepes and sprinkle with ground almonds. Roll carefully, tucking in the ends. Place crepes in a buttered bake-and-serve dish. Pour on the melted butter and sprinkle with 2 tbsp. sugar and slivered almonds.
5. Bake at 375 F. for several minutes.
6. Just before serving, pour warmed cognac over crepes. Set aflame and bring flaming to the table. Spoon flaming liquor over crepes until fire subsides.

Apricot Crepes

18 dessert crepes
½ lb. dried apricots
2/3 C. sugar
4 tbsp. butter
rum
vanilla ice cream

1. Soak apricots in 2 C. water overnight. Bring to a boil and cook until tender. Sieve or blend to make a purée.
2. Combine sugar and ½ C. water and boil for 5 minutes. Add ¼ C. rum and the purée. Keep warm.
3. Melt the butter in a skillet or chafing dish. Add 2 tbsp. rum and heat the crepes. Then fill crepes with the purée and fold. Top with vanilla ice cream. Serve immediately.

Crepes Suzette

12 dessert crepes
2 oranges
2 pieces lemon peel
2/3 C. sugar
2/3 C. butter
6 tbsp. orange liqueur

1. Peel oranges and reserve the peel. Squeeze out juice and combine with

chopped lemon and orange peels. Combine with sugar, butter and orange liqueur.

2. Place ½ the mixture in a chafing dish and heat 1 crepe at a time by placing a pale, or uncooked, side of the crepe in the dish. Cook 1 side, then the other. Fold into quarters and draw to side of the dish. Repeat until all crepes have been heated through. You may have to add more of the sauce in order to heat all the crepes.

3. Douse crepes with remaining sauce and ignite. Serve immediately.

Crepes with Nuts and Butter

10 dessert crepes
¼ C. butter
¼ C. sugar
1 C. ground nuts
grated sweet chocolate
chocolate sauce

1. Place crepes in oven to warm.
2. Combine butter and sugar. Spread on 1 side of each crepe. Sprinkle with nuts and a little grated chocolate. Fold and serve topped with ready-made chocolate sauce.

Variations

1. Substitute any fruit sauce for the chocolate sauce.
2. Serve topped with whipped cream instead of chocolate sauce.
3. Serve topped with coffee or vanilla ice cream.

Additional Dessert Crepe Fillings

Alsatian

Fill crepes with currant jelly or raspberry jam. Fold and sprinkle with sugar. Glaze in a hot oven.

Breton

Fill crepes with glacéed chestnuts flavored with rum. Fold and sprinkle with sugar. Glaze in a hot oven.

Apple and Chestnut

Use 5 or 6 slices of apple for each crepe. Cook them in butter and sugar until tender. Fill crepes with apples and a ½ slice glaceéd chestnut. Fold and sprinkle with sugar. Glaze in a hot oven.

Fruit

Fill crepes with compote of fresh fruits steeped in brandy. Fold and top with vanilla ice cream just before serving.

Macaroon

Use 2 crushed macaroons for each crepe. Combine with currant jelly and fill crepes. Fold and sprinkle with sugar. Glaze in a hot oven.

The German Dessert Crepe

6 eggs, beaten
¼ tsp. salt
1 tbsp. sugar
2 C. milk
1½ C. flour, sifted
½ lb. butter, melted

1. Add salt, sugar and milk to beaten eggs. Beat well and add the flour. Refrigerate for at least 2 hours.

2. Use a 12" skillet for these crepes. Melt 1 tbsp. butter for frying each crepe individually, and use about 4 tbsp. batter for each crepe. Fry as usual for crepes. Makes 6 to 8 crepes.

The Filling

cinnamon
sugar
currant jelly, or blueberry, raspberry or lingonberry sauce
2 tbsp. lemon juice
rum, cognac, kirschwasser or other fruit brandy

1. Sprinkle each crepe with cinnamon, sugar and lemon juice. Place some jelly on each crepe and roll. Place in a serving dish and sprinkle with rum. Ignite and serve immediately.

BLINI

Blini are simply Russian crepes or pancakes. Serve them stacked on an attractive platter which has been kept warm on a hot-tray and covered with a cloth. It is fun to offer a variety of sauces and spreads when you serve blini. Try a few of these: red or black caviar (lumpfish is less expensive), sour cream, cognac mixed with Roquefort cheese, hard-cooked eggs, mashed sardines, herring, smoked salmon, melted butter and onions. The traditional way to serve blini is with caviar, onions and sour cream. But we think variety is diverting and tends to produce an atmosphere of conviviality, especially when vodka or cognac is also served.

The Basic Blini

2 eggs
pinch of salt
1 tsp. sugar
2 C. milk
1 C. flour, sifted
butter for frying

1. Beat the eggs, salt and sugar for 2 minutes. Gradually add the milk. Stir this mixture into the flour. Beat into a runny batter, making certain there are no lumps. This batter can be made very quickly in a blender. It should be refrigerated for a few hours, or until it is well-chilled, before frying the blini.
2. Smear a small frying pan with butter and heat it. When it is hot, drop in about 2 tbsp. of batter. Fry 1 side only until it is golden brown. Remove and place on a floured plate and fill. Fold and keep warm until time to serve. Makes 30 blini. Serves 10.

Another way, which we prefer, is to fry both sides of the blini and stack them in a warm oven. When all are cooked, we then serve them with a choice of fillings.

Note: Blini can be prepared ahead of time and frozen. To freeze, place waxed paper between them and then wrap completely to avoid their drying out. When you wish to use them, simply remove the number you need, thaw them and heat in the oven.

The Buckwheat Blini

Here is an interesting and more traditional alternate recipe for blini. They can be made either in a skillet or poured onto a griddle like pancakes. The buckwheat flour can be purchased in health food stores. These blini must rise like bread before they are cooked, and they are always served filled with caviar, onions and sour cream. (You can of course substitute the less expensive lumpfish for the caviar.)

1 package dry yeast
1 C. lukewarm water
2 C. lukewarm milk
2 C. buckwheat flour, sifted
3 eggs, separated
2 tbsp. butter
1 tsp. sugar
salt to taste

1. Dissolve the yeast in ½ C. lukewarm water. Combine remaining water and ½ C. lukewarm milk and add to the yeast.
2. Add 1 C. flour and mix well. Cover the bowl and place in a warm, draft-free place for 3 hours.

3. Beat the egg yolks and add remaining milk, butter, sugar and salt. Add to the yeast mixture along with the remaining cup of flour.
4. Beat the egg whites until they hold stiff peaks. Fold into batter. Cover and allow to stand about 1 hour.
5. Without stirring, ladle the batter onto a greased griddle. Brown on both sides. Use about ¼ C. batter for each blini. Makes 30 blini. Serves 10.

BLINTZES

Blintzes are a type of crepe that are especially popular among the Jewish people of Eastern Europe. They can be served for lunches, first courses, snacks, late suppers and even for desserts. Today, of course, they are well-known all over the world.

Bessie Kaufman's Blintzes

1 recipe The Basic Crepe
3 C. pot cheese
1 C. farmer cheese
1 egg, beaten
4 tsp. sugar
5 tbsp. sour cream
butter

1. Combine the cheeses, egg, sugar and sour cream. The resulting mixture should be creamy but not overly loose. If the mixture is too dry, add more sour cream. More sugar can be added if you prefer a sweeter filling.
2. Divide the filling and spread on the crepes. Fold the sides of each crepe slightly inward and roll like a jellyroll. The finished blintz should be about 4½" long.
3. Fry blintzes in butter until they are golden on both sides. Serve topped with additional sour cream. Makes about 30 blintzes.

Note: Blintzes can be frozen filled and later heated when needed.

Alternate Cheese Filling

4 C. drained cottage cheese
2 eggs, beaten
4 tsp. sugar
½ tsp. cinnamon

1. Combine ingredients and proceed as in Bessie Kaufman's Blintzes for filling and frying.

The Fruit Filling

4 C. fruit, washed and drained
½ C. sugar, or to taste
½ C. water
2 tbsp. cornstarch

1. Use apples, blueberries, cherries, peaches, apricots or plums.
2. Place in a pan with the water and sugar. Cook until fruit is tender. Add cornstarch to thicken. Proceed as before for filling and frying blintzes.

KNISHES

Knishes are another kind of delicious filled pancake that originated among the Jewish people, but are now a universal treat. They can be served hot or cold; for lunches, snacks or whenever you please.

The Knish Dough

1 package dry yeast
1¼ C. lukewarm water
3½ C. flour
2 tbsp. sugar
1 tsp. salt
2 eggs, beaten
4 tbsp. butter
melted butter (for brushing knishes)

1. Dissolve the yeast in lukewarm water. Combine the rest of the

ingredients and add to the yeast.
2. Cover and stand in a warm, draft-free place for 3 hours.
3. Place the dough on a lightly-floured surface and punch down. Knead until it becomes smooth and elastic.
4. Pinch off pieces of dough the size of golf balls and roll them out to 1/8" thick. Cover these rounds with a cloth and let stand for 1 hour or more.
5. Fill the rounds. Fold over and seal edges. Brush with melted butter.
6. Bake at 350 F. until browned. Makes 30 knishes.

The Knish Fillings

Each of the filling recipes makes enough to fill 30 knishes.

Cheese

2 lb. cottage cheese
2 eggs
1/3 C. sugar
1 tbsp. lemon juice
1/3 C. bread crumbs
salt to taste

1. Combine all ingredients and fill knishes. Bake as directed.

Fruit

2 to 3 cans cherry, blueberry or apple pie fillings, drained

1. Use drained fruit to fill knishes. Bake as directed.

Fruit and Cheese

1½ to 2 cans drained pie filling
1 recipe Cheese Filling

1. Use 1 tbsp. drained pie filling on top of the cheese mixture when filling knishes. Bake as directed.

Chicken Liver

1½ lb. chicken livers
2 onions, chopped
butter (for sautéing)
1/3 C. bread crumbs
2 medium potatoes, boiled and mashed (optional)

1. Sauté livers and onion in butter and add bread crumbs and potatoes. Fill knishes. Bake as directed.

Mashed Potato

2 onions, chopped
butter (for sautéing)
1/3 C. bread crumbs
2 C. mashed potatoes

1. Sauté onion in butter and add bread crumbs.
2. Add mashed potatoes. Mix and fill knishes. Bake as directed.

KREPLACH

Kreplach are Jewish dumplings. They are delicious when served with sour cream. Serve them for lunch or for snacks.

The Kreplach Dumpling

1 egg
2/3 C. flour
¼ tsp. salt
2 tsp. milk

1. Combine all ingredients and knead on a lightly-floured board until a

mass is formed. Roll out and cut into 2½" squares. Makes 10 to 12 dumplings.

The Filling

1 lb. cottage cheese
2 egg yolks
1½ tsp. sugar
½ tsp. cinnamon
salt to taste

1. Combine all filling ingredients and divide among the squares. Fold to form triangles and press edges with a fork to seal.
2. Drop triangles 1 at a time into boiling water. Boil for 10 minutes. Reduce heat and cook an additional 5 minutes.

APPLE DUMPLINGS

The Dumpling Dough

2 C. flour, sifted
1 tbsp. baking powder
1 tbsp. sugar
salt to taste
4 tbsp. butter
2/3 C. milk

1. Combine the flour, baking powder, sugar and salt. Cut in the butter with a pastry blender. When the mixture is coarse and crumbly, add the milk.
2. Knead the dough on a lightly-floured board for 3 minutes. Refrigerate for at least 2 hours.
3. Prepare The Filling and The Syrup.

The Filling

3 apples, cored, peeled and diced
1 tsp. lemon juice
¼ C. raisins
¼ C. sugar
½ tsp. cinnamon

1. Combine all filling ingredients and set aside.

The Syrup

1 C. sugar
1 C. brown sugar
4 tbsp. butter
2 C. water

1. Combine all syrup ingredients and boil for 5 minutes. Pour into a 9" x 12" pan.
2. Remove the dough from refrigerator and roll out on a lightly-floured board into a large square.
3. Cut the dough into 4 squares. Divide the filling among them and fold each to form a triangle. Press the edges together with a fork.
4. Place the triangles in the syrup and sprinkle with additional sugar.
5. Bake at 400 F. for 25 minutes. Serves 4.

SOUFFLE ROLL WITH BROCCOLI

Here is one of the most unusual and interesting recipes we know—an omelette soufflé roll stuffed with broccoli in a creamy cheese sauce. It is impressive to serve and can be a first course for the most elegant dinner, a luncheon or even a main dish.

The Roll

4 tbsp. butter
½ C. instant blending flour
¼ tsp. salt
2 C. milk
4 eggs, separated
2 packages frozen broccoli
1/3 C. grated Swiss cheese

1. Grease a 10" x 15" jellyroll pan and line it with waxed paper. Grease the waxed paper and dust it with flour.
2. Melt the butter over low heat and add flour and salt. Stir in the milk and cook until mixture thickens.
3. Beat the egg yolks and add to the mixture. Beat the egg whites until stiff and fold into the mixture. Spread into the pan.
4. Bake at 325 F. for 45 minutes. The roll should be golden and spring back when touched.
5. While the roll is baking, cook and drain the broccoli. Cut it into 1" pieces.

The Sauce

1/3 C. butter
1/3 C. instant blending flour
2 C. hot milk
salt and pepper to taste
3 oz. grated Swiss cheese

1. Melt the butter and add flour and milk. Season and stir. Add the cheese and stir until the sauce thickens.
2. To remove roll from the pan, cover it with waxed paper and flip it over on a flat surface. Peel off the waxed paper which lined the pan.
3. Arrange the broccoli and cheese on top of the roll and pour ½ The Sauce on top. Lift the end and roll like a jellyroll. Place on a serving platter and top with remaining sauce. Serves 4 to 6.

Alternate Filling

3 tbsp. chopped onion
6 mushrooms, sliced
2 tbsp. butter
1 C. chopped cooked spinach
1 C. chopped boiled ham
1 tbsp. tangy prepared mustard
¼ tsp. nutmeg
2 3-oz. packages cream cheese, softened
salt and pepper to taste

1. Sauté onion and mushrooms in butter until tender. Cook until all liquid has been absorbed.
2. Combine with the rest of the filling ingredients and place on the roll. Roll and top with The Sauce. Serves 4 to 6.

V. SPOTLIGHT CENTER STAGE MAIN COURSES:

Meats, Poultry and Pastas

Cocktails and delectable hors d'oeuvres have been served, the atmosphere is one of mellowness blended with a soupçon of pleasurable expectancy. Now it is time for your great moment—the presentation of the main course. At this time, you should be able to offer your central attraction in as blithe a manner as if a phantom caterer had somehow descended into your kitchen, worked her magic and unobtrusively disappeared. All you have to do right now is ready yourself—to accept with cool poise the barrage of compliments on your prepared-in-advance rolled and stuffed creation.

What will you choose? Here is an array of gourmet delights. If veal suits you, we have offered a baker's dozen of terrific ideas from which to choose. There are hearty, stuffed beef roasts, regal and mouth-watering things to do with boned lamb and numerous pungent varieties of chicken and beef roulades. We have also included budget-stretching stuffed pastas, and a compendium of stuffing ideas for fowl.

Mix and match. Vary and combine. Do let your imagination roam, for your own fun and that of your fortunate guests!

MAIN COURSE SERVING TIPS

1. Delightful fare is all the more so when spiced with a dash of romance. If you have a separate dining room, close the doors and keep your resplendent table a surprise. If the dining area is part of the living room, dress it to the hilt anyway–with your prettiest cloth, matching napkins, your best silver or stainless, water goblets and wine glasses. Use separate salad plates, colorful baskets lined with folded linen napkins for bread or rolls; and candles, which you will light with a flourish as the guests come to the table. Flowers are a must. But remember to keep the vase small enough–it should not dominate the table or impede conversation.

2. Make your own place cards and be as elaborate as you like. People will appreciate your flights of fancy and enjoy the surprise of finding where you have placed them at the table. This also avoids any last-minute awkward scramble if you are hastily obliged to assign places while seeing to other tasks. Attractive place-card holders may be obtained in any good department store or specialty shop.

3. Handwritten menus will heighten festivity. Everyone likes to know what is being served, and a menu adds anticipation for the next course. Besides, a name imparts a special aura to anything–even if it is a self-created concoction.

4. For extra fun, we recommend interesting napkin folding as a specially-folded napkin adds dash to any setting.

5. For efficiency, set up your own silent butler–a small serving table or shelf near the dining table. This should contain clean linens, dishes and silver for the next course, and an electric hot-tray if you have one. You can then officiate without having to dash back and forth to the kitchen.

6. Attractive cook-and-serve ware and interesting trivets for bubbling casseroles make excellent aids. In addition, it is wise to acquire some miniature matching china ash trays and cigarette holders that go well with your dishes. In deference to your guests, the cigarette holders should be filled. You should also have attractive, filled receptacles for salt and pepper.

7. Cultivate a sense of theme, color and balance. As an artist creates a canvas, plan your menu with a central theme. From hors d'oeuvres to dessert, your choices should be complementary. Avoid repeating. For example, if you have determined on a tomato hors d'oeuvre, don't serve a stuffed tomato, however delightful, as a side dish; or a main dish with tomato sauce.

Subordinate minor themes to the major one. If the main course is richly sauced, plan simpler accompaniments–an unadorned appetizer or perhaps a frank dessert of fruit and cheese. And, for an absolutely drop-dead effect, try to please the eye as well as the palate. Remember that color is important! Try to imagine what the plates will look like once they are filled. And, of course, use plates and serving dishes which complement the food. Stuffed tomatoes and eggplant surrounding startling white fish fillets on a colorful platter will create keen anticipation.

8. Whatever you choose, serve wine! As a simple rule of thumb, dry red wines should be served with red meats, mainly beef or lamb. White wines and pink or rosé wines, can be served with chicken, veal or pork. Normally, white wines are preferred with fish. The wine need not be expensive. If it is well-chosen, however, it will add an indefinable ingredient of verve and festivity to your central attraction, and help to produce a truly memorable moment.

ROULADEN GALORE!

Here is zesty rouladen, Germany's great gift to the gastronome, served in a variety of different styles. Quite simply, rouladen is top round of beef, sliced very thinly, and then stuffed and treated in a number of delectable ways.

Rouladen Heidelberg

6 slices round steak
Dijon mustard
salt and pepper
6 strips of bacon
6 slices of onion
6 strips of sour pickle
1 whole onion, sliced
1½ tbsp. butter, or margarine
1½ tbsp. oil
¾ C. water
1 tbsp. dry red wine, or dry sherry
2 tbsp. ketchup
1 tsp. cornstarch

1. Pound meat slices until very thin. (Your butcher may do this for you.)
2. Spread mustard on each steak slice and sprinkle with salt and pepper. Add 1 strip of bacon, 1 slice of onion and 1 strip of pickle. Roll and tie securely with string.
3. Sauté rolls in a mixture of butter and oil with the whole, sliced onion until well-browned.
4. Add water and cook covered for 1 hour. If rolls seem dry, add a bit more water.
5. Remove rolls and place on a heated platter. Remove the string. Add the wine and ketchup to the pan juices. To thicken gravy, mix cornstarch in a little cold water and add to the pan mixture. Pour hot gravy over the rolls. Serves 6.

Rouladen Hongroise–Hungarian Style

1 2-lb. round steak, cut into 6 to 8 slices
1 package instant mashed potatoes
(approximately 4 servings)
shortening
1 4-oz. can mushrooms
1 medium onion, chopped
½ tsp. rosemary
½ tsp. thyme
3 tbsp. flour
½ tsp. salt
1/8 tsp. pepper
1 cube beef bouillon
1 C. hot water
½ C. sour cream
2 tsp. dry sherry
1 tsp. chervil

1. Pound meat slices until very thin.
2. Prepare potatoes according to package directions. Sauté mushrooms and onion and add to the potatoes. Add ¼ tsp. rosemary and ¼ tsp. thyme. Spread this mixture on each steak slice. Roll and tie with string.
3. Combine flour, salt and pepper. Dip rolls in this mixture and fry until brown.
4. Dissolve bouillon cube in the hot water. Add remaining rosemary and thyme and pour over rolls. Cook covered about 45 minutes.
5. Remove rolls from the pan and remove string from the rolls. Skim off all fat and blend sour cream into the pan gravy. Heat to boiling point and add sherry and chervil. Pour hot gravy over rolls and serve. Serves 6 to 8.

Rouladen à la Flamande–Flemish Style

2-lbs. beef round, cut into 8 slices
½ lb. bulk sausage meat (no casing)
2 tbsp. chopped onion
¼ C. dry bread crumbs
salt and pepper to taste
8 strips of bacon
2 tbsp. butter, or margarine

6 small white onions, halved
¼ C. flour
2 12-oz. cans beer
3 cubes beef bouillon
1 4-oz. can mushroom stems and pieces, drained
2 tbsp. chopped fresh parsley
cooked hot noodles

1. Pound meat slices until very thin. Sprinkle with salt and pepper.
2. Combine sausage, chopped onion and bread crumbs in a mixing bowl. Blend well. Divide mixture equally among beef slices.
3. Shape sausage mixture into a long, thin roll at one end of each beef slice. Roll to enclose filling. Wrap a bacon strip around each roll. Tie with string.
4. Brown rolls in butter in a Dutch oven. Add white onion halves and brown. Mix flour with ½ C. beer. Pour over meat and add remaining beer. Add bouillon cubes and stir to blend.
5. Cover and simmer over low heat for 1½ hours, or until beef is tender. Add mushrooms and parsley and simmer another 12 minutes.
6. Remove string and place rouladen on a platter lined with hot noodles. Skim excess fat from gravy. Spoon gravy over meat. Serves 4.

Rhenish Beef Rouladen–Rhineland Style

1 2-lb. flank steak
½ tsp. salt
¼ tsp. pepper
meat tenderizer
1 onion, finely chopped
1 scallion, chopped
1 garlic clove, minced
½ lb. sweet Italian sausage (casing removed)
¼ lb. ground beef
1 tbsp. chopped fresh parsley
1 tbsp. chopped chives
2 slices white bread, soaked in milk
½ C. heavy cream
3 strips of bacon
¼ C. flour
2 tbsp. butter
2 large onions, thinly sliced
2 carrots, thinly sliced
½ tsp. thyme
1 bay leaf
1 1-lb. can tomatoes
1 C. dry red wine
1 C. beef bouillon

1. Pound flank steak until very thin. Sprinkle with salt, pepper and tenderizer. Set aside for 30 minutes.

2. Combine chopped onion, scallion, garlic, sausage, ground beef, parsley, chives, bread (crumbled) and cream. Spread on steak. Roll to enclose filling. Wrap bacon strips around roll. Tie with string.
3. Sprinkle with flour and brown in butter in a Dutch oven. Put sliced onion, carrots, thyme and bay leaf into the pot while the meat is browning.
4. Add tomatoes, wine and bouillon. Cover and place in 350 F. oven for 1½ to 2 hours, or until meat is tender.
5. Remove rouladen from the oven and remove string. Purée sauce in a blender. Pour over rouladen and serve. Serves 4.

Note: The sauce should be carefully skimmed of all fat while cooking. You may skim ½ C. or more during cooking. This rouladen is ideally made in advance and served on the second day. You will need to remove fat that has solidified during overnight refrigeration.

Czechoslovakian Rouladen

1 2-lb. round steak, cut into 4 slices
tangy prepared mustard
8 strips of bacon, halved
1 sour pickle, cut into fourths
3 small onions, sliced
salt and pepper to taste
1 tbsp. instant blending flour
1½ C. sour cream
cooked noodles

1. Pound steak slices until very thin. Spread mustard on each slice. Place 4 half-strips of bacon and 1 piece of pickle on each slice. Roll and skewer. Season with salt and pepper.
2. Place rolls in a deep skillet and sear for 2 minutes. Add onion slices and ½ C. water to the pan. Cover and simmer about 1½ hours. Keep pan covered and do not turn rolls.
3. Remove rolls from the pan. Allow juices to cool slightly, then add the flour and sour cream. Replace rolls and simmer 30 minutes longer.
4. Serve on a bed of boiled noodles. Serves 4.

Broiled Flank Kebobs

1 1½- to 2-lb. flank steak
3/4 C. dry red wine
¼ C. oil
2 garlic cloves, crushed
¼ tsp. rosemary
1 tsp. Worcestershire sauce
salt and pepper to taste
¼ tsp. oregano
¼ tsp. basil
8 small pearl onions

1. Slice the steak along the grain into 8 pieces.
2. Combine all other ingredients, except the pearl onions. Place in a non-metallic dish with the steak and marinate at least 5. hours in the refrigerator. Be sure that the dish is securely covered.
3. Remove steak from the marinade and roll each slice around a pearl onion. Skewer to secure.
4. Broil rolls to desired degree of doneness. This steak is also an excellent barbecue dish when basted with the marinade. Serves 4.

Rolled Flank Steak with Pineapple

2 1½- to 2-lb. flank steaks
1 C. oil
2/3 C. water
¼ C. soy sauce
2 tsp. Worcestershire sauce
1/8 tsp. chili pepper, crushed
2 tsp. lemon pepper
1 1-lb. can water-packed pineapple chunks

1. Slice each steak along the grain into 8 slices.
2. Combine all other ingredients, except the pineapple. Place in a non-metallic dish with the steak and marinate at least 5 hours in the refrigerator. Be sure that dish is securely covered.
3. Remove steak from the marinade and roll each slice around a pineapple chunk. Skewer to secure.

4. Broil to desired degree of doneness. Or barbecue, basting frequently with the marinade. Serves 8.

Pepper-Stuffed Steak

1 2-lb. sirloin steak, 1½" thick
1 tbsp. butter
½ C. chopped green pepper
1 garlic clove, minced
salt and pepper to taste
¼ C. dry red wine
2 tbsp. soy sauce

1. Trim excess fat from meat. Slash each side of steak almost to bone.
2. Sauté green pepper and garlic in butter and season with salt and pepper to taste.
3. Fill each of the slashes with sautéed mixture and skewer closed.
4. Combine wine and soy sauce and brush over steak.
5. Grill over coals to desired degree of doneness. Serves 4.

Beef-Stuffed Flank Steak

1 2½-lb. flank steak
salt and pepper to taste
4 tbsp. butter
1 onion, chopped
¼ lb. mushrooms, sliced
1 lb. ground beef
¼ C. heavy cream
½ tsp. oregano
¼ C. chopped fresh parsley
½ C. beef bouillon
½ C. red wine

1. Slice steak about 3/4 of the way through and open like a book. Season with salt and pepper.
2. Sauté onion and mushrooms in 2 tbsp. butter until tender.
3. Combine ground beef, cream, oregano, parsley and sautéed vegetables. Blend well and spread inside the steak. Close steak and roll tightly. Tie with string.
4. Melt remaining 2 tbsp. butter in a skillet and brown the roll lightly. Add bouillon and wine and simmer about 1½ hours, or until meat is tender.
5. Remove string. Slice to serve. Serves 4 to 6.

Stuffed Flank Steak Marengo

2 1½- to 2-lb. flank steaks
½ lb. fresh mushrooms, sliced
2 stalks celery, chopped
¼ C. chopped onion
1 C. chopped green pepper
1 package prepared stuffing
dash of garlic powder
salt and pepper to taste
flour
4 tbsp. butter
½ C. dry red wine
2 C. tomato sauce

1. Sauté mushrooms, celery, onion and green pepper. Prepare stuffing as directed on package and add the sautéed vegetables. Add seasonings.
2. Pound the steaks as flat as possible. Divide the filling and place on top of each steak. Roll tightly and skewer.
3. Dredge in flour and season outside with salt and pepper.
4. Melt butter in a large skillet. Brown rolls on all sides.
5. Mix wine and tomato sauce. Pour over rolls and simmer about 1 hour, or until meat is tender. Serves 8.

Les Oiseaux sans Têtes

This is a beef version of the famous French classic that is normally made with veal.

12 slices round steak,
6" square and ¾" thick
butter
1 onion, chopped
6 mushrooms, chopped
½ tsp. thyme
3 tbsp. chopped fresh parsley
1 garlic clove, chopped
1½ C. unflavored bread crumbs
salt and pepper to taste
1 egg, beaten
12 slices prosciutto ham
oil
flour
1 C. beef bouillon
½ C. dry red wine

1. Brown onion and mushrooms in butter. Add thyme, parsley, garlic, bread crumbs and salt and pepper. Beat egg and add to the mixture with about ¼ C. melted butter.
2. Pound steak slices as thinly as possible. Spread stuffing on each piece and top with slice of prosciutto. Roll and tie with string.
3. Place 3 tbsp. butter and 3 tbsp. oil in a skillet. Dredge each roll in flour and brown on all sides. Add bouillon and wine to the skillet. Cover and simmer 1½ to 2 hours.
4. Remove string. Serve with the gravy. Serves 6.

Variations

1. Omit prosciutto and use bacon on top of the stuffing.
2. Add 1 C. sour cream to the gravy before serving.

Bracciole

4 thinly-sliced minute steaks
salt and pepper to taste
butter
12 strips sweet red pepper
4 hard-cooked eggs, sliced
16 slices pepperoni sausage (casing removed)
2 garlic cloves, minced
1 tsp. oregano
½ tsp. basil
½ C. grated Parmesan cheese
3 C. tomato sauce

1. Pound steaks as thinly as possible. Season with salt and pepper.
2. Cook strips of red pepper in butter until tender.
3. Place 3 slices of pepper on each steak. Add egg slices, sausage and seasonings. Sprinkle cheese on top. Roll and tie with string.
4. Place in a casserole. Pour tomato sauce over rolls. Cover.
5. Bake at 350 F. for 1 hour. Remove string. Serves 4.

Genovese Beef Roll

1 2-lb. round steak
½ lb. ground veal
¼ lb. diced prosciutto ham
¼ C. grated Parmesan cheese
1 egg, beaten
¼ C. chopped fresh parsley
½ tsp. basil
½ tsp. oregano
¼ tsp. thyme
salt and pepper to taste
olive oil
butter
3/4 C. chopped onion
1 garlic clove, chopped
3 tbsp. cognac
½ C. dry red wine
1 C. beef bouillon
½ 6-oz. can tomato paste

1. Pound the steak as thinly as possible.
2. Combine veal, prosciutto, cheese, egg, parsley and seasonings.
3. Spread stuffing on the steak. Roll and tie with string.
4. Place a little olive oil and butter in a skillet. Sauté the onion and garlic. Place roll in the skillet and brown. Add the cognac and simmer for 3 minutes. Add the wine and simmer for 5 minutes. Add bouillon and tomato paste and simmer covered until tender. Serves 4.

STUFFED CABBAGE

Almost every culture has produced some version of this marvelous dish. It is economical, simple to prepare, and freezes well. Stuffed cabbage is both a hearty main dish and an attractive first course. And it makes a nice appetizer.

To prepare cabbage for stuffing, core it and separate the leaves. Parboil the leaves in salted water for 5 minutes. Place stuffing in the center of the leaf, fold two sides inward, and roll.

Jewish Stuffed Cabbage

1 head of green cabbage
3 tbsp. oil
½ C. chopped onion
1 garlic clove, minced
1 lb. ground beef
2 C. cooked rice
1 tsp. salt
¼ tsp. ground pepper
1 C. tomato sauce
1 C. beef bouillon

1. Prepare cabbage according to directions.
2. Heat oil in a skillet. Add onion and garlic and cook lightly. Add ground beef and brown. Add the rice, salt and pepper. Divide and stuff and roll cabbage leaves.
3. Place rolls in a large pot and cover with tomato sauce and bouillon. Cover. Cook over medium heat for 1 hour. Serves 6.

Austrian Stuffed Cabbage

1 head of green cabbage
½ lb. bulk sweet sausage meat (no casing)
1 lb. ground veal
1 egg
1 tbsp. chopped fresh parsley
½ tsp. dried dill
1 garlic clove, chopped
1 small onion, minced
salt and pepper to taste
2 C. beef bouillon
1 6-oz. can tomato paste

1. Prepare cabbage according to directions.
2. Combine meats, egg, seasonings and onion. Stuff and roll cabbage leaves.
3. Place rolls in a large pot with bouillon and tomato paste. Simmer covered about 1¼ hours. Add more liquid if necessary. Serves 6.

Italian Stuffed Cabbage

1 head of green cabbage
½ lb. ground beef, cooked
2 eggs
1 C. chopped cooked spinach
½ C. grated Romano cheese
1 tbsp. chopped fresh parsley
salt and pepper to taste
5 tbsp. olive oil

1. Prepare cabbage according to directions.
2. Combine meat, eggs, spinach, cheese, parsley, salt and pepper. Stuff and roll cabbage leaves.
3. Place rolls in a baking dish. Add olive oil. Bake covered at 350 F. for 25 minutes. Add a little water during baking if pan gets too dry. Serves 6.

Greek Stuffed Cabbage

The use of cinnamon with meat is unique to the Near East. Cinnamon produces an exotic flavor that is not to everyone's taste, but it is nevertheless worth trying. (The cinnamon can be omitted without harming this dish at all.)

1 large head of green cabbage
½ C. olive oil
1 8-oz. can tomato sauce
1 bay leaf, crushed
2 C. beef bouillon

Stuffing

½ lb. ground beef
½ lb. ground lamb
1 egg
1 onion, chopped
½ tsp. oregano
½ tsp. mint
¼ tsp. cinnamon
salt and pepper to taste
3/4 C. raw rice
2 tbsp. tomato sauce
3 tbsp. olive oil
½ C. dry white wine.

1. Prepare cabbage according to directions.
2. Combine all stuffing ingredients. Stuff and roll cabbage leaves. Place rolls in layers in a large pot. Sprinkle each layer with olive oil, tomato sauce and bay leaf.
3. Add the bouillon to the pot with enough water to cover. Cover and simmer over low heat for 1 hour. Serves 6.

Sweet and Sour Stuffed Cabbage

1 head of green cabbage
1½ lb. ground beef
1 C. cooked rice
½ C. raisins
1 small onion, finely chopped
1 egg, beaten
salt and pepper to taste
1 can beef bouillon, undiluted
2 tsp. cornstarch
2 tsp. cider vinegar
½ C. tomato sauce
1 tbsp. brown sugar
¼ C. water

1. Prepare cabbage according to directions.
2. Combine beef, rice, raisins, onion, egg and salt and pepper. Mix well and stuff and roll cabbage leaves. Place rolls in a pot with beef bouillon and simmer covered for 45 minutes.
3. Remove rolls. Add a little of the pot liquid to the cornstarch. When it is lump-free, return it to the pot. Add vinegar, tomato sauce, sugar and water. Boil until sauce is clear.
4. Pour sauce over cabbage rolls and serve. Serves 6.

American Stuffed Cabbage

1 head of green cabbage
½ C. milk
1 can condensed cream of mushroom soup
1 lb. cooked ground beef
1 C. frozen peas
1 C. cooked rice
1 egg, beaten
1 tsp. onion powder
salt and pepper to taste

1. Prepare cabbage according to directions.
2. Combine milk and soup. Add 1 C. of this mixture to ground beef. Then add peas, rice, egg, onion powder, salt and pepper. Stuff and roll cabbage leaves.
3. Place rolls in a baking dish. Pour remaining soup over rolls. Bake covered at 350 F. for 1 hour. Serves 4.

Polynesian Stuffed Cabbage

From the islands of the Pacific, here is a most unusual recipe for stuffed cabbage. The coconut cream that is used in this recipe can be purchased in any store that sells Caribbean foods.

1 medium head of green cabbage
½ lb. ground pork
½ lb. cleaned cooked shrimp, chopped
½ lb. white fish fillet, cooked and flaked
1 C. finely chopped onion
salt and pepper to taste
3/4 C. coconut cream
aluminum foil

1. Prepare cabbage according to directions.
2. Chop 2 of the cabbage leaves and combine with pork, shrimp, fish fillet, onion, salt and pepper. Divide filling and place on leaves. Spoon 2 tbsp. of coconut cream over each. Stuff and roll cabbage leaves.
3. Place each roll in a sheet of aluminum foil. Seal foil well and place on a rack over a pan of water in the oven.
4. Bake covered at 350 F. for 1 hour. Serves 8.

BEEF MEDLEY

Beef Pie

1½ recipes "The Dough"
2 tbsp. butter
1 medium onion, chopped
4 tbsp. instant blending flour
1½ C. beef bouillon
1 package frozen mixed vegetables, thawed
2 large potatoes, boiled and cubed
2 C. diced leftover meat, or 3/4 lb. cooked ground beef
salt and pepper to taste

1. Roll out "The Dough" for a 9" pie crust, reserving about 1/3 for the top crust.
2. Sauté onion in butter. Add the flour and blend well. Add bouillon and cook until smooth and thick. Add vegetables, potatoes, meat, salt and pepper. If filling is too dry, add a little more bouillon.
3. Place filling in prepared pie crust and cover with the top crust. Prick top with a fork. Bake at 400 F. for 30 to 35 minutes, or until top is browned. Serves 8.

Ground Beef Roll

1lb. ground round beef
1 small onion, chopped
1 garlic clove, chopped
3/4 C. soft bread crumbs
¼ C. light cream
2 eggs, beaten
¼ C. chopped fresh parsley
½ tsp. basil
salt and pepper to taste
1 6-oz. can tomato paste
3 slices boiled ham
1½ C. chicken bouillon
1 bay leaf, crumbled
¼ tsp. rosemary

1. Sauté onion and garlic. Combine with bread crumbs, cream, eggs, parsley, basil, salt and pepper, and ½ the tomato paste. Add ground beef and blend well.
2. Turn mixture out onto a large sheet of waxed paper. Form into a large rectangle. Place ham slices on top and roll tightly and carefully.
3. Brown the roll on all sides. Dilute remaining tomato paste in bouillon and pour over the roll. Add bay leaf and rosemary.
4. Simmer covered for about 1 hour, basting frequently with pan juices. Serves 6.

South American Pot Roast

1 4-lb. beef rump roast, boned
1 medium jar stuffed green olives, sliced
4 strips of bacon, cooked and crumbled
1 garlic clove, minced
½ C. instant blending flour
½ C. dry red wine
2 8-oz. cans tomato sauce

1. Make 3 lengthwise slits in the roast. Combine olives and bacon and stuff the slits. Skewer slits closed.
2. Place roast on a large sheet of heavy-duty aluminum foil. Combine remaining ingredients and pour over the roast. Fold foil over top of roast and seal well.
3. Bake at 325 F. for 2 to 2½ hours. Serves 6.

STUFFED PORK CHOPS

Here is a variety of interesting, internationally inspired preparations to dress up the simple, unprepossessing pork chop.

Stuffed Pork Chops with Raisins

6 rib pork chops, thickly cut
salt and pepper to taste
2 tbsp. butter
3/4 C. raisins
1 small onion, chopped
½ C. finely chopped celery
1/3 C. hot water
1½ C. seasoned stuffing mix
1½ C. orange juice
1/8 tsp. mace
1/8 tsp. ground clove
1½ tsp. cornstarch

1. Slit each chop almost 3/4 of the way through. Season with salt and pepper.
2. Sauté ½ C. raisins with onion and celery in butter until soft. Mix water with stuffing and add to sautéed mixture. Stuff the chops and skewer closed.
3. Place the chops in a skillet and add orange juice, mace and clove. Cook over low heat for 1 hour. Add more orange juice if pan is too dry.
4. Mix cornstarch with a little water and add to the sauce with remaining ¼ C. raisins. Simmer until thick. Serves 6.

Floridian Stuffed Pork Chops

8 loin pork chops, thickly cut
¼ C. butter
1 small onion, chopped
2½ C. crumbled corn muffins
½ C. orange juice
3 tbsp. chopped nuts
2 tsp. grated orange rind
salt and pepper to taste
½ C. light corn syrup
½ tsp. mace

1. Slit each chop almost 3/4 of the way through.
2. Sauté onion in butter until tender. Add corn muffin crumbs. Add orange juice, nuts and 1 tsp. orange rind. Season with salt and pepper. Stuff chops and skewer closed.
3. Combine syrup, remaining orange rind and mace. Brush this mixture lightly over chops. Place chops in a baking dish. Cover and bake at 375 F. for 1 hour.
4. Pour remaining glaze over chops and bake uncovered for 30 minutes longer. Serves 8.

Italian Stuffed Pork Chops

6 loin pork chops, thickly cut
1 C. soft bread crumbs
1½ C. grated mozzarella cheese
½ tsp. oregano
½ tsp. thyme
salt and pepper to taste
¼ C. chicken bouillon
2 tbsp. olive oil
2 tbsp. butter
3/4 C. tomato sauce
¼ C. dry white wine

1. Slit each chop almost 3/4 of the way through.
2. Combine bread crumbs, cheese and seasonings. Add a little chicken bouillon and blend. Stuff the chops and skewer closed.

3. Heat oil and butter in a large skillet. Brown the chops on both sides. Drain excess fat and add tomato sauce, remaining bouillon and white wine.
4. Cover tightly and simmer for 1 hour. Serves 6.

Pork Chop Surprise

8 loin pork chops, thickly cut
1 large can apricot halves
8 blanched whole almonds
salt and pepper to taste
¼ C. ketchup
1 tbsp. lemon juice
½ tsp. onion powder
½ tsp. dry mustard
2 tbsp. butter

1. Slit each chop almost 3/4 of the way through. Reserve apricot syrup. Place an apricot half and 1 almond in each chop. Skewer closed and season with salt and pepper.
2. In a blender, blend remaining apricots and ½ C. of apricot syrup. Place in a saucepan and add ketchup, lemon juice, onion powder, mustard and butter. Bring to a boil and simmer covered for 20 minutes. Place chops in a casserole and pour the sauce over them.
3. Cover and bake at 375 F. for 1 hour. Uncover and bake for 20 minutes longer. Serves 8.

STUFFED SPARE RIBS

2 2-lb. racks of pork spare ribs
¼ C. butter
1 medium onion, finely chopped
½ C. chopped celery
1 C. chopped peeled apple
1¼ tsp. salt
¼ tsp. pepper
4 C. prepared stuffing mix
1 C. milk

1. Sauté onion in butter. Add celery, apple, salt, pepper, stuffing mix and milk to the pan. Blend well.

2. Place 1 rack of ribs on a cookie sheet. Spread with the stuffing. Place second rack on top, aligning ribs so that you will be able to cut through both layers.
3. Cover and bake at 350 F. for 1 hour.

The Glaze

½ C. apricot or plum jam
¼ C. soy sauce
¼ tsp. ground ginger
¼ tsp. black pepper

1. Combine jam, soy sauce, ginger and pepper. Spread this glaze over the ribs.
2. Bake uncovered for 30 minutes longer. Serves 6.

ELEGANT HAMS

The French do it with puff paste and paté. We have Americanized and streamlined the process, so that you can have a magnificent ham creation in no more than 15 minutes. All of these pastry-wrapped hams are ideal for buffets and larger groups. They also make dramatic main courses for a formal dinner.

Ham en Croûte

1 3-lb. canned ham
2 tbsp. butter
1 small onion, chopped
½ lb. fresh mushrooms, sliced
1/8 tsp. thyme
1/8 tsp. rosemary
salt and pepper to taste
1½ recipes "The Dough", or 1½ C. biscuit mix and 3 oz. milk
1 egg, beaten

1. Remove all gelatin from surface of the ham and wipe dry with paper towel.

2. Sauté onion and mushrooms in butter with thyme, rosemary, salt and pepper. Cool slightly and place on top of ham.
3. Roll out "The Dough" on a lightly-floured board. Reserve a small portion to be used for decoration.
4. Carefully wrap ham in the dough, joining the crust on the bottom. Seal any cracks in the dough by smoothing edges together with fingers that have been dipped in water.
5. Roll out reserved dough and cut into stems, leaves or flowers. Secure to ham by brushing one side with beaten egg. Brush entire ham with egg. Prick lightly in the center.
6. Bake at 400 F. for 30 to 35 minutes. If crust browns too quickly, turn heat down to allow ham to heat through. Serves 6.

Ham en Croûte Savannah

1 5-lb. canned ham
3/4 C. chopped dried apricots
½ C. chopped almonds, pecans or walnuts
½ small can crushed pineapple, drained
1/8 tsp. thyme
2 recipes "The Dough", or 2 C. biscuit mix and ½ C. milk
1 egg, beaten

1. Follow general directions for preparation of the ham and dough given in "Ham en Croûte" recipe.
2. Combine apricots, nuts, pineapple and thyme. Place on top of the ham and wrap as directed. Brush with beaten egg.
3. Bake at 400 F. for 35 to 45 minutes. If crust browns too quickly, turn heat down to allow ham to heat through. Serves 10.

The Savannah Sauce

½ can apricot nectar
¼ C. honey
¼ tsp. ground allspice

1. Combine apricot nectar, honey and allspice in a saucepan. Bring to

a boil and simmer 15 minutes. Use as sauce for the ham.

Ham en Croûte with Cheese

1 5-lb. canned ham
3 oz. diced cheddar, Swiss or Monterey Jack cheese
2 tbsp. dry mustard
2 recipes "The Dough", or 2 C. biscuit mix and ½ C. milk
1 egg, beaten

1. Follow general directions for preparation of the ham and dough given in "Ham en Croûte" recipe.
2. Slash top of ham at ½" intervals and stuff with cheese.
3. Sprinkle dry mustard over the top and wrap as directed.
4. Bake at 400 F. for 45 minutes. If crust browns too quickly, turn heat down to allow ham to heat through. Serves 10.

ROLLED AND STUFFED HAM

Ham Rolls

8 ½" slices boiled ham
2 C. unflavored bread crumbs
2/3 C. melted butter
½ C. chopped raisins
½ tsp. salt
1/8 tsp. pepper
½ tsp. sage
½ C. chopped walnuts
chicken bouillon

1. Combine bread crumbs, butter, raisins, salt, pepper, sage and walnuts.
2. Spread on ham slices. Roll and skewer.

3. Place rolls in a baking dish. Cover with chicken bouillon.
4. Bake at 350 F. for 30 minutes. Serves 4.

Stuffed Ham Cones

This makes a particularly nice luncheon dish.

6 slices boiled ham
½ tsp. unflavored gelatin
1 can beef bouillon, undiluted
1 C. frozen mixed vegetables, cooked
6 cone-shaped paper cups

1. Dissolve the gelatin in the bouillon and add cooked vegetables.
2. Place in refrigerator until mixture thickens.
3. Line each paper cup with a slice of ham and fill with thickened vegetable mixture. Return to refrigerator until cones are firm. Unmold before serving. Serves 6.

Mousse-Stuffed Ham

1 3-lb. canned ham
2 packages unflavored gelatin
½ C. cold water
¼ C. chopped celery
¼ C. combined mixture of minced olives, green peppers, chives and pimientos
1 C. sour cream
1 C. mayonnaise

1. Remove all gelatin from surface of ham and wipe dry with paper towel. Remove a 1" horizontal slice from the top of the ham. Scoop out center of ham, leaving a 1" thick shell on bottom and sides.
2. Grind scooped out ham in a food mill or grinder.
3. Dissolve gelatin in the water and place in a double boiler. Cook until all gelatin particles are absorbed. Combine gelatin with all other ingredients. Fill the ham. Replace top slice and chill until firm. Serves 6.

Ham Turnovers

1½ recipes "The Dough"
2 C. ground cooked ham
2/3 C. finely chopped onion
2 hard-cooked eggs, chopped
2 tbsp. chopped peeled cucumber
1 tbsp. tangy prepared mustard
2 tbsp. chopped fresh parsley

1. Prepare "The Dough" according to directions. Roll out on a lightly-floured board. Cut into four 6" circles, using a plate as a guide.
2. Combine all filling ingredients and divide evenly among the 4 circles. Fold over and press edges, sealing with fingers that have been dipped in water.
3. Bake at 375 F. until golden. Serves 4.

Ham Rolls Mandarin

This is a famous northern Chinese classic–and a knockout!

8 thin slices boiled ham
1 C. minced cooked chicken
1 tsp. minced garlic clove
1 tbsp. sesame oil
1 tsp. monosodium glutamate (MSG), optional
½ tsp. cornstarch
salt and pepper to taste
oil for frying

1. Combine chicken, garlic, sesame oil, MSG and cornstarch. Mix well and add salt and pepper.
2. Divide mixture and spread on ham slices. Roll tightly and secure with toothpicks. Fry in hot oil for 3 to 5 minutes until brown but not crisp. Drain and remove toothpicks.

The Mandarin Sauce

1 tbsp. cooking oil
½ C. bamboo shoots
¼ lb. fresh mushrooms, sliced
1 small onion, sliced

¼ C. chopped walnuts
1 tsp. sugar
2 tbsp. ketchup
¼ C. dry sherry
½ can chicken broth
1 tsp. cornstarch

1. Sauté bamboo shoots, mushrooms and onion in oil until tender. Add walnuts, sugar, ketchup, sherry and broth. Simmer for 3 minutes. Add cornstarch and mix well. Pour over ham rolls and serve. Serves 4.

VARIED VEAL BIRDS

Here follows a collection of classic preparations from many countries. If you prefer–for economy or other reasons–in most of these cases you can substitute a chicken breast, a slice of beef bracciole or a pork cutlet for the ubiquitous thin slice of veal. So, improvise, mix and match, and have fun!

Veal Birds Genovese–Italian Style

12 veal cutlets, pounded thin
12 thin slices prosciutto ham
12 slices Gruyère, or Swiss cheese
2 tbsp. butter or margarine
½ C. dry white wine
2 tbsp. tomato paste
1 bay leaf
¼ tsp. basil
½ tsp. oregano
¼ tsp. thyme
salt and pepper to taste

1. Place a slice of prosciutto and a slice of cheese on each cutlet. Roll carefully, tucking ham around the cheese so it will not leak out during cooking. Skewer rolls well with toothpicks. Brown in butter.
2. Combine remaining ingredients. Pour over rolls. Cover and simmer for about 20 minutes. Mashed potatoes and sautéed zucchini are nice accompaniments. Serves 6.

Veal Birds à la Greque–Greek Style

12 veal cutlets, pounded thin
butter or margarine
12 scallions, finely chopped
3 tbsp. finely chopped fresh parsley
1 garlic clove, finely chopped
12 chopped artichoke hearts, canned or cooked frozen
2 8-oz. cans tomato sauce
salt and pepper to taste
2 tbsp. instant blending flour
dry sherry

1. Sauté scallions, parsley, garlic and artichoke hearts in 6 tbsp. butter. Add 4 tbsp. tomato sauce to mixture and season with salt and pepper.
2. Blend flour into mixture. Simmer 5 minutes. Add 4 tbsp. sherry.
3. Place 1 tbsp. or so of mixture on each veal slice. Roll and skewer.
4. Brown rolls in 4 tbsp. butter. Place in a casserole. Pour butter from skillet over rolls. Add remaining tomato sauce and 1 C. sherry.
5. Bake covered at 350 F. until tender. Serves 6.

Oiseaux sans Têtes–Veal Birds French Style

6 veal cutlets, pounded thin
½ lb. ground pork
salt and freshly ground pepper to taste
½ C. finely chopped onion
1 tsp. minced garlic clove
1 tbsp. chopped chives
¼ tsp. dried marjoram
1 C. fresh bread crumbs
2 eggs, beaten
1 tbsp. dried parsley, or ¼ tsp. dried savory

1. Cook the pork in a saucepan and add salt and pepper. Stir to break up pieces. Add onion, garlic, chives, marjoram, bread crumbs, eggs and parsley. Mix well.
2. Add equal part of filling mixture to the center of each cutlet. Roll carefully, tucking all edges in. Tie securely with string.

The Sauce

4 tbsp. butter
½ C. finely chopped onion
1 tsp. minced garlic clove
1 tbsp. chopped chives
¼ tsp. marjoram
1 tbsp. dried parsley, or ¼ tsp. dried savory
1 C. chopped peeled tomatoes
1 C. finely chopped mushrooms
1½ C. canned beef gravy
1 bay leaf
3 tbsp. dry white wine
cooked rice

1. Heat 2 tbsp. butter and add onion, garlic, chives, marjoram and parsley. Add tomatoes, mushrooms, gravy and bay leaf. Cover and simmer for 10 minutes.
2. Heat remaining 2 tbsp. butter and brown rolls on all sides. Place rolls in a baking dish. Add sauce and wine and cover. Bake in pre-heated oven at 350 F. for 45 minutes. Remove string from the rolls. Serve with rice. Serves 3.

Roman Veal Birds

8 veal cutlets, pounded thin
1/3 lb. salt pork
¼ C. chopped fresh parsley
½ tsp. oregano
2 tbsp. Parmesan or Romano Cheese
8 slices boiled ham
2 tbsp. olive oil
2 tbsp. butter
2 C. tomato sauce

1. Combine pork, parsley and oregano in a chopping bowl. Chop as finely as possible and blend in the cheese.
2. Place a slice of ham on each cutlet. Spread stuffing on ham. Roll and tie with string.

3. Brown the rolls in a combination of butter and olive oil. Pour tomato sauce over rolls and simmer covered until tender. Remove string from the rolls. Serves 4.

Veal Birds Florentine

6 veal cutlets, pounded thin
2 tbsp. butter
1 medium onion, chopped
¼ lb. mushrooms, chopped
1 10-oz. package frozen spinach, thawed
¼ tsp. oregano
¼ tsp. basil
salt and pepper to taste
¼ C. grated Parmesan cheese
½ tsp. grated lemon rind
¼ C. olive oil
1 C. chicken bouillon

1. Melt the butter in a skillet and cook onion and mushrooms until tender.
2. Drain spinach well so there is no liquid remaining in the leaves. Add to the onion and mushrooms. Combine remaining ingredients, except olive oil and bouillon and add to cooking mixture. Simmer covered about 10 minutes.
3. Divide filling mixture and place on cutlets. Roll and tie with string.
4. Sauté rolls in olive oil until brown on all sides. Drain off oil and add bouillon. Cook slowly for 45 minutes. Remove string from rolls. Serves 3.

Veal Birds Venetian Style

6 veal cutlets, pounded thin
2 tbsp. cream cheese
3 large mushrooms, finely chopped
2 tbsp. chopped celery
4 tbsp. butter
1/3 C. port wine
salt and pepper to taste
½ tsp. instant blending flour

1. Combine cream cheese, mushrooms and celery. Place a little in the center of each slice of veal. Roll and tie with string.

2. Melt ½ the butter in a skillet and sauté the rolls until browned on all sides. Add the wine and cook for 20 minutes. Remove rolls from the skillet and the string from the rolls.
3. Add remaining butter and flour to the pan juices. Cook until sauce thickens. Pour over rolls. Serves 3.

Veal Birds Versailles

12 veal cutlets, pounded thin
½ lb. ground pork
2 tbsp. dried parsley
2 eggs, beaten
½ tsp. marjoram
1 C. soft bread crumbs
butter
1 large onion, chopped
3 garlic cloves, minced
2 tbsp. chopped chives
4 large tomatoes, peeled and chopped
½ lb. mushrooms, chopped
1 bay leaf

1. Place pork in a saucepan and cook over high heat until browned. Add parsley, eggs and marjoram. Remove from heat and add bread crumbs.
2. Sauté onion, garlic and chives in 1 tbsp. butter until tender. Add tomatoes, mushrooms and bay leaf. Simmer covered while making Brown Béchamel Sauce.
3. Combine the pork with simmering vegetables. Divide among cutlets. Roll and tie with string.
4. Melt 1 tbsp. butter in a skillet and brown rolls on all sides. Remove string from the rolls.

The Brown Béchamel Sauce

5 tbsp. butter
4 tbsp. instant blending flour
1½ C. beef bouillon
salt and pepper to taste
4 tbsp. dry white wine

1. Melt butter in a saucepan. Add flour and blend well. Add bouillon. Cook until sauce is thick and creamy. Season with salt and pepper. Combine wine with the sauce. Pour over rolls and simmer covered for 1 hour. Serves 6.

Veal Birds with Capers

6 veal cutlets, pounded thin
¼ C. butter
½ onion, finely chopped
2 tbsp. chopped celery
½ C. chopped cooked ham
salt and pepper to taste
heavy cream
1½ C. fresh bread crumbs
flour
1 C. chicken bouillon
1 bay leaf, crumbled
2 tbsp. capers, well-drained

1. Melt ½ the butter and cook onion and celery until tender. Add ham, salt and pepper, 2 tbsp. cream and bread crumbs. Mix well.
2. Divide filling among the cutlets. Roll and tie with string. Dredge in flour and brown in remaining butter.
3. Place rolls in a baking dish. Pour bouillon over rolls and add bay leaf.
4. Bake at 350 F. for 45 minutes. Remove rolls from the baking dish and the string from the rolls.
5. Add ½ C. cream to pan juices and bring to a boil. Season with salt and pepper and add capers. Pour over rolls and serve. Serves 3.

Veal Birds with Anchovies

12 veal cutlets, pounded thin
½ C. diced Gruyère cheese
12 anchovies
salt and pepper to taste
1/3 lb. butter
1/3 C. dry white wine

1. Place a little cheese and 1 anchovy fillet on each cutlet. Season with salt and pepper. Roll and tie with string.
2. Brown rolls in butter until brown on all sides. Cook for 10 minutes. Add the wine and cook covered for 10 minutes longer. Remove string from the rolls. Serve with sauce from the pan. Serves 6.

Veal Birds with Oysters

8 veal cutlets, pounded thin
1½ C. soft bread crumbs
¼ tsp. thyme
1 egg, beaten
2 tbsp. chopped fresh parsley
butter
salt and pepper to taste
8 oysters
flour
¼ C. dry white wine
½ C. chicken bouillon
½ C. heavy cream

1. Combine bread crumbs, thyme, egg, parsley and 4 tbsp. melted butter. Season with salt and pepper. Blend well and form balls, with 1 oyster inside each ball.
2. Place balls on cutlets. Roll and tie with string.
3. Dredge rolls in flour and brown them in 3 tbsp. butter. Add wine and bouillon. Simmer covered for 30 minutes. Remove the rolls from the pan and the string from the rolls.
4. Add cream to the pan juices. Cook for 2 minutes. Pour sauce over rolls. Serves 4.

Veal Birds Scandinavian

12 veal cutlets, pounded thin
½ C. butter
1 C. chopped fresh parsley
2 onions, quartered
2 carrots, sliced
salt and pepper to taste
2 C. beef bouillon
3/4 C. heavy cream
1 tbsp. instant blending flour

1. Melt ½ the butter and sauté parsley lightly. Spread parsley on cutlets. Roll and tie with string.

2. Melt remaining butter and sauté onion and carrots. Add rolls and brown. Season with salt and pepper. Add bouillon and simmer covered for 45 minutes.
3. Remove rolls from the pan and string from the rolls. Add cream and flour to the pan juices. Stir until sauce thickens. Pour over rolls. Serves 6.

Veal Birds with Vegetable Purée

6 veal cutlets, pounded thin
6 tbsp. butter
2 garlic cloves, minced
1 carrot, thinly sliced
1 small onion, chopped
¼ C. dry white wine
½ C. water
1 bay leaf, crumbled
4 tbsp. tomato paste
salt and pepper to taste
6 thin slices prosciutto
2 tbsp. flour

1. Sauté garlic, carrot and onion in 2 tbsp. butter until tender. Add wine, water, bay leaf and tomato paste. Simmer covered for 15 minutes. Season with salt and pepper. Purée.
2. Place 1 slice of prosciutto on each cutlet. Roll and tie with string.
3. Dredge rolls in flour and brown in 4 tbsp. butter.
4. Place rolls in vegetable purée and simmer covered for 45 minutes. Remove string from the rolls. Serves 3.

Veal and Ham Rolls

1 1½-lb. veal steak
6 thin slices boiled ham
1 onion, chopped
1 C. cooked rice
¼ tsp. basil

¼ tsp. thyme
¼ tsp. oregano
butter

1. Remove bone from veal. Cut into 6 slices and pound very thin. Top each slice with 1 slice of ham.
2. Sauté onion. Combine with rice and herbs. Spread on ham. Roll and tie with string.
3. Brown rolls in butter in a frying pan. Place rolls in a baking dish. Make The Sauce.

The Sauce

2 cubes chicken bouillon
1½ C. hot water
1 tbsp. tomato paste
¼ tsp. basil
¼ tsp. oregano
¼ tsp. thyme
1 bay leaf
¼ tsp. grated lemon peel
½ tsp. chervil
¼ C. Parmesan cheese

1. Combine all ingredients except the cheese. Pour over the rolls.
2. Bake covered at 350 F. for 35 minutes. Just before serving, remove string from rolls and sprinkle rolls with cheese. Serves 6.

STUFFED VEAL

Here is a variety of intriguing creations made with breast or shoulder of veal. Breast of veal is far more economical than veal cutlets, and can be just as tasty and dramatic when dressed up in the various ways we suggest.

(You may wish to ask your butcher to assist in boning or pocketing the veal, as specified in the recipes.)

Stuffed Veal Shoulder in Tomato Sauce

1 3½-lb. shoulder of veal, boned
½ lb. cooked ground pork
1 large onion, chopped
1 garlic clove, minced
6 strips of bacon, cooked and crumbled
¾ C. chopped cooked chicken
¼ C. pine nuts
¼ C. chopped celery
½ C. soft bread crumbs
salt and pepper to taste
1 egg, beaten
butter
2 C. marinara sauce
½ C. dry white wine
½ tsp. tarragon

1. Cook the pork until well-done with the onion and garlic. Remove from heat and add bacon, chicken, nuts, celery and bread crumbs. Season with salt and pepper. Add egg and mix well.
2. Spread the filling on the veal. Roll and skewer closed. Brown in butter on both sides.
3. Add 2 tbsp. butter to the marinara sauce and mix well. Add wine and bring to a boil. Add tarragon. Pour mixture over veal and simmer covered for 1 to 1½ hours, or until veal is tender. Serves 6 to 8.

Veal Stuffed with Cheese

1 3½-lb. shoulder of veal, boned
4 tbsp. butter
salt and pepper to taste
1 C. grated Parmesan cheese
5 garlic cloves, minced
juice of 1 lemon
½ C. dry white wine

1. Cut shoulder open to form 1 long strip. Rub with 1 tbsp. butter. Season to taste with salt and pepper. Sprinkle with cheese and garlic. Roll and tie with string.
2. Brown rolls in remaining butter. Add lemon juice and wine.
3. Cover and cook slowly until meat is tender. (If more liquid is needed, add chicken bouillon.) Remove string before serving. Serves 6 to 8.

Pork-Stuffed Breast of Veal

1 2- to 2½-lb. breast of veal
4 tbsp. butter
4 tbsp. olive oil
1 onion, chopped
½ lb. ground pork
3 heaping tbsp. rice soaked in ¼ C. water for ½ hour
1 tomato, peeled and chopped
1 egg, beaten
1 tbsp. chopped fresh parsley
¼ C. pine nuts
salt and pepper to taste
1 tbsp. lemon juice
½ C. dry white wine
½ C. water

1. Sauté onion and pork in 2 tbsp. butter and 1 tbsp. oil. Brown pork well. Remove from heat and add rice, tomato, egg, parsley, nuts, salt and pepper.
2. Cut a pocket in the veal. Stuff and skewer closed.
3. Heat remaining butter and oil and brown veal. Add lemon juice, wine and water and cook covered 1 to 1½ hours. Serves 4 to 6.

Deviled Breast of Veal

1 3-lb. breast of veal, boned
1 can deviled ham
1 onion, chopped
1½ C. flavored bread crumbs
4 tbsp. butter
salt and pepper to taste
1½ C. hot beef bouillon
1 tsp. chervil
½ C. light cream
2 tsp. cornstarch

1. Pound veal flat with boned side up. Spread with deviled ham.
2. Sauté onions. Combine with bread crumbs and 2 tbsp. butter, melted. Spread on top of deviled ham. Roll veal and tie with string.

3. Melt 2 tbsp. butter in a heavy skillet. Brown veal well and season with salt and pepper. Pour bouillon over veal and add chervil. Simmer covered for about 1½ hours. Remove veal from the pan and string from the veal.
4. Add cream to the pan juices. Cook for 5 minutes. Add cornstarch that has been dissolved in a little water. Cook until sauce is thick. Pour over veal. Serves 6.

Stuffed Breast of Veal Jewish Style

1 5-lb. breast of veal
oil
3/4 C. diced celery
1 medium onion, chopped
1 C. matzoh meal
2 tbsp. chopped fresh parsley
3/4 C. hot water
1 egg, beaten
salt and pepper to taste
2 8-oz. cans tomato sauce
1 tomato sauce can of water
¼ lb. mushrooms, sliced

1. Sauté celery and onion in a little oil. Add matzoh meal, parsley, hot water, egg, salt and pepper.
2. Cut a pocket in the veal. Stuff and skewer closed.
3. Place the veal in a roasting pan. Add tomato sauce and water. Sauté mushrooms and add to the pan.
4. Cover and roast at 350 F. for 2 hours. Uncover and roast for 30 minutes longer. Baste with pan juices. Serves 8.

Veal Pot Roast

1 1½-lb. shoulder of veal, boned
salt and pepper to taste
2 garlic cloves, chopped
2 tbsp. finely chopped fresh parsley
3 slices boiled ham

6 slices mozzarella cheese
3 tbsp. butter
3 tbsp. olive oil
4 tbsp. dry white wine
2 tbsp. tomato paste, diluted in ½ C. hot water

1. Pound veal as thinly as possible. Season with salt and pepper.
2. Spread veal out and sprinkle with garlic and parsley. Place the ham and cheese on top. Roll and tie with string.
3. Put the butter and olive oil in a pan and brown veal on all sides. Add the wine and tomato paste. Cook covered for 1½ hours. Remove string before serving. Serves 4.

STUFFED LAMB

Stuffed lamb is always a delight, and here are some interesting ways to make it–with onions, peppers, spinach or eggplant. There is also a curried lamb of Middle Eastern origin and a splendid Royal Roast Lamb. Lamb should always be served well-done. When prepared with wine and spices, and served with a dry red wine, it can be a truly regal dish. (You may wish to ask your butcher to assist in boning or pocketing the lamb, as specified in the recipes.)

Lamb Rolls

1 1¼-lb. lamb steak
salt and pepper to taste
2 garlic cloves, sliced
1 medium onion, sliced
4 tbsp. olive oil
¼ tsp. rosemary
½ C. dry white wine

1. Cut lamb steak into ¼" slices and then into 3" square pieces. Season with salt and pepper. Place a slice of garlic and a slice of onion on each

piece. Roll and skewer closed.
2. Heat oil in a skillet and brown rolls on all sides. Add rosemary and wine and cook covered about 25 minutes. Serves 4.

Curried Shoulder of Lamb

1 5-lb. shoulder of lamb, boned
2 tbsp. butter
1 medium onion, chopped
2 tbsp. chopped fresh parsley
1 garlic clove, minced
2 tsp. curry powder
½ tsp. turmeric
½ C. raw rice
¾ C. water
salt and pepper to taste

1. Melt butter in saucepan and sauté onion and parsley. Add garlic, curry powder and turmeric to the mixture. Blend well and simmer for 3 minutes.
2. Cook the rice in the water until tender. Add to the curried mixture. If too dry, add a little melted butter. Season with salt and pepper.
3. Open lamb out and pound thin. Spread with curried rice. Roll and skewer closed. Rub outside of lamb with a little butter or oil.
4. Place on a rack in a roasting pan. Roast uncovered at 350 F. for about 3½ hours, or about 40 minutes per pound. Serves 8.

Royal Rolled Roast Lamb

This is truly a dish fit for kings. Its origin seems to date back to times when nutmeg, cinnamon and cloves were infused into meats as preservatives.

1 whole leg of lamb, boned
olive oil
1 jar Italian roasted red peppers, drained
1 lb. chopped fresh spinach, cooked and drained
¼ tsp. ground nutmeg
salt and pepper to taste

1. Open lamb and rub both sides with a little olive oil. Place peppers on lamb. Spread spinach on top and season with nutmeg, salt and pepper. Roll and tie with string.

2. Place on a rack in a roasting pan. Roast uncovered at 350 F. for about 40 minutes per pound. Remove string before serving. Serves 6.

Stuffed Shoulder of Lamb with Eggplant

1 5-lb. shoulder of lamb, boned
olive oil
1 small eggplant, peeled and thinly sliced
1 onion, chopped
1 garlic clove, chopped
1 tsp. oregano
1 tbsp. chopped fresh parsley
salt and pepper to taste
1 C. dry white wine
juice of 1 lemon

1. Brown eggplant in olive oil with onion, garlic, oregano and parsley.
2. Spread out lamb and place eggplant mixture on top. Season with salt and pepper. Roll and tie with string.
3. Place in a roasting pan and pour ½ the wine over. Roast uncovered at 450 F. for 15 minutes. Lower heat to 325 F. and roast 2½ hours longer. Baste the lamb with a mixture of olive oil and lemon juice.
4. When lamb is cooked, remove it from the pan and remove the string. Skim off all fat from the pan juices. Add remaining wine and simmer for 5 minutes. Pour sauce over the lamb. Serves 6 to 8.

Stuffed Lamb with Chicken Liver

1 5- to 6-lb. shoulder of lamb
4 tbsp. butter
3/4 lb. chicken livers
1 medium onion, chopped
4 heaping tbsp. raw rice
3 tbsp. pine nuts
¼ tsp. rosemary
¼ tsp. thyme
3 tbsp. cognac
1 tbsp. tomato paste, dissolved in 2 tbsp. water
2 tbsp. raisins
salt and pepper to taste
lemon juice
oil

1. Sauté livers and onion in butter for 5 minutes over fairly high heat. Add rice, nuts, rosemary, thyme, cognac, tomato paste, raisins, salt and pepper. Cook until all the liquid is absorbed.
2. Make a pocket in the lamb. Stuff and skewer to close. Rub outside of lamb with a mixture of lemon juice and oil.
3. Place on a rack in a roasting pan. Roast uncovered at 350 F. for about 2 hours, or about 40 minutes per pound. Serves 8.

Stuffed Shoulder of Lamb with Pasta

1 4- to 5-lb. shoulder of lamb
olive oil
1 small eggplant, peeled and cubed
½ C. chopped celery
½ lb. ground lamb
½ C. cooked macaroni
½ tsp. oregano
¼ C. grated Parmesan cheese
2 tbsp. chopped fresh parsley
1 6-oz. can tomato paste
salt and pepper to taste

1. Sauté eggplant and celery in a little olive oil until golden.
2. In a separate pan, sauté ground lamb until well-browned. Then add to the eggplant mixture. Combine remaining ingredients.
3. Make a pocket in the lamb. Stuff and skewer closed.
4. Place on a rack in a roasting pan. Roast uncovered at 325 F. for 2 to 2½ hours, or about 40 minutes per pound. Serves 6 to 8.

ROLLED AND STUFFED CHICKEN BREASTS

Chicken breasts are almost interchangeable with veal cutlets and can certainly be depended upon to help stretch your budget. Aside from economy, however, chicken breasts that are artfully filled and sauced lend a festive aura to a menu at any time.

Chicken Breasts with Prosciutto

3 whole chicken breasts, boned, skinned and halved
salt and pepper to taste
1/3 C. flour
6 thin slices prosciutto ham
6 thin slices Gruyère cheese
8 tbsp. butter
4 tbsp. dry sherry
½ C. dry white wine
3/4 lb. thinly sliced mushrooms

1. Pound chicken flat. Sprinkle with salt and pepper and dredge in flour.
2. Place 1 slice of prosciutto and 1 slice of cheese on each piece of chicken. Roll and skewer to close.
3. Brown in 4 tbsp. butter until done. Remove chicken and keep warm on a hot-tray or warm platter. Add the sherry and wine to the skillet and simmer to reduce, about 7 minutes.
4. Sauté mushrooms in remaining 4 tbsp. butter. Arrange on chicken and top with sauce. Serves 6.

Chicken Breasts with Cheese and Bacon

4 whole chicken breasts, boned, skinned and halved
8 slices Gruyère cheese
4 strips of bacon, halved and cooked
4 tbsp. Italian style salad dressing
salt and pepper to taste
½ C. butter

1. Pound chicken flat. Place 1 slice of cheese on four of the pieces. Top with 2 ½-strips of bacon and 1 tbsp. salad dressing. Place a second slice of cheese on top and then a second piece of chicken. Skewer to hold.
2. Season with salt and pepper. Brown in ½ the butter. Cook about 20 minutes, turning frequently. Use remaining butter to insure that chicken does not stick while cooking. Serves 4.

Chicken Breasts with Cheese and Nuts

3 whole chicken breasts, boned, skinned and halved
cognac
6 slices prosciutto ham
¼ C. grated Swiss cheese
½ C. pine nuts
5 tbsp. butter
½ C. dry white wine
1/3 C. chicken bouillon

1. Pound chicken flat. Cut a pocket in each piece. Rub a little cognac inside and stuff with a slice of prosciutto.
2. Combine cheese and pine nuts and add to prosciutto in the pockets. Skewer closed with toothpicks.
3. Melt butter and sauté chicken until well-browned on both sides. Add wine and simmer covered for 15 minutes.
4. Remove chicken and add bouillon to the pan. Bring to a boil and simmer 3 minutes. Pour over chicken. Serves 6.

Chicken Breasts Cordon Bleu

One of the incomparable delights of classic French cuisine.

2 whole chicken breasts, boned, skinned and halved
1 3-oz. package cream cheese
¼ lb. bleu cheese
¼ tsp. paprika
¼ tsp. pepper
¼ tsp. thyme
¼ tsp. rosemary
¼ C. butter
4 slices Swiss cheese
1 egg white, beaten
bread crumbs

1. Slice each piece of chicken almost 3/4 of the way through. Open and pound flat.
2. Combine cream cheese, bleu cheese, spices, herbs and butter. Make 4 rolls out of this mixture and wrap a slice of Swiss cheese around each one.

Place 1 roll on each piece of chicken and fold over. Secure edges with skewers.
3. Dip each piece of chicken in egg white and roll in bread crumbs.
4. Sauté in additional butter until well-browned on both sides. Serves 4.

Chicken Kiev

This recipe from Czarist Russia is not for the faint-hearted. It is quite possibly one of the richest combinations of ingredients ever assembled in one course.

4 whole chicken breasts, boned and skinned
½ lb. sweet butter
½ lb. cream cheese
¼ lb. cheddar cheese, grated
2 oz. grated Parmesan cheese
2 tbsp. chopped fresh parsley
2 tbsp. chopped chives
1 tbsp. chopped shallots
2 eggs, beaten
bread crumbs

1. Open chicken breasts and pound flat.
2. Combine butter, cheeses, parsley, chives and shallots. Divide and place on opened breasts. Roll and skewer closed.
3. Dip rolls in egg and dredge in bread crumbs. Place in the refrigerator for 2 hours.
4. Cook in additional butter so that all sides of each roll are nicely browned, or about 10 to 15 minutes. Serves 4.

Rolled Chicken Breasts in Cheese Sauce

8 whole chicken breasts, boned, skinned and halved
butter
2 small cans sliced mushrooms
flour
2 C. sour cream
2 C. grated cheddar cheese
2 eggs, beaten
bread crumbs

1. Melt a little butter in a skillet and sauté 1 can of mushrooms. Add 1

tbsp. of flour and stir over low heat. Add 1 cup of sour cream and 1 C. of cheese. Stir well and cook until cheese is melted.
2. Pour mixture into a square dish and refrigerate until it is hard. This should take about 3 to 4 hours. Then cut it into 16 squares.
3. Pound the chicken flat. Place 1 square of filling on each piece. Roll and skewer with toothpicks.
4. Dip rolls in flour, egg and bread crumbs. Brown in butter and place in a flat-bottomed casserole. Bake covered at 350 F. for 30 minutes.
5. Make a second batch of sauce, combining sautéed mushrooms, 1 tbsp. flour, 1 C. sour cream and 1 C. cheese. Pour hot over the rolls and serve. Serves 8.

Barbecued Chicken Breasts

6 whole chicken breasts, boned but not skinned
salt and pepper to taste
¼ C. chopped celery
¼ C. chopped fresh parsley
1 C. seasoned stuffing mix
½ lb. small shrimp, cooked, cleaned and chopped
1 egg, beaten
4 tbsp. butter, melted

1. Season inside of breasts with salt and pepper.
2. Combine celery, parsley, stuffing, shrimp and beaten egg.
3. Stuff breasts and skewer tightly so that no stuffing will escape during grilling.
4. Grill over coals and brush frequently with butter. Serves 6.

Paté-Stuffed Chicken Breasts in Aspic

3 whole chicken breasts, boned, skinned and halved
1½ C. chicken bouillon
1 small can paté
1 tsp. lemon juice
1 package unflavored gelatin

3/4 C. mayonnaise
4 black olives, minced
1 small can mushrooms, sliced

1. Place chicken in a skillet and cover with bouillon. Simmer slowly until done and let cool in the bouillon.
2. Remove chicken and cut each piece in half horizontally. Spread 6 pieces with paté and top with a second piece of chicken.
3. Remove ½ the chicken bouillon from skillet and add lemon juice and gelatin. Simmer until gelatin dissolves.
4. Combine with mayonnaise, olives and mushrooms. Mound on top of chicken pieces and refrigerate until firm. Serves 6.

Chicken on a Mountain

3 whole chicken breasts, boned, skinned and halved
1 C. butter
1 onion, chopped
¼ C. chopped celery
4 cooking apples, cored, peeled and diced
½ C. chopped walnuts
½ C. raisins, plumped in boiling water
1 C. soft white bread crumbs
1 tsp. lemon juice
½ tsp. rosemary
½ tsp. oregano
salt and pepper to taste
flour

1. Melt ½ the butter and sauté onion and celery until tender.
2. Combine with apple, walnuts, raisins, bread crumbs, lemon juice, herbs, salt and pepper. Blend well and form into 6 dome-shaped "mountains." Place on a lightly-greased cookie sheet.
3. Dredge chicken in flour and brown in remaining butter. Put 1 piece of chicken on each "mountain." Cover with aluminum foil.
4. Bake at 350 F. for 15 minutes. Remove foil and bake 10 minutes longer. Serves 6.

Chicken Birds on Rice

2 whole chicken breasts, boned, skinned and halved
1 medium onion
2 chicken livers
1 tsp. chopped fresh parsley
1 tsp. chopped chives
¼ C. bread crumbs
salt and pepper to taste
6 tbsp. butter
8 mushroom caps
flour
½ C. chicken broth
½ C. heavy cream
2 tbsp. instant blending flour
cooked rice

1. Grind onion and livers together and combine with parsley, chives, bread crumbs, salt and pepper.
2. Pound chicken flat. Divide stuffing and spread on chicken. Roll and skewer closed.
3. Melt butter and sauté mushroom caps and set them aside. Dredge rolls in flour and brown in melted butter.
4. Add broth and bake covered at 350 F. for 45 minutes.
5. Remove rolls and add cream to the broth. Bring to a boil and add 2 tbsp. instant blending flour. Cook until sauce thickens.
6. Place rolls on a bed of cooked rice. Place mushroom caps on rolls. Pour sauce over all. Serves 4.

Chicken en Croûte

2 recipes "The Dough" made with butter
8 chicken thighs, skinned
2 tbsp. butter
½ C. chicken bouillon
½ C. water
3 tbsp. instant blending flour
salt and pepper to taste

1 C. light cream
¼ lb. mushrooms, finely chopped
¼ C. dry white wine
4 slices cooked ham, halved
1 egg, beaten

1. Melt the butter and brown thighs well on all sides. Add bouillon. Cover and simmer for 30 minutes. Remove chicken and cool. Bone chicken, being careful that thighs retain their shape.
2. Add ½ C. water to skillet. Add flour, salt and pepper. Stir in cream. Cook over high heat until sauce thickens. Add mushrooms and wine.
3. Roll ½ slice of ham and place inside each thigh.
4. Roll out "The Dough" on a lightly-floured board. Cut into 8 large triangles. Place a thigh on each and top with 1 tbsp. sauce. Roll thigh in triangle in crescent fashion. Tuck in ends and seal all edges with fingers that have been dipped in water. Brush each crescent with beaten egg.
5. Bake uncovered at 400 F. for 30 minutes. Heat sauce and pour over crescents. Serves 4.

Chicken Breasts à la Greque

8 filo leaves
2 large whole chicken breasts, boned, skinned and halved
¼ lb. butter
1 medium onion, chopped
2 tbsp. minced fresh parsley
2 garlic cloves, minced
½ package frozen spinach, cooked and drained
1 tbsp. instant blending flour
¼ C. dry white wine
salt and pepper to taste
2 tbsp. olive oil
2 tbsp. butter
melted butter (for brushing filo leaves)

1. Sauté onion, parsley and garlic in ¼ lb. butter until tender. Combine with spinach. Add flour and wine, stirring until sauce thickens. Season with salt and pepper.

2. Pound chicken flat. Sauté chicken in 2 tbsp. butter mixed with 2 tbsp. olive oil until browned.
3. Place each piece of chicken on a double sheet of buttered filo and top with ¼ of the sauce. Fold in sides and roll. Brush tops with melted butter.
4. Bake on a cookie sheet at 350 F. for 35 minutes. Serves 4.

Note: Leftover filo can be frozen in plastic wrap in your freezer.

ROAST STUFFED CHICKEN

Stuffed Chicken with Nuts

1 4-lb. roasting chicken, reserve liver
2 tbsp. butter
½ small onion, chopped
salt and pepper to taste
2 tbsp. brandy
¼ C. ground almonds
1/8 C. ground walnuts
2 tbsp. chopped fresh parsley
3 tbsp. bread crumbs
2 eggs, beaten

1. Chop chicken liver and sauté with onion in 1 tbsp. butter. Season with salt and pepper. Add brandy and simmer 5 minutes.
2. Combine with nuts, parsley, bread crumbs and eggs.
3. Stuff the chicken and rub the outside with remaining butter. Skewer closed.
4. Roast uncovered at 350 F. for 1½ hours. Serves 4 to 6.

Sausage-Stuffed Chicken

1 3-lb. roasting chicken
6 oz. sweet Italian sausage, casing removed
3/4 C. bread crumbs
¼ C. chicken bouillon
¼ C. chopped onion
1 garlic clove, minced
¼ C. chopped celery

½ tsp. oregano
½ tsp. basil
¼ tsp. rosemary
1 egg, beaten
salt and pepper to taste

1. Cook sausage over high heat until browned. Add bread crumbs and bouillon and simmer 5 minutes.
2. Add remaining ingredients. Stuff chicken. Skewer closed.
3. Roast uncovered at 350 F. for 1¼ to 1½ hours. Serves 4.

Peking Roast Chicken

In former times, the Chinese had no ovens in their homes. All meats had to be sent out to be roasted, and therefore what a treat chicken like this must have been.

1 4-lb. roasting chicken
1 bunch scallions
oil
½ tsp. ground, or 3 to 4 slices fresh ginger
¼ lb. fresh mushrooms, sliced
salt
1 C. chicken bouillon
¼ C. dry sherry
1 tsp. sugar
2 tbsp. soy sauce
1 tbsp. cornstarch

1. Cut scallions into 2" lengths. Wash and dry them.
2. Sauté ginger, scallions and mushrooms in a little oil. Sauté 3 minutes only as they must not brown. Cool.
3. Clean chicken and rub inside and outside with salt. Stuff with sautéed mixture. Skewer closed. Place in roasting pan.
4. Combine bouillon, sherry, sugar and soy sauce. Pour over chicken.
5. Roast uncovered at 350 F. for 1½ hours. Baste frequently.
6. When chicken is done, thicken ½ C. of pan juice with cornstarch. Pour over chicken when it is served. Serves 4 to 6.

DUCK STUFFED WITH FRUIT

1 5-lb. duck
salt and pepper
1 onion, chopped
2 apples, peeled, cored and coarsely chopped
1 C. seedless grapes
½ C. coarsely chopped dried apricots
1 C. chopped nuts
1 C. soft bread crumbs
½ tsp. coriander
2 to 3 tbsp. madeira

1. Season the duck inside and outside with salt and pepper.
2. Combine remaining ingredients and stuff duck. Skewer closed.
3. Place the duck on a rack in a roasting pan. Roast uncovered at 450 F. for 20 minutes. Turn heat to 350 F. and roast for 1½ hours. Prick often with a fork to allow fat to escape. Serves 4.

MANICOTTI SPECIALS

Pre-cook all manicotti al dente—just slightly chewy—and leave in cold water until ready to stuff.

Three-Cheese Chicken Bake

1 lb. manicotti
1½ C. cream-style cottage cheese
2 C. shredded cheddar cheese
½ C. grated Parmesan cheese
3 C. diced cooked chicken
Mushroom Sauce

1. Combine cheeses and chicken and stuff manicotti.

The Mushroom Sauce

3 tbsp. butter
½ C. chopped onion
½ C. chopped green pepper
1 can condensed cream of chicken soup
½ C. milk
1 small can sliced mushrooms
¼ C. chopped pimiento
½ tsp. basil

1. Sauté onion and pepper in butter until tender. Add remaining sauce ingredients. Simmer 10 minutes.
2. Place stuffed manicotti in a baking dish. Pour sauce over them.
3. Bake uncovered at 350 F. for 45 minutes. Serves 8 to 10.

Manicotti Bolognese

1 lb. manicotti
6 strips of bacon, cooked and fat reserved
1 stalk celery, chopped
1 carrot, diced
¼ lb. chicken livers, chopped
1½ lb. ground beef
¼ C. tomato sauce
½ C. dry white wine
1 C. sliced mushrooms
½ tsp. basil
½ tsp. oregano
½ tsp. thyme
salt and pepper to taste

1. Sauté bacon. Remove from pan and sauté celery, carrot and liver in fat.
2. In a separate skillet, sauté beef over fairly high heat until all liquid is absorbed. Stir frequently to prevent sticking.

3. Add sautéed liver mixture to meat. Add tomato sauce, wine, mushrooms, crumbled bacon, herbs, salt and pepper. Simmer covered for 30 minutes.
4. Stuff manicotti and place in a baking dish.

The Sauce

3 tbsp. butter
3 tbsp. instant blending flour
1 C. milk
1 C. cream
1 C. grated Parmesan cheese
¼ tsp. nutmeg
salt and pepper to taste

1. Melt butter. Add flour and blend well. Add milk and cream and cook until sauce is thick and creamy. Add cheese, nutmeg, salt and pepper.
2. Pour sauce over stuffed manicotti and bake uncovered at 350 F. for 45 minutes. Serves 8 to 10.

Tuscan Manicotti

For this recipe, you will need to make The Sauce first.

½ lb. manicotti
2 tbsp. butter
½ lb. mushrooms, finely sliced
2 C. cooked diced chicken
5 to 6 tbsp. The Sauce
½ C. grated Parmesan cheese

1. Sauté mushrooms in butter. Add chicken and 5 to 6 tbsp. The Sauce. Stuff manicotti and place in a baking dish.

The Sauce

6 tbsp. butter
6 tbsp. instant blending flour
½ C. milk
1 C. light cream
salt and pepper to taste
1 egg yolk

1. Melt butter in a saucepan and add flour. Blend well. Add milk and cream, stirring until sauce is thick. Cook 3 minutes and add salt and pepper. Remove from heat and add egg yolk. Stand saucepan in hot water and cover so that no film will form on sauce.
2. Pour sauce over manicotti and sprinkle with grated cheese. Bake uncovered at 375 F. for 20 minutes. Serves 4.

Cheese-Stuffed Manicotti

½ lb. manicotti
1½ C. grated Parmesan cheese
1-3/4 C. ricotta cheese
4 tbsp. Basic Bèchamel Sauce
1 egg, beaten
1/8 tsp. nutmeg

1. Combine all stuffing ingredients and stuff manicotti. Place in a baking dish and top with any of your favorite sauces.
2. Bake uncovered at 375 F. for 20 minutes. Serves 4.

Note: Any remaining Béchamel Sauce can be saved in the refrigerator for later use.

Sausage-and-Ricotta-Stuffed Manicotti

½ lb. manicotti
4 sweet Italian sausages (casing removed)
2 C. ricotta cheese
5 tbsp. Parmesan cheese
1 egg, beaten
salt and pepper to taste

1. Cook sausage meat until well-browned. Combine with remaining ingredients and stuff manicotti. Place in a baking dish and top with any of your favorite sauces.
2. Bake uncovered at 375 F. for 20 minutes. Serves 4.

Lasagne Rolls

1 lb. lasagne, cooked and left in cold water
1 lb. ground beef
2 eggs
1 garlic clove, chopped
¼ C. bread crumbs
salt and pepper to taste
1½ 16-oz. jars marinara sauce
grated Parmesan cheese

1. Sauté ground beef until cooked. Add eggs, garlic, bread crumbs, salt and pepper.
2. Place a portion of stuffing on each lasagne strip. Roll, using a toothpick to secure the edge.
3. Half fill a baking dish with marinara sauce. Place the rolls in the sauce side by side. Top with remaining sauce and a heavy sprinkling of cheese.
4. Bake uncovered at 350 F. for 20 minutes. Serves 6 to 8.

Stuffing Variations

The above filling and these variations can also be used for manicotti and for tufoli, the giant pasta shells. Use 1 lb. of manicotti or 1 lb. of tufoli.

1. Substitute 1 lb. well-cooked sweet sausage meat for the ground beef.
2. Use ½ lb. ground beef and ½ lb. sweet sausage meat, both well-cooked.
3. Use ½ lb. ground beef, ½ lb. ricotta cheese and ¼ C. diced mozzarella cheese.

DELECTABLE STUFFINGS FOR ROAST FOWL

Here is a delightful variety of stuffings for fowl of all kinds. Mix them, match them and savor them!

Citrus

¼ C. butter, melted
½ C. diced celery with leaves
5 tangerines, or 2 medium oranges, or 3 lemons
1 8-oz. package seasoned bread crumbs
1 C. diced walnuts
3 C. cooked rice
½ C. chicken stock or bouillon
½ tsp. poultry seasoning

1. Cook celery in melted butter for about 10 minutes.
2. Peel fruit, remove membranes and cut into pieces.
3. Combine all ingredients and stuff fowl.
4. This makes enough for a 10-lb. goose, or 2 5-lb. ducks or chickens.

Tart Apple

¼ C. butter
¼ C. chopped onion
1 C. peeled, cored and chopped tart apples
1 C. chopped dried apricots
5 C. bread crumbs
½ tsp. salt
1/8 tsp. pepper

1. Heat butter and add onion. Cook until tender.
2. Combine all ingredients and stuff fowl.
3. This makes enough for a 10-lb. goose, a 10- to 12-lb. turkey, or 2 5-lb. ducks or chickens.

Risotto

4 tbsp. butter
1 C. raw rice, unwashed
2¼ C. chicken stock or bouillon
2 stalks celery with leaves, finely diced
1 medium onion, diced

¼ C. white raisins
¼ C. pine nuts
2 broiled and chopped chicken livers
½ C. dry sherry
½ tsp. sage
½ tsp. rosemary
½ tsp. thyme
salt and pepper to taste

1. Melt 2 tbsp. butter in a heavy saucepan. Add rice and stir with a wooden spoon over moderate heat for about 3 minutes. The rice will become translucent, then milky white.
2. When rice is white, add about ½ C. stock and lower heat. When stock is absorbed, add another ½ C., keeping rice at a slow simmer. Continue with remaining stock, stirring occasionally until rice is tender. Do not add more stock until former amount is absorbed.
3. Sauté celery and onion in 2 tbsp. butter until onion is golden. Add remaining ingredients and simmer 10 minutes.
4. Mix rice and vegetables together and season with salt and pepper.
5. This makes enough for an 8- to 10-lb. turkey, or 2 4-lb. chickens.

Ham and Olive

4 C. cooked rice
4 C. bread crumbs
4 eggs, beaten
1 C. diced cooked ham
2/3 C. chopped green olives
½ C. chopped fresh parsley
1 C. chopped onion
1 C. diced celery
1 tsp. sage
1 tsp. marjoram
¼ tsp. garlic powder
1 tsp. salt
½ tsp. black pepper

1. Combine all ingredients. Stuff fowl.
2. This makes enough for a 21-lb. turkey or other very large bird. This

recipe can be cut for smaller fowl.

Fabulous Spinach

3 10-oz. packages frozen chopped spinach, thawed
3 tbsp. butter
1 medium onion, finely chopped
1 lb. bulk sausage meat (no casing)
2 eggs
2 packages instant brown gravy mix
1½ C. freshly-grated Parmesan cheese
3 C. unseasoned bread crumbs
water (optional)

1. Squeeze all moisture from thawed spinach. Place in a heavy skillet and sauté in butter, draining off excess moisture. Set aside in a large mixing bowl to cool.
2. In same skillet, sauté onion. Then add spinach. Break up sausage and fry in same skillet until brown and done. Reserve a small amount of the drippings, discarding the rest.
3. Place mixture in a bowl. Add eggs, instant gravy mix, cheese, bread crumbs and enough water to moisten. Omit the water if you wish. Let cool.
4. This makes enough for a 12- to 14-lb. turkey.

Noodle

¼ lb. fine egg noodles, cooked al dente (slightly chewy)
2 tbsp. butter
¼ C. chopped fresh parsley
½ C. bread crumbs
¼ C. pine nuts, or walnuts
¼ C. chopped fennel, or celery
½ tsp. oregano
salt and pepper to taste

1. Toss cooked noodles with butter and combine with remaining ingredients. Let cool.

2. This makes enough for a 10-lb. turkey, or 2 5-lb. chickens.

Walnut

½ C. butter
1 C. chopped onion
1 C. chopped celery
½ C. diced chicken liver
8 C. cubed white bread
1 C. chopped walnuts
1 tbsp. poultry seasoning
½ C. water
½ C. brandy
1½ tsp. salt
pepper to taste

1. Sauté onion and celery in butter until tender. Add liver. Cook 3 minutes. Combine with remaining ingredients.
2. This makes enough for an 18- to 20-lb. turkey.

Potato

½ C. melted butter
2 medium onions, chopped
¼ C. chopped fresh parsley
½ tsp. sage
2 tsp. salt
½ tsp. pepper
6 cooked potatoes, diced

1. Place all ingredients, except potatoes, in a blender and blend until smooth. Pour over potatoes and mix.
2. This makes enough for a 12-lb. turkey.

Wild Rice

¼ C. butter
½ C. chopped onion
¼ lb. mushrooms, sliced
½ lb. chicken livers
5 C. water

2 packages long grain and wild rice mix
8 strips of bacon, cooked and crumbled

1. Sauté onion and mushrooms in butter for 5 minutes. Add livers and cook until done.
2. Add water and rice. Bring to a boil and add bacon. Cook covered until all water is absorbed and rice is tender. Let cool.
3. This makes enough for a 10-lb. fowl.

Clam

30 clams, in shells
¼ lb. butter
1 onion, chopped
¼ C. chopped celery
2 packages herb stuffing
1 C. water
1 egg, beaten

1. Scrub clams well under running water to remove all sand. Place in a large pot with about 2" water. Cover and boil until shells open. Remove clams, reserving 2 C. of the broth.
2. Chop clam meat well.
3. Sauté onion and celery in butter. Add clams, stuffing, water and egg. Pour in enough clam broth to moisten stuffing. Let cool.
4. This makes enough for a 12- to 14-lb. fowl.

Oyster

24 oysters, in shells
2 tbsp. olive oil
1 tbsp. chopped fresh parsley
2 tsp. chopped chives
4 C. bread crumbs
1 tsp. thyme
salt and pepper to taste

1. Scrub oysters well under running water to remove all sand. Place in a large pot with about 2" of water. Cover and boil until shells open. Remove

oysters, reserving about 2 C. of the broth.
2. Chop oyster meat well.
3. Sauté parsley and chives in olive oil until wilted. Add oysters, bread crumbs, thyme, salt and pepper. Add enough oyster broth to moisten stuffing. Cool.
4. This makes enough for a 10-lb. fowl.

Matzoh

3 tbsp. vegetable oil, or chicken fat
giblets from fowl, chopped
2 onions, finely chopped
½ tsp. thyme
½ tsp. sage
¼ tsp. ground ginger
salt and pepper to taste
8 matzohs
4 eggs, beaten

1. Sauté giblets and onion in oil and add seasonings.
2. Soak matzohs in hot water until soft. Squeeze out all moisture and add to sautéed mixture. Cook 5 minutes and add eggs.
3. This makes enough for an 8-lb. fowl.

Bread

¼ C. butter, melted
1 onion, chopped
1 C. finely diced celery
3½ C. soft bread crumbs
1 tbsp. chopped fresh parsley
½ tsp. marjoram
½ tsp. thyme
salt and pepper to taste

1. Sauté onion and celery in 1 tbsp. of the butter. Combine with remaining ingredients.

2. This makes enough for a 10-lb. fowl.

Bread Stuffing Variations

Add 1 or more of the following ingredients to the Bread Stuffing:

1. *2 tbsp. chopped green pepper*
2. *1 C. sliced mushrooms, sautéed*
3. *½ C. well-browned bulk sausage meat*
4. *½ C. diced boiled ham*
5. *½ C. cooked crumbled bacon*
6. *½ C. chopped nuts*
7. *½ C. chopped apple*
8. *½ C. white raisins soaked in madeira or sherry*
9. *1 lb. boiled, skinned and chopped chestnuts*
10. *Substitute crumbled corn bread for the bread crumbs.*

VI. SPOTLIGHT CENTER STAGE
MAIN COURSES

Rolled and Stuffed Fruits de Mer

Although ours is primarily a meat culture, fish and seafoods, especially rolled and stuffed creations, can be as elegant, gracious and nutritious as meats. Exciting fish dishes can serve equally well as first courses or as hearty, yet delicate, main dishes. They can add flair, variety and heightened interest to your menus. Also important, fish is an excellent source of protein yet is low in calories and in cholesterol.

The proper preparation of fish, and its presentation with appropriate wines and sauces, is a simple, yet high art, that has developed dramatically over the centuries. It is perhaps interesting and somewhat romantic to note that in a number of ancient cultures fishermen were considered as gods. The famous god-musician Orpheus, who had power over the beasts and forests, also had power to charm the denizens of the sea and induce them to multiply. Long ago an eloquent Greek poet extolled the merits of rolled and stuffed fish cookery as follows:

For spring the chromius is best
The anthias in winter
But of all fish the daintiest
Is a young shrimp in fig leaves

As history proceeded, Roman gourmets and gastronomes were famed for the delightful, artfully prepared fish dishes they served. Emperors even maintained special fleets for the sole purpose of having fresh fish daily. Later, the importance of fish to French cuisine can be appreciated by the legendary tale of Louis XIV's famous chef, Vatel, who killed himself, at the age of 36, because the fishmonger could not deliver his order on time. Ironically, the fish supposedly arrived only a few minutes after Vatel's death.

So, if the grand kings of history have always enjoyed great fish cookery, why not you and your honored guests?

Here we have collected for you a varied cornucopia of unusual fish recipes from the four corners of the globe. There is a fascinating and delicate Mousse-Stuffed Trout from France and an exotic Portuguese Stuffed Fish. We have also included original versions of lobster stuffed with a sherried filling, zesty curried fillets and mouth-watering mackerel with almond stuffing. For the economy-minded gourmet, there is a roster of savory tuna dishes and a rare Polynesian creation–cabbage stuffed with spiced pork and diced fish fillet. Among the other originals are bass with oyster stuffing, shrimp stuffed with crab meat, an elegant stuffed halibut in cucumber sauce, and a fillet of sole named after the daring Roman Empress Messalina.

We have concluded the chapter with a medley of fish stuffings, which can be made mostly from leftovers and frozen ahead of time. Then all you have to do when you have a fish to stuff, is to take some of the filling from the freezer.

Fresh fish is, of course, preferable to frozen. And we have an abundance of fresh fish in this country–from two oceans, the Gulf of Mexico, from many rivers and lakes. Frozen fish will do, however, if the fresh is unavailable.

Ask your fish dealer to clean and prepare the fish you need. If you wish to be extra economical, save the heads, tails and bones, and cook them to make a stock that can be used as the base for sauces and chowders.

Whenever you serve fish, remember that a bottle of chilled, dry white wine always adds the perfect complement to a savory creation from the sea.

THE LORDLY LOBSTER

If boiled lobsters are unavailable, cook live ones by placing them head first into a very large pot with boiling salted water. The water should reach approximately the ¼ level. Place a weight on the lid. Boil for about 15 minutes. The shells will turn a bright red-orange.

Sherried Stuffed Lobster

2 1-lb. boiled lobsters
2 tbsp. butter
2 tbsp. instant blending flour
1 C. light cream
2 egg yolks, beaten
2 tbsp. dry sherry
¼ C. sliced mushrooms
½ C. flavored bread crumbs
2 tbsp. melted butter

1. Split each lobster and clean everything from shells. Crack claws and remove all meat. Chop meat coarsely.
2. Melt butter in a saucepan and add flour. Blend well and add the cream. Simmer until sauce is thick and remove from heat.
3. Add some of the sauce to beaten egg yolks. Add sherry. Mix well and return to the saucepan. Combine remaining ingredients, except the melted butter, and add to the sauce.
4. Stuff lobster shells and brush with melted butter.
5. Bake at 400 F. for 15 minutes. Serves 2.

Stuffed Lobster with Parmesan Cheese

2 1-lb. boiled lobsters
2 C. soft bread crumbs
3 tbsp. melted butter
¼ tsp. onion powder
¼ tsp. garlic powder
salt and pepper to taste
grated Parmesan cheese

1. Split each lobster and clean everything from shells. Crack claws and remove meat. Chop meat coarsely.
2. Combine all stuffing ingredients, except cheese, with the lobster meat. Stuff shells and top with grated cheese.
3. Bake at 400 F. for 20 minutes. Serves 2.

Fabulous Scallop-Stuffed Lobster

8 ¼-lb. lobster tails, cooked
¼ C. butter
1 tbsp. chopped chives
dash of cayenne
1 tsp. salt
¼ C. instant blending flour
1 C. milk
1 C. light cream
1 lb. bay scallops
3/4 C. soft bread crumbs
butter

1. Split bottoms of shells so that they will not curl while cooking. Remove meat and chop coarsely.
2. Melt ¼ C. butter in a saucepan. Add chives, cayenne and salt. Add flour and blend well. Slowly add milk and cream to form a thick sauce. Add the scallops and lobster meat. Simmer together for 3 minutes.
3. Stuff shells and sprinkle with bread crumbs. Dot with additional butter.
4. Bake at 450 F. for 20 to 25 minutes. Serves 4.

FISH FILLETS WITH A FLAIR

Although seemingly simple, fish fillets can indeed be elegant, exciting and versatile when dressed and stuffed. Here is a roster of recipes from all over the world to suit your moods and needs. Fillets of flounder, cod, halibut, or whatever, are amazingly interchangeable–so don't be afraid to experiment.

Among special tips for fine fillet cookery we might add the following: any fish fillet can be spread with a little anchovy paste, or rolled around shrimps, oysters or clams before baking. A stuffed fillet can be baked in a sauce of melted butter, white wine, parsley, chives, chervil, tarragon, onion, minced shallots or scallions, a few tablespoons of lemon juice, some slivered almonds–or any combination. Any simple fish fillet will taste richer when spread with a white sauce mixed with cheese and a dash of wine. Follow your moods and use your imagination!

Mousse-Stuffed Trout

12 frozen trout fillets, thawed and drained
½ lb. flounder, fluke, sole or turbot fillets
1 egg white
3 C. heavy cream
½ tsp. thyme
dash of cayenne
salt and pepper to taste
¼ lb. butter, cubed
3 scallions, finely chopped
¼ C. chopped fresh parsley
¼ lb. mushrooms, sliced
4 oz. tomato sauce
2 tbsp. lemon juice
1 C. dry white wine
2 tbsp. butter
2 tbsp. instant blending flour

1. To make the mousse, cube ½ lb. fish fillets and place in a blender. Add egg white and blend until smooth. Add 1 C. cream, thyme, cayenne, salt and pepper and blend well.
2. Place 6 trout fillets in a lightly-greased, oven-proof dish. Divide the mousse among them and spread on top. Cover each with another trout fillet.
3. Sprinkle cubed butter on top of fillets. Add scallions, parsley and mushrooms. Cover.
4. Bake at 425 F. until sauce is boiling. Turn heat down and bake at 400

F. for 20 minutes.
5. Remove fish from oven. Extract all liquid and reserve. This can easily be done with a baster. Return trout to oven that has been lowered to a warming temperature.
6. Place fish liquid in a saucepan. Add tomato sauce, lemon juice and wine. Bring to a boil. Cook down to 1/3. Add 2 C. cream and simmer 10 minutes more. Add 2 tbsp. butter. Remove ¼ C. of sauce and combine with instant blending flour. When this mixture is free of lumps, return to pan. Stir well and pour over fish. Serve. Serves 6.

Curried Fillets in a Pancake

This unusual recipe comes from the northern regions of India's coast.

4 firm-fleshed fish fillets
½ C. flour
3/4 C. cold water
2 tsp. curry powder
salt and pepper to taste
oil for frying
1 lemon, sliced

1. Mix flour and water into a batter and add curry powder, salt and pepper. Dip fillets in batter and allow to stand in refrigerator for 15 minutes.
2. Heat oil in a frying pan and fry fish until it flakes. Remove fish. Pour remaining batter into the same pan and cook it well. Turn and cook the other side.
3. Place the "pancake" on a serving dish. Place fish on top and fold. Garnish with lemon slices. Serves 4.

Fillets Thermidor

3 lbs. fish fillets; cod, flounder or sole
2¼ C. milk
1½ tsp. salt
1/8 tsp. pepper
½ C. butter
½ C. instant blending flour
½ lb. cheddar cheese, grated
½ C. dry sherry
paprika

1. Roll fillets and stand on end in a shallow baking dish.

2. Pour milk over fish and add salt and pepper. Bake at 350 F. for 30 minutes.
3. Remove fish from oven. Carefully extract milk from the pan and reserve.
4. Melt butter in a double boiler and stir in the flour and reserved milk. Cook until thick. Add cheese and sherry. Sprinkle in the paprika.
5. Pour sauce over fish and brown quickly under broiler. Serves 6 to 8.

Cheesy Fish Rolls

2 lbs. firm white fish fillets
¼ C. butter
¼ C. instant blending flour
salt and pepper to taste
2 C. milk
¼ C. chopped chives
1½ tbsp. chopped fresh parsley
1 tsp. grated lemon rind
3 tbsp. lemon juice
1 can cheddar cheese soup
3/4 lb. cooked cleaned shrimp, chopped

1. Melt butter in a saucepan. Add flour and blend well. Add salt and pepper. Add milk, cooking slowly until sauce is thick. Then add chives, parsley, lemon rind and lemon juice. Add the soup and mix well.
2. Spoon chopped shrimp down the center of each fillet. Roll fillets and skewer to close.
3. Place rolls in a lightly-greased baking dish and carefully pour sauce over.
4. Bake at 350 F. for 20 minutes. Serves 6.

Fillet of Sole Messalina

2 lbs. sole fillets
1 tbsp. butter
¼ lb. mushrooms, sliced
salt and pepper to taste
3/4 C. dry white wine
1 tbsp. tomato paste
1 1-lb. can tomatoes, sieved
½ tsp. oregano
4 tbsp. melted butter

1. Use 1 tbsp. butter to grease bottom of baking dish. Place mushrooms on bottom.
2. Roll fillets and place on top of mushrooms. Sprinkle with salt and pepper and cover with wine. Bake at 375 F. for 20 to 25 minutes.
3. Carefully drain liquid from fish. Place in a saucepan and add tomato paste, tomatoes, salt and pepper and oregano. Bring to a boil and simmer ½ hour, or until thick. Remove from heat and add 4 tbsp. melted butter.
4. Place rolls on a serving dish and garnish with mushrooms and sauce. Serves 4.

Rolled Fish Fillets Piquant

1 lb. fillets; sole or flounder
2 medium onions, thinly sliced
1 large lemon, thinly sliced
½ tsp. salt
dash of pepper
1 garlic clove, minced
2 tbsp. prepared mustard
½ tsp. sage
butter
1 C. sour cream

1. Place onion and lemon slices in the bottom of a baking dish.
2. Mix salt, pepper, garlic, mustard and sage to form a paste.
3. Coat 1 side of each fillet with paste. Roll and skewer to close. Top with butter.
4. Place rolls in the baking dish and bake at 350 F. for 25 minutes.
5. Add dollops of sour cream and bake 10 minutes longer. Serves 3 to 4.

Onion-Filled Flounder

8 flounder fillets
1 8-oz. bottle French dressing
1 package onion soup mix
1 C. soft bread crumbs
chopped fresh parsley

1. Brush white side of fillets with French dressing. Sprinkle each with dry onion soup mix and bread crumbs.
2. Roll fillets and place side by side in a buttered baking dish. Pour over remaining French dressing.

3. Bake in a pre-heated oven at 350 F. for 25 to 30 minutes, or until fish flakes easily with a fork.
4. Just before serving, sprinkle rolls with fresh parsley. Serves 4 to 6.

Double Fish Roll-Ups

6 fillets; sole or flounder
1 1-lb. can salmon
3/4 tsp. salt
½ tsp. Tabasco sauce
¼ C. butter
2 tbsp. minced onion
¼ C. instant blending flour
2 C. milk

1. Dry fillets carefully and place flat on a work surface.
2. Remove skin and bone from salmon chunks. Chop and mix with ¼ tsp. salt and ¼ tsp. Tabasco. Divide mixture and spread on fillets. Roll and secure with toothpicks.
3. Melt butter in a large, deep skillet. Gently sauté onion, stir in flour and add ½ tsp. salt and ¼ tsp. Tabasco. Slowly add milk, stirring constantly until sauce is smooth and thick.
4. Add rolls to sauce and cover skillet. Simmer gently about 15 minutes, or until fish flakes easily with a fork. Turn rolls during cooking. Serves 4 to 6.

Flipped Fillets

6 good-sized fish fillets
salt and pepper to taste
6 scallions, each 4" long
12 strips green pepper
12 strips dill pickle
3/4 C. Italian salad dressing

1. Season each fillet with salt and pepper. In the center of each fillet, place 1 scallion, 2 green pepper strips and 2 dill pickle strips. Roll and secure with toothpicks.
2. Pour salad dressing into a small bowl. Dip each roll in dressing to coat completely and place in a baking dish.
3. Bake at 400 F. for 15 minutes, or until fish flakes easily with a fork. Serves 4 to 6.

Flounder Kiev

This is a variation on the delectable haute cuisine classic so commonly prepared with chicken.

6 to 8 flounder fillets
½ C. soft butter
2 tbsp. chopped fresh parsley
1 tsp. lemon juice
3/4 tsp. Worcestershire sauce
¼ tsp. Tabasco sauce
1 garlic clove, finely chopped
½ tsp. salt
1/8 tsp. freshly ground black pepper
2 tbsp. water
2 eggs, lightly beaten
½ C. flour
3 C. soft bread crumbs
fat or oil for deep frying

1. Mix butter, parsley, lemon juice, Worcestershire, Tabasco and garlic. Place on wax paper and form into a roll. Chill until firm.
2. Season fillets with salt and pepper. Cut chilled butter mixture into same number of pieces as there are fillets. Place 1 piece on the end of the dark side of each fillet and roll, tucking in edges carefully so butter will not run out during cooking. Secure with toothpicks.
3. Combine water and eggs. Coat rolls with flour, dip in egg and then in bread crumbs. Make sure each roll is coated well. Repeat dipping if necessary. Chill for one hour or longer.
4. Deep fry rolls in fat. Serve immediately. Serves 6.

Pompano en Papillotte

Pompano is one of America's greatest contributions to the seafood gastronomy of the world. Most of our finest pompano comes from our southern waters, particularly off the coast of Florida. The traditional way to prepare this delicate, yet regal, gift from the sea, is to bake it in sauce in parchment. Today it is efficiently and easily baked in aluminum foil and should be served in its wrapping or "papillotte."

Interesting sauces go well with this distinctive fish and almost any dry white wine complements it. We have recommended condensed cream of shrimp soup, but mushroom, celery, cheddar cheese, or any other cream soup of your choice will do as well.

4 pompano fillets
4 tbsp. margarine
3 tbsp. chopped onion
½ lb. sliced mushrooms
aluminum foil
1 can condensed cream of shrimp soup
1 can small shrimp, washed and drained (not obligatory if other soups are used)
1/3 C. dry white wine

1. Sauté onion and fish in margarine until lightly browned on each side. Remove fish from the pan. Sauté mushrooms until limp.
2. Cut 4 aluminum foil hearts, about 8" long and 12" wide. Grease them well with margarine.
3. Mix soup and shrimp with cooked onion and wine. Place 1 tsp. in each heart. Cover with 1 fillet. Add more sauce and then some mushrooms.
4. Fold ½ the heart onto the other and squeeze edges together to seal.
5. Bake at 450 F. for 20 minutes. (If you use parchment, bake 15 minutes.)
6. Serve in "papillotte." Open at the table to delight all! Serves 4.

Oyster-Stuffed Bass

1 4-lb. bass, filleted
½ lb. butter
½ C. chopped celery
¼ C. chopped chives
1 tsp. dried celery
12 oysters, finely chopped
1½ C. flavored bread crumbs
salt and pepper to taste
5 strips of bacon

1. Heat butter and sauté celery, chives and dried celery until tender.
2. Combine oysters and bread crumbs and add to sautéed mixture. Place

all stuffing on 1 fillet. Top with second fillet and skewer tightly to prevent stuffing from escaping.
3. Place in an oiled baking dish and top with bacon. Bake at 350 F. for about 40 minutes, basting with pan juices. Serves 6 to 8.

Almond-Stuffed Mackerel

2 2½-lb. mackerel, filleted
6 tbsp. butter
1 small onion, chopped
3/4 C. chopped celery
3¼ C. soft fresh bread crumbs
1 C. chopped toasted almonds
1 tsp. sage
salt and pepper to taste
3 strips of bacon, halved

1. Melt butter in a skillet and sauté onion and celery. Blend in bread crumbs, almonds, sage, salt and pepper.
2. Place 2 fillets in a greased baking dish. Top each with ½ the stuffing. Place remaining 2 fillets on top of stuffing. Gash the backs of each 3 times and place ½ a bacon strip in each gash.
3. Bake at 375 F. for 45 minutes. Serves 4 to 6.

TUNA TREATS

Fish en Croûte

Many foods can be made en croûte–in a pastry crust. And this includes fish. The crusting idea can certainly be applied to tuna or salmon as we have done here, to make a splendid–and economical–dish. It has always been a sure-fire crowd pleaser for us.

1 large can tuna, or salmon, drained of oil
1 C. biscuit mix
¼ C. milk
2 tbsp. bread crumbs
1 small onion, chopped
2 tsp. salad dressing
½ green pepper, seeded and chopped
½ tsp. dry mustard
dash of Worcestershire sauce

1. Combine biscuit mix and milk to make a dough. Roll dough out on a lightly-floured surface to make a rectangle ½" thick.
2. Mix remaining ingredients well and spread on rectangle. Roll carefully and place on a greased cookie sheet, seam side down.
3. Bake at 400 F. for 15 minutes, until crust is browned. Slice roll and serve with sauce. Serves 4 to 6.

Sauce Suggestions

1. Cream of mushroom soup, diluted with a little milk if desired.
2. Cream of celery soup, diluted with a little milk if desired.
3. About 1 C. Béchamel Sauce.

Note: In making sauces with canned soups, follow sauce directions on can.

Variations of Fish en Croûte

1 C. biscuit mix
½ package dry onion soup mix
1 7-oz. can tuna, or whatever canned fish you have
1/3 C. garlic salad dressing
½ tsp. dry mustard
dash of Worcestershire sauce
1 can condensed cheddar cheese soup
¼ C. milk

1. Make biscuit dough per package directions. Add dry onion soup

and mix well. Roll dough out on a lightly-floured surface to make a large rectangle.
2. Combine fish, salad dressing, mustard and Worcestershire. Spread on dough. Roll carefully and place on a greased cookie sheet, seam side down.
3. Bake at 400 F. for 15 minutes, or until dough is browned.
4. Mix soup and milk and heat. Pour hot over roll and serve. Serves 4 to 6.

Tuna-Stuffed Cabbage

This is a Scandinavian specialty that makes an interesting change from the usual meat-stuffed cabbage. It is also quite economical.

2 7-oz. cans tuna
1 C. cooked rice
½ C. chopped celery
1 small onion, chopped
1 egg, beaten
1 tbsp. tangy prepared mustard
½ tsp. white horseradish
12 large cabbage leaves
2 tbsp. butter
1 tbsp. brown sugar
2 C. chicken bouillon
2 tbsp. instant blending flour
½ C. light cream
salt and pepper to taste

1. Combine tuna, rice, celery, onion, egg, mustard and horseradish.
2. Parboil cabbage leaves in boiling salted water for 3 minutes.
3. Divide stuffing and place in center of each leaf. Fold sides inward and roll. Secure with toothpicks.
4. In a large, deep skillet, melt the butter and sauté the rolls. Add sugar and bouillon. Simmer covered for 35 minutes.
5. Remove rolls from skillet and carefully remove toothpicks. Keep rolls warm in a serving dish.
6. Combine flour and cream and add to the bouillon juice in skillet. Season to taste and pour over rolls. Serves 6.

Tuna-Onion Pie

An extremely attractive, inexpensive, and easy to assemble tuna gem.

The Filling

2 tbsp. butter
1 small onion, chopped
¼ C. instant blending flour
¼ C. vegetable or chicken bouillon
1 small can evaporated milk
½ tsp. dry mustard
dash of Worcestershire sauce
1 tbsp. chopped fresh parsley
salt and pepper to taste
2 7-oz. cans tuna, well-flaked

1. Melt butter in a frying pan and sauté onion until tender. Add flour and blend well. Add bouillon. Blend together and add evaporated milk, mustard, Worcestershire, parsley, salt and pepper. Cook until mixture thickens. Add tuna. Cool.

The Pie Crust

1½ recipes "The Dough," or 2 C. biscuit mix combined with ½ C. milk
½ C. grated sharp cheddar cheese

1. Mix cheese into flour and blend in the margarine. Chill well. Add ice water and roll out for a 2-crust pie.
2. If you use the biscuit mix, blend cheese with mix and add milk. Then roll out dough for a 2-crust pie.
3. Line a 9" pie tin with 2/3 of the dough. Spoon in filling. Top with remaining dough and crimp edges. Prick with fork in center to allow steam to escape.
4. Bake at 400 F. for 30 minutes, or until crust is browned. Serves 4 to 6.

STUFFED WHOLE FISH

When you have your fish dealer prepare a whole fish for stuffing, have him clean it, scale it, and remove the head and tail.

Portuguese Stuffed Fish

Portuguese cuisine is little known in this country, and here is an authentic and especially exciting dish from this land bordered by the sea, where fish is indeed a very important part of the national diet.

1 5-lb. fish, prepared for stuffing
salt and pepper to taste
4 tbsp. butter
2 tbsp. instant blending flour
1 C. milk
2 egg yolks, beaten
1 tbsp. lemon juice
¼ C. dry bread crumbs
1 C. cooked, cleaned baby shrimp
¼ C. dry white wine
2 C. chopped cooked beets
2 C. cooked peas

1. Salt inside of fish.
2. Melt 2 tbsp. butter in a saucepan. Add flour, salt and pepper and stir until all butter is absorbed. Add milk and cook over low heat until mixture is thick.
3. Add some of the sauce to egg yolks, blend well and return to remaining sauce. Stir and add lemon juice.
4. Combine ½ the sauce with bread crumbs and shrimp. Stuff the fish and skewer closed.
5. Place in a lightly-greased baking dish. Combine remaining sauce, wine and remaining butter and pour over fish. Bake at 350 F. for 40 minutes.
6. To serve, garnish with warm peas and beets. Serves 6 to 8.

Bacon-Stuffed Trout

1 4-lb. trout, prepared for stuffing
salt and pepper to taste
4 strips of bacon
1 small onion, minced
1 egg, beaten
2 C. soft bread crumbs
1 tsp. lemon juice
1 tbsp. chopped fresh parsley
1/8 tsp. nutmeg
2 tbsp. milk
¼ tsp. thyme

1. Cook bacon and onion together until tender. Remove from fat.
2. Combine egg and bread crumbs. Add remaining ingredients. Combine

with bacon and onion.
3. Season inside of fish with salt and pepper. Stuff and skewer closed.
4. Place in a lightly-greased baking dish and bake at 350 F. for 30 minutes. Serves 4 to 6.

Bluefish with Caper Stuffing

1 5-lb. bluefish, prepared for stuffing
salt and pepper to taste
3 tbsp. capers
1 sour pickle, chopped
1 tbsp. melted butter
2 C. cooked rice
½ C. chopped celery
1 medium onion, sliced
1 lemon, sliced
½ C. boiling water

1. Salt and pepper inside of fish.
2. Combine capers, pickle, butter, rice and celery. Stuff fish. Arrange onion and lemon slices on top and place in a baking dish.
3. Pour ½ C. boiling water over fish. Bake at 350 F. for 50 minutes. Serves 6 to 8.

Whole Stuffed Mackerel

3 1-lb. mackerel, prepared for stuffing
6 tbsp. cooking oil
¼ C. chopped mushrooms
1 small onion, chopped
1 C. seasoned bread crumbs
¼ C. Parmesan cheese
½ tsp. marjoram
salt and pepper to taste
1 lemon, sliced

1. Heat 3 tbsp. oil and sauté mushrooms and onion until tender.
2. Combine bread crumbs, cheese, marjoram, salt and pepper with sautéed mixture. Stuff fish and skewer to close.
3. Brush remaining oil over fish and place in a baking dish.
4. Bake at 400 F. for 15 minutes. Reduce heat to 300 F. and bake 15 minutes longer. Serve garnished with lemon slices. Serves 4 to 6.

Stuffed Sardines

Delicately stuffed and elegantly sauced with tomato and wine, this is a tasty treatment for sardines.

2 lbs. fresh sardines, prepared for stuffing
1½ C. flavored bread crumbs
1 small onion, chopped
4 tbsp. olive oil
¼ C. grated Parmesan cheese
1 garlic clove, finely chopped
salt and pepper to taste

1. Combine all filling ingredients. Stuff fish and skewer or tie with thread.
2. Place in a large frying pan or Dutch oven and cover with The Sauce.
3. Cook over low heat about 15 minutes. Serves 4 as a main course, or 6 as an appetizer.

The Sauce

3 tbsp. olive oil
1 garlic clove, chopped
1 6-oz. can tomato paste
½ C. dry white wine
1 tsp. basil
salt and pepper to taste

1. Combine all ingredients in a saucepan and simmer 20 minutes. Pour over stuffed fish.

Herb-Stuffed Bass

1 4-lb. striped bass, prepared for stuffing
5 tbsp. oil
1 medium onion, chopped
½ C. chopped celery
1 garlic clove, chopped
¼ C. grated cheddar cheese
2 C. unflavored bread crumbs

juice of 1 lemon
2 tbsp. chopped fresh parsley
½ tsp. basil
½ tsp. thyme
½ tsp. marjoram
salt and pepper to taste
1/8 C. dry white wine
1/8 C. water

1. Sauté onion and celery in 2½ tbsp. oil for 3 minutes. Add garlic and cook until tender.
2. Combine remaining ingredients, except wine, water and remaining oil, and mix with sautéed mixture. Stuff fish and skewer to close. Rub with remaining oil.
3. Place fish in a shallow pan and pour wine and water over. Use to baste fish while cooking. Bake at 400 F. for 10 minutes. Reduce heat to 350 F. and bake for 20 minutes longer. Serves 4 to 6.

Italian Stuffed Bass

1 4-lb. bass, prepared for stuffing, but do not remove tail
3 C. chicken broth
1 C. raw rice
¼ lb. butter
1 C. chopped onion
1 C. chopped celery
salt and pepper to taste
5 tbsp. chopped fresh parsley
½ C. blanched almonds
½ C. raisins, soaked in madeira
1 small can clams, minced
juice of 1 lemon
½ C. olive oil
1 C. dry white wine
1 tbsp. oregano

1. Cook rice in 2½ cups of broth until tender.
2. Melt butter and sauté onion and celery. Season with salt and pepper

and add almonds, raisins, clams and 3 tbsp. parsley. Add remaining broth, to moisten. Stuff fish and skewer to close.
3. Place fish in shallow pan and season with lemon juice. Combine oil, wine, oregano and remaining parsley. Pour around fish.
4. Bake at 375 F. for 45 minutes. Serves 6 to 8.

Stuffed Bass with Cucumber Sauce

1 3-lb. striped bass, prepared for stuffing
¼ C. butter
½ C. chopped onion
4 tbsp. chopped celery
½ lb. cooked crab meat
2 tbsp. chopped fresh parsley
salt and pepper to taste
1 C. bread crumbs
¼ C. milk, or cream

1. Melt butter and cook onion and celery until tender.
2. Add crab meat, parsley, salt, pepper, bread crumbs and milk. Mix well together. Stuff fish and skewer closed. Place in a buttered baking dish and dot with additional butter.
3. Bake at 400 F. for about 35 minutes, or until fish flakes easily.
4. Serve covered with Cucumber Sauce. Serves 4 to 6.

The Cucumber Sauce

3 tbsp. butter, or margarine
3 tbsp. flour
¼ C. clam juice
1 C. milk
¼ C. cream
½ C. chopped cucumber

1. Melt butter and stir in flour. Add clam juice and milk. Stir until sauce thickens.
2. Simmer 5 minutes, stirring occasionally. Just before serving, stir in cream and cucumber.

Stuffed Red Snapper

1 2½- to 3-lb. red snapper, prepared for stuffing
4 tbsp. butter
1 large onion, minced
½ green pepper, seeded and chopped
3/4 C. chopped celery
3 C. mashed potatoes (1½ lbs. when raw)
1/8 tsp. sage
¼ tsp. thyme
salt to taste
¼ tsp. black pepper

1. Cook onion, green pepper and celery in 2 tbsp. butter until onion is transparent. Mix with potatoes and seasonings. Stuff fish and skewer to close.
2. Place fish in a buttered baking dish. Score skin lightly in a few places. Melt remaining butter and sprinkle over fish.
3. Bake in a pre-heated oven at 375 F. for about 35 minutes, or until fish flakes easily. Serves 4.

Stuffed Red Snapper Biscayne

1 4- to 5-lb. red snapper, prepared for stuffing
salt
6 tbsp. margarine
½ medium onion, minced
1 C. bread crumbs
½ C. cracker crumbs
½ tsp. dried dill
3 tsp. chopped fresh parsley
salt and black pepper to taste
1 grapefruit, sectioned, with juice
1 orange, sectioned

1. Sprinkle fish inside and out with salt.
2. Melt 4 tbsp. margarine and cook onion until it is transparent.
3. Add bread and cracker crumbs, dill, parsley, salt and pepper. Mix well. Stuff fish.

4. Place fish in a greased, foil-lined pan. Bake in a pre-heated oven at 400 F. for about 40 minutes, or until fish flakes easily. Brush often during baking with a mixture of grapefruit juice and remaining margarine.
5. A few minutes before removing fish from oven, put grapefruit and orance sections on top of it and brush with remaining margarine mixture or additional margarine. Serves 6 to 8.

Crab-Stuffed Halibut with Cucumber Sauce

1 4-lb. piece of halibut, prepared for stuffing
¼ C. butter
½ lb. mushrooms, chopped
¼ C. chopped onion
2 tbsp. chopped fresh parsley
½ lb. cooked crab meat, flaked
1½ C. cooked rice
¼ C. light cream
salt and pepper to taste

1. Sauté mushrooms and onion in a small portion of the butter until tender. Add remaining ingredients. Stuff fish and skewer to close.
2. Place in a baking dish and cover with remaining butter. Bake at 350 F. for 1 hour. Cover with Cucumber Sauce from page 189. Serves 6 to 8.

Noodle-Stuffed Halibut with Cold Cucumber Sauce

1 4-lb. piece of halibut, prepared for stuffing
butter
1 large onion, chopped
2 tbsp. minced fresh parsley
3/4 C. chopped celery
2 tsp. basil
½ tsp. oregano
½ tsp. thyme
2 tbsp. lemon juice
3 C. cooked fine noodles
salt and pepper to taste

1. Sauté onion and celery in a small amount of butter until tender. Add remaining ingredients. Stuff fish and skewer to close.
2. Place fish in a lightly-greased baking dish. Bake at 350 F. for 1 hour. Serve covered with Cold Cucumber Sauce. Serves 6 to 8.

The Cold Cucumber Sauce

½ C. sour cream
½ C. mayonnaise
1 C. finely diced cucumber
1 tsp. lemon juice
¼ tsp. salt
dash of Tabasco sauce

1. Combine all ingredients and chill well. Pour over fish before serving.

SQUID MEDITERRANEAN

Here is an interesting preparation of squid, a fish popular in many Mediterranean countries, particularly in Italy, and in Greece. For a touch of intrigue, serve this with ouzo, a well-known, anise-flavored Greek apéritif wine. The ouzo is quite strong and should be mixed with a little water.

1 2-lb. squid
¼ C. olive oil
1 bunch scallions, chopped
1 garlic clove, minced
1 tbsp. chopped fresh parsley
¼ tsp. oregano
½ C. dry white wine
1 C. frozen chopped spinach, thawed and well-drained
½ C. cooked rice
juice of 1 lemon
½ C. clam broth
1¼ C. chicken bouillon

1. Clean and prepare squid for stuffing, removing ink bag and tentacles. Reserve tentacles.
2. Heat olive oil and brown scallions, garlic, parsley and oregano. Add wine and tentacles. Braise slightly for 5 minutes.
3. Add chopped spinach and rice and simmer for 20 minutes.
4. Stuff squid and place in a skillet. Add lemon juice and a bit more olive oil if desired. Add clam broth and bouillon and simmer for 30 minutes.
5. Cool and slice to serve. Serves 4.

STUFFED SHRIMP SUPREME

The French call them "crevettes," the Germans call them "krabben" and the Spanish call them "camarones." But whatever you call them, shrimp are universally popular. Our name for them was supposedly derived from the habit they have of curling up or shrinking when caught. A large proportion of the shrimp consumed in this country comes from the Gulf Coast region, especially from Louisiana.

Most shrimp can be cooked in about 4 minutes and should never be overcooked, or they will become tough. (It is always a good idea to keep cooked shrimp in sealed plastic bags in your freezer, ready for thawing and use whenever you need them.)

Shrimp with Crab Stuffing

1 lb. raw jumbo shrimp (12 to 15 in a pound)
1 small onion, finely chopped
½ green pepper, seeded and chopped
¼ C. melted butter
2 slices white bread, cubed
1 lb. cooked crab meat, well-flaked
2 tbsp. mayonnaise
1 tsp. Worcestershire sauce
1 tsp. tangy prepared mustard

1. Clean and devein shrimp. On deveined side, slit shrimp 3/4 of the way through and spread out butterfly fashion.
2. Sauté onion and pepper in a small portion of melted butter.
3. Combine bread, crab meat, mayonnaise, Worcestershire, mustard and sautéed onion and pepper.
4. Divide stuffing among the shrimp. Fold. Place stuffing side down on a greased baking dish. Brush with remaining butter.
5. Bake at 400 F. for 15 minutes, or until golden. Serves 2 to 3.

Stuffed Jumbo Shrimp Creole

2½ lbs. raw jumbo shrimp (12 to 15 in a pound)
3 tbsp. olive oil
1 small onion, chopped
1 garlic clove, minced
¼ C. finely chopped green pepper
1 7-oz. can water-packed tuna, drained
1 egg, beaten
1 C. cooked rice
2 tbsp. tomato sauce
¼ tsp. salt
dash of pepper

1. Clean and devein shrimp. On deveined side, slit shrimp 3/4 of the way through and spread out butterfly fashion.
2. Sauté onion, garlic and green pepper in olive oil until tender. Drain off oil and reserve.
3. Combine tuna, egg, rice, tomato sauce and salt and pepper with sautéed mixture.
4. Divide stuffing among shrimp. Fold and place stuffing side down in a broiling pan that has been lightly oiled with some of the reserved oil. Brush tops with oil.
5. Broil 5 to 7 minutes, or until well-cooked. Serves 6 to 8.

STUFFED CRABS

Despite their name, crabs are delicious and fun too. Our first recipe is from the Basque country of northern Spain, and it can be made with our own large, Maryland crabs. This dish is perfect served with plain boiled rice, or even with saffron rice.

The other two recipes, one from Spain and one from France, can be made with frozen or canned crab meat. Of course, if you have an old-fashioned fish market nearby, fresh crab meat is always preferable. It is delicate in flavor and the chunks are usually large. But it will be necessary to pick it over well to remove all pieces of shell and cartilage.

Basque Stuffed Crab

4 large live crabs
4 tbsp. olive oil
2 medium onions, minced
2 garlic cloves, minced
2 tomatoes, peeled and chopped
3 tbsp. chopped fresh parsley
1 C. dry white wine
2 tsp. salt
2 tsp. sugar
½ C. dry bread crumbs
¼ C. butter

1. Cook crabs by plunging them live into boiling salted water to cover. Boil for 30 minutes. Remove and allow to cool.

2. To clean, break off claws, remove back and scrape out all soft parts underneath. Cut out small oval-shaped section on underside of crab. Crack legs and scrape out meat. Remove meat from shell. Drain and save juices. All of this can be done in advance so that only the final preparation for the shells is left to do. Save body shells.
3. Fry onion and garlic slowly in olive oil. As they are browning, increase heat. Add tomatoes and cook until liquid evaporates. Add parsley and wine. Cook over high heat for 2 to 3 minutes, until alcohol has evaporated.
4. Put internal parts of crab and juices through a colander. Blend into the sauce with salt and sugar. This can all be done in advance and refrigerated.
5. Before serving, heat crab meat in sauce and fill body shells. Sprinkle tops with bread crumbs, dot with butter. Brown in 400 F. oven. Serves 4.

Spanish Stuffed Crab

2 live hard-shelled crabs, or ¼ lb. canned crab
1 medium onion, chopped
2 tbsp. olive oil
1 garlic clove, minced
2 small tomatoes, peeled and chopped
½ tsp. paprika
¼ C. cognac
4 tbsp. bread crumbs
2 tbsp. margarine

1. Cook crabs by plunging them live into boiling salted water to cover. Boil for 15 minutes. Allow to cool.
2. To clean, break off claws, remove back and scrape out all soft parts underneath. Cut out small oval-shaped section on underside of crab. Crack legs and scrape out meat. Remove meat from shell. Drain and save juices. All of this can be done in advance so that only the final preparation for the shells is left to do. Save body shells.
3. Heat olive oil and fry onion. When onion becomes golden, add garlic and brown. Add tomatoes. Remove from heat and stir in paprika. Return to heat, pour in cognac and cook until alcohol evaporates.
4. Add crab meat and juice from shell (or can). Fill crab shell with the mixture. Sprinkle tops with bread crumbs and dot with margarine. Place in a hot oven for about 10 minutes, or until browned and golden.

5. If live crab is not available, use individual ramekins or scallop shells in place of crab shells. Serves 2.

Caribbean Crab

A basically French recipe with Caribbean overtones.

3 firm avocados
6 tbsp. garlic vinegar
2 tbsp. margarine
2 tbsp. instant blending flour
1 C. cream, scalded
salt and pepper to taste
1½ C. cooked crab meat
1 tbsp. capers, drained
dash of Worcestershire sauce
6 tbsp. grated cheddar cheese

1. Cut avocados in half lengthwise and remove pits, but do not peel. Sprinkle each half with 1 tbsp. vinegar. Let stand for 30 minutes.
2. Melt margarine and blend in flour. Add scalded cream. Cook, stirring constantly until sauce is smooth and thickened. Add salt, pepper, crab meat, capers and Worcestershire.
3. Stuff avocado halves with crab mixture and sprinkle each with 1 tbsp. cheese. Bake in a pre-heated oven at 375 F. until thoroughly warmed, or about 20 minutes. Serves 6.

FABULOUS FISH STUFFINGS

The following roster of recipes provides a wide selection of delicious all-purpose fish and shellfish stuffings. Each one is enough to stuff a 4-lb. fish, and the seasonings used can be altered to suit any palate. All of them are quick and easy to prepare and can be made in advance and frozen. So, you can always have a good supply of interesting fish stuffings on hand. Simply thaw the one you like and go to work. If you use a smaller fish, simply halve the amounts. As a general rule, bake at 350 F. until done.

The Basic Fish Stuffing

2 tbsp. butter
1 small onion, minced
3 C. soft bread crumbs
¼ C. milk
¼ tsp. rosemary
½ tsp. thyme
salt and pepper to taste

1. Melt butter in a skillet and sauté onion until tender. Add onion to remaining ingredients. Mix and stuff fish.

Variations

1. Celery–omit milk and add 1 C. cooked chopped celery
2. Cheese–add 1 C. grated Cheese
3. Green pepper–omit milk and add ½ C. cooked, chopped green pepper
4. Mushroom–add ¼ lb. cooked sliced mushrooms

Herb and Wine Stuffing

1 tbsp. butter
1 small onion, chopped
1½ C. soft bread crumbs
¼ C. cooked chopped celery
¼ C. dry white wine
½ tsp. basil
1/8 tsp. rosemary
salt and pepper to taste

1. Melt butter in a skillet and sauté onion until tender. Combine remaining ingredients and add onion. Mix and stuff fish.

Shellfish Variation

1. Add 1 C. cooked crab, lobster or shrimp to basic Herb and Wine Stuffing.

Hawaiian Stuffing

2 C. cooked rice
1 egg, beaten
1 C. crushed pineapple, drained
½ C. coconut flakes
2 tbsp. lemon juice
2 strips of bacon, cooked and crumbled
salt to taste

1. Combine all ingredients and stuff fish.

Wild Rice and Mushroom Stuffing

¼ C. butter
1 medium onion, chopped
1 C. sliced fresh mushrooms
2½ C. cooked long grain and wild rice mixture
½ C. canned cream of mushroom soup
1 egg, beaten
¼ tsp. rosemary
½ tsp. thyme
salt to taste

1. Sauté onion and mushrooms in butter until tender. Combine with remaining ingredients and stuff fish.

Sour Cream Stuffing

¼ C. butter, melted
1 small onion, chopped
1½ C. chopped celery
5 C. soft bread crumbs
½ C. sour cream
2 tbsp. milk
1 egg, beaten
½ tsp. poultry seasoning
salt to taste

1. Sauté onion and celery in a small amount of butter. Combine with remaining ingredients and blend well. Stuffs a 5-lb. fish.

SHELLFISH STUFFINGS

Clam Stuffing

2 8-oz. cans clams in broth
2 tbsp. butter
1 small onion, chopped
½ tsp. thyme
¼ tsp. basil
dash of paprika
salt and pepper to taste
1 egg, beaten
2½ C. dry bread crumbs

1. Drain and clean clams. Reserve broth.
2. Sauté onion in butter and add seasonings.
3. Combine egg with bread crumbs. Add onion and herb mixture. If too dry, add a little clam broth. Stuff fish.

Variations

Use the basic Clam Stuffing recipe, but omit the clams.

1. Crab–1 C. cooked flaked crab meat. Use 2 tbsp. milk instead of clam broth.
2. Lobster–1 C. cooked diced lobster. Use 2 tbsp. milk instead of clamb broth.
3. Oyster–1 pint of oysters in broth. Follow recipe.
4. Shrimp–1 C. diced cooked shrimp. Use 2 tbsp. milk instead of clam broth.

Herbed Shellfish Stuffing

1 C. diced cooked shellfish
3 tbsp. butter
1 celery stalk, minced
1 small onion, chopped
2 scallions, minced
1 garlic clove, minced
1 egg, beaten
3 C. dry bread crumbs
¼ tsp. rosemary
¼ tsp. thyme
¼ C. dry sherry
salt and pepper to taste

1. Sauté celery, onion, scallions and garlic in butter until tender.
2. Combine egg and bread crumbs and all remaining ingredients. Stuff fish.

VII. INTRIGUING ACCOMPANIMENTS

The World of Vegetables

An exotic vegetable dish can often make the difference between a main course that is ordinary or even excellent, and one that is truly inspired. Savory rolled and stuffed vegetables can dramatize and complement your center-stage fare and can go far to enhance the simplicity of a roast or even enliven a platter of cold, sliced meat. Or, if you have a particularly exciting vegetable creation in mind, you might want to adopt the French custom of making an intriguing vegetable an accented first course. In this case, the potatoes (or pasta or rice) and salad should be served with the main course.

Although modern food experts tout vegetables as being extremely healthful and nutritious, and although vegetables have so increased in popularity in recent years that even zucchini has become fairly common, our ancestors virtually ignored the world of vegetables. Very old menus list no vegetables of any sort. Vast quantities of game, meat, poultry and sweets were the mainstays, and winter was definitely a time without fresh produce. Eventually elaborate kitchen gardens began to flourish, however, and vegetables joined meats on the menu.

We hope you will become as adept with vegetables as the Chinese and the French, who are famed the world over for their expertise with legumes as well as other cookery. In China, and in most of the Orient actually, asparagus, snow peas, young green bamboo shoots and other vegetables are cooked gently and served just underdone. The French excel, of course, in using various herbs and spices with their vegetables.

In the creative spirit of the Chinese and French, therefore, here is a greatly varied world of fresh new ideas in vegetable savoir faire for the adventurous cook. We have offered a number of ways to fill a plump purple eggplant, tender green zucchini, a crisp fresh pepper, tomato or onion. You can heap mixtures of meat, fish or shellfish into vegetables for an exciting main course, or you can embellish your legumes with spices, cheeses, dashes of other vegetables, rice, seasoned bread crumbs, crumbled bits of bacon and sausage, croutons, splashes of wine–what you will–to achieve a delightful and totally new taste experience.

Thin slices of white onion enhance many other vegetables, such as carrots, peas and many kinds of beans. Crisp slivers of toasted almonds, hazelnuts, macadamia nuts or pine nuts dress up many vegetables, including Brussels sprouts, spinach and broccoli. A sprinkling of caraway seed is a fillip you shouldn't ignore, and parsley goes with absolutely everything. Garlic is a very important accent in vegetable cookery, even though temple priests of the ancient world considered it an abomination and forbade anyone with garlic on his breath to enter their precincts. Nevertheless, people continued to use garlic and, in fact, Aristotle, Pliny and some oriental physicians even praised its medicinal properties. In haute cuisine, or in any cuisine with imagination, its delicate application is indispensable.

Enjoy experimenting! Don't be afraid of artichokes, leeks, or a host of aromatic spices. Following our general pattern, learn to combine your own leftovers to create exciting new dishes. Spice them, sauce them and interchange. As with our other recipes, most of the vegetable stuffers are scandalously simple, can be prepared ahead, and often can be frozen.

The judicious use of stuffed vegetables, especially if you think about them as candidates for main dishes, can be an excellent way of paring down your food budget. Eggplants, zucchini and peppers, for example, can be economical as well as delicious and filling when they are stuffed.

Note: Most Americans generally boil vegetables until they are tasteless and then forget about them–which perhaps they should be if cooked too long. Vegetables should be undercooked, if anything. In other words, if it doesn't crunch, don't serve it!

Note: The portion notations given with the vegetable recipes are approximate, and depend upon whether you plan to serve them as main dishes or as side dishes.

NEW ACCENTS ON TOMATOES

Tomatoes, called "pommes d'amour" or love apples in former times, were, strangely enough, a gift to the world from the Americas, along with the potato, green pepper, corn and beans. Before Columbus, Europeans were not acquainted with tomatoes. Our own puritanical forefathers considered tomatoes poisonous and refused to eat them, probably because they thought this dramatic-looking vegetable might have some sinful effect. Europeans, on the other hand, readily adopted tomatoes and their use spread rapidly throughout the Mediterranean countries. Curiously enough, one variety of tomato, the Italian plum tomato, has traveled back across the Atlantic to become popular in this country.

Here then is a rich potpourri of ideas for making a simple tomato into a masterpiece of culinary art.

Tomatoes with Rice Stuffing

6 to 8 large tomatoes
½ C. olive oil
2 onions, finely chopped
3 oz. raw rice
3 tbsp. chopped fresh parsley
1 tbsp. white raisins
salt and pepper to taste
2 tbsp. boiling water
2 tbsp. flavored bread crumbs

1. Slice off tops of the tomatoes. Scoop out the pulp and sieve it. Invert the tomatoes to drain.

2. Heat ¼ C. oil in a skillet and fry the onion and rice. Add ½ the tomato pulp, parsley, raisins, salt and pepper and boiling water. Cover pan and simmer until no liquid is left.
3. Stuff tomatoes and place them in an oven-proof dish. Sprinkle with bread crumbs. Pour remaining oil on top.
4. Bake at 350 F. for 20 to 25 minutes. Serves 6 to 8.

Baked Eggs in Tomatoes

This is an intriguing idea for breakfast, brunch, or even luncheon.

tomatoes
eggs
salt and pepper to taste
Parmesan cheese
cooked bacon

1. Slice off tops of as many tomatoes as there are persons to be served. Scoop out the pulp and invert tomatoes to drain.
2. Break 1 egg into each tomato and season with salt and pepper.
3. Bake at 350 F. for 15 minutes, or until egg whites are set.
4. Sprinkle with Parmesan and brown quickly under broiler. Serve with bacon.

Ham 'n Eggs Baked Tomato

tomatoes
diced cooked ham
eggs
salt and pepper to taste
buttered bread crumbs

1. Slice off tops of as many tomatoes as there are persons to be served. Scoop out the pulp and invert tomatoes to drain.
2. Place some diced ham in the tomatoes. Break 1 egg into each tomato and season with salt and pepper. Top with buttered bread crumbs.
3. Bake at 350 F. for 15 minutes, or until firm.

Cucumber-Stuffed Tomatoes

6 tomatoes
2 cucumbers, peeled and cubed
2 tbsp. grated onion
2 tsp. lemon juice
¼ C. butter
½ C. water
salt and pepper to taste
buttered bread crumbs

1. Slice off tops of the tomatoes. Scoop out the pulp and invert tomatoes to drain.
2. Place cucumbers in a pan and add onion, lemon juice, butter, water, salt and pepper. Simmer for 5 minutes.
3. Stuff tomatoes with cucumber mixture and top with bread crumbs.
4. Bake at 350 F. for 10 minutes. Serves 6.

Tomatoes Stuffed with Pickled Cucumbers

6 tomatoes
2 cucumbers, peeled and very thinly sliced
½ C. red wine vinegar
½ tsp. tarragon
½ tsp. dried dill
1/3 C. salad oil
2 tsp. sugar

1. Combine vinegar, tarragon, dill, oil and sugar. Pour over cucumbers and marinate for several hours in refrigerator.
2. Slice off tops of the tomatoes. Scoop out the pulp and invert tomatoes to drain.
3. Fill tomatoes with cucumber mixture and use marinade as salad dressing. Serves 6.

Tomatoes with Spinach Purée

6 tomatoes
1 C. hot cooked spinach, well-drained
¼ tsp. nutmeg
bread crumbs
salt and pepper to taste

1. Slice off tops of the tomatoes. Scoop out the pulp and invert tomatoes to drain.

2. Place spinach in a blender with a little of the liquid in which it was cooked. Blend until spinach is puréed. Season with nutmeg, salt and pepper.
3. Fill tomatoes with spinach and top with bread crumbs.
4. Bake at 350 F. for 10 minutes. Serves 6.

Stuffed Tomatoes with Chicken

6 tomatoes
2 tbsp. butter
½ tbsp. finely chopped onion
½ C. cooked diced chicken
½ C. flavored bread crumbs
1 egg, beaten
salt and pepper to taste
buttered bread crumbs

1. Slice off tops of the tomatoes. Scoop out the pulp and reserve. Invert tomatoes to drain.
2. Sauté onion in butter and add chicken, flavored bread crumbs and tomato pulp. Add beaten egg, salt and pepper and cook for 1 minute.
3. Fill tomatoes with the mixture and top with buttered bread crumbs.
4. Bake at 400 F. for 20 minutes. Serves 6.

Variations

Substitute any of the following for the chicken: veal, shrimp, crab meat or lobster.

MEDLEY OF TOMATO STUFFINGS

Here are some additional, interesting stuffings for tomatoes. All of these are enough for 6 large tomatoes, and you should reduce or increase the amounts as needed. The first thing to do is slice off the tops of the tomatoes, remove the pulp and invert the tomatoes to drain. Then prepare your stuffings. All stuffed tomatoes in this section should be baked at 350 F. for 15 minutes.

Ham and Mushroom Stuffing

½ C. sliced mushrooms
½ onion, chopped
1 shallot, sliced
oil
1 C. chopped cooked ham
¼ tsp. nutmeg
salt and pepper to taste
bread crumbs

1. Sauté mushrooms, onion and shallot in a little oil. Combine with ham, nutmeg, salt and pepper.
2. Fill tomatoes. Top with bread crumbs and a little oil.

Sausage-Stuffed Tomatoes

1½ C. bulk sausage meat, cooked
1 small onion, chopped
1 garlic clove, chopped
oil
salt and pepper to taste
bread crumbs
2 tbsp. chopped fresh parsley

1. Sauté onion and garlic in a little oil until tender. Combine with sausage, salt and pepper, 2 tbsp. bread crumbs and parsley.
2. Fill tomatoes and top with bread crumbs.

Egg-and-Sausage-Stuffed Tomatoes

Follow directions for Sausage-Stuffed Tomatoes, but use only 1 C. sausage and add 2 chopped hard-cooked eggs.

Variations

You can add 2 tbsp. chopped sautéed green pepper or 2 tbsp. chopped sautéed mushrooms to any recipe. Also, you can add a variety of other seasonings, such as ½ tsp. curry powder, ½ tsp. oregano or ½ tsp. basil.

STUFFED CUCUMBERS

Cucumbers with Feta Cheese

Feta cheese is the famous crumbly white cheese of Greek origin. It has a tangy flavor and part of its distinctive taste comes from its being preserved in brine. It can be purchased in fine cheese shops or in markets specializing in Greek foods. This recipe is a variation of a well-known Greek dish.

4 cucumbers, peeled and cut in half lengthwise
1 tbsp. mayonnaise
½ C. crumbled feta cheese
1/8 tsp. Worcestershire sauce
1 tbsp. chopped fresh parsley

1. Scoop out centers of cucumbers. Chill cucumbers.
2. Combine mayonnaise, feta and Worcestershire. Stuff cucumbers and sprinkle with parsley. Serve cold. Serves 4 to 6.

Ham-Stuffed Cucumbers

2 large cucumbers, peeled and cut into 2" slices
4 tbsp. flavored bread crumbs
4 tbsp. finely chopped cooked ham
2 tbsp. grated Parmesan cheese
dash of cayenne
salt and pepper to taste
2 oz. tomato sauce
3/4 C. chicken bouillon
buttered bread crumbs

1. Remove seeds from cucumber slices.
2. Combine flavored bread crumbs, ham, Parmesan, cayenne, salt and pepper. Moisten this mixture with tomato sauce.
3. Stuff cucumbers and place in a baking dish. Pour bouillon around them. Sprinkle with buttered bread crumbs.
4. Bake at 350 F. for 20 minutes. Serves 4 to 6.

Braised Shrimp-Stuffed Cucumbers

6 small cucumbers, peeled and cut in half lengthwise
1 C. diced cooked shrimp
1 egg, beaten
1½ tsp. cornstarch
oil
1 tsp. soy sauce
3/4 C. chicken bouillon
2 tbsp. dry sherry

1. Remove seeds from the cucumber halves.
2. Combine shrimp, egg and ½ tsp. cornstarch. Stuff the cucumbers.
3. Fry cucumbers in oil, stuffing side down, until golden. Add soy sauce, bouillon and sherry. Cover and cook slowly for 15 minutes.
4. Remove cucumbers from the liquid. Add remaining 1 tsp. cornstarch to 2 tbsp. of the liquid and mix to lump-free consistency. Pour this back into the pan and cook over high heat until sauce is thick and clear.
5. Pour over cucumbers to serve. Serves 6.

Chicken-Stuffed Cucumbers

3 large cucumbers, peeled and cut into 2" slices
¼ C. butter
2 tbsp. finely chopped scallions
¼ C. bread crumbs
½ C. diced cooked chicken; or turkey, veal or ground beef
1 tbsp. pine nuts
¼ tsp. thyme
salt and pepper to taste
¼ C. bouillon

1. Remove seeds from cucumber slices. Place slices in boiling salted water for 3 minutes. Drain well.
2. Sauté scallions in 2 tbsp. of the butter. Add bread crumbs, chicken, nuts, thyme, salt and pepper. Moisten the mixture with a little bouillon.
3. Stuff cucumber slices and place in a buttered baking dish. Melt remaining butter and pour over cucumbers. Add enough bouillon to cover the cucumbers about half way.
4. Bake at 375 F. for 20 minutes. Serves 3.

ASPARAGUS ROLL-UPS DANSK

The French often give the lordly asparagus a separate place on the menu, generally following the meat. But they also serve it as a first course. Here is a tempting asparagus preparation from Denmark that can easily double as an appetizer or hors d'oeuvre with drinks, or as an elegant and unusual first course.

20 cooked asparagus spears (canned may be used)
10 thin slices white bread, crusts removed
¼ C. butter or margarine, softened
½ lb. cooked cleaned shrimp, finely chopped
1 3-oz. package cream cheese, softened
½ tsp. soy sauce
2 drops Tabasco sauce
½ tsp. white horseradish
½ tsp. prepared mustard

1. Drain asparagus and set aside. Use a rolling pin to flatten bread slices and then carefully butter them, making sure entire surface is covered.
2. Combine shrimp, cream cheese, soy sauce, Tabasco, horseradish and mustard. Blend well. Spread on buttered bread. Place 2 asparagus spears on each slice.
3. Roll each slice like a jellyroll and secure end with a toothpick. These may be prepared ahead of time, refrigerated and covered with foil. Serve cold. Serves 5.

STUFFED ZUCCHINI

As a general rule, the tender white flesh of the zucchini can always be made more tasty by a hint of garlic, a sprinkling of bacon or Parmesan cheese, a touch of onion, tomatoes, or a dusting of buttered bread crumbs. The following recipes offer further embellishments for the popular zucchini.

Mushroom-Stuffed Zucchini

10 zucchini
10 strips of bacon
1 C. finely chopped onion
2 C. finely chopped celery
3/4 lb. finely chopped mushrooms
2 tbsp. tomato sauce
2 tbsp. Parmesan cheese
1 C. bread crumbs
½ tsp. oregano
½ tsp. basil
salt and pepper to taste

1. Slice zucchini in half lengthwise and place in boiling salted water for 5 minutes. Scoop out the pulp, chop and reserve for stuffing mixture.
2. Fry bacon and remove from the pan. Sauté onion and celery in bacon fat.
3. Combine remaining ingredients, except bacon, and stuff zucchini. If the stuffing seems too dry, add a little more tomato sauce. Crumble bacon on top of the stuffed zucchini and place in an oven-proof dish.
4. Bake at 350 F. for 20 minutes. Serves 10.

Zucchini Florentine

4 medium zucchini
2 packages frozen spinach; or 1 lb. fresh spinach, cooked and drained
olive oil
1 onion, chopped
1 garlic clove, chopped
2 tbsp. chopped fresh parsley
salt and pepper to taste
bread crumbs
2 tbsp. grated Parmesan cheese

1. Slice zucchini in half lengthwise and place in boiling salted water for 5 minutes. Scoop out the pulp and reserve for stuffing mixture.
2. Sauté onion, garlic and parsley in a little oil until tender. Season with

salt and pepper. Combine with spinach and zucchini pulp, and stuff zucchini.

3. Top with bread crumbs and Parmesan, and drizzle a little oil over them. Place in an oven-proof dish.
4. Bake at 350 F. for 25 minutes. Serves 8.

Zucchini Niçoise

4 medium zucchini
oil
1 small onion, chopped
1 garlic clove, chopped
2 C. rice, cooked in bouillon
2 tbsp. tomato paste
¼ C. pitted black olives, chopped
salt and pepper to taste
bread crumbs
2 tbsp. Parmesan cheese

1. Slice zucchini in half lengthwise and place in boiling salted water for 5 minutes. Scoop out the pulp and reserve.
2. Chop pulp and sauté in oil with onion and garlic until tender.
3. Combine rice, tomato paste, sautéed mixture, olives, salt and pepper. Stuff zucchini.
4. Top with bread crumbs and Parmesan and drizzle a little oil over them. Place in an oven-proof dish.
5. Bake at 350 for 25 minutes. Serves 8.

Russian Stuffed Zucchini

3 medium zucchini
1½ C. rice, cooked in bouillon
¼ lb. cooked ground lamb
½ small onion, chopped and sautéed
¼ tsp. garlic powder
salt and pepper to taste
1 C. beef bouillon
3 tbsp. tomato paste

1. Peel zucchini and cut into 1½" lengths. Scoop out seeds.
2. Combine rice, lamb, onion, garlic, salt and pepper. Stuff centers of zucchini pieces and place in a large skillet.

3. Combine bouillon and tomato paste and add to skillet to ½-way point. Cook slowly until tender. Serves 6.

Israeli Zucchini

4 medium zucchini
½ lb. ground beef
½ C. instant rice
1 tbsp. olive oil
1/8 tsp. turmeric
1/8 tsp. cumin
1/8 tsp. coriander
1 tsp. salt
pepper to taste
1½ 8-oz. cans tomato sauce

1. Slice zucchini in half lengthwise and place in boiling salted water for 5 minutes. Scoop out the pulp, chop and reserve for stuffing mixture.
2. Combine zucchini pulp, ground beef, rice and olive oil. Add seasonings and stuff zucchini. Leave room for stuffing to expand during cooking. Place zucchini in a baking dish and pour tomato sauce over all. (If there is any extra meat mixture, form meat balls and cook in sauce with zucchini.)
3. Bake at 350 F. for 45 minutes. Serves 4.

ESPECIALLY STUFFED SQUASH

These hearty crowd-pleasers hail from New England and are especially good when the cool days of autumn come.

Autumn Acorn

3 acorn squash, halved
3 tbsp. butter
2 C. chopped onion
½ lb. thinly sliced mushrooms
2 tbsp. chopped fresh parsley
salt and pepper to taste
1 tbsp. seasoned bread crumbs
1 C. grated American cheese

1. Remove fibers and seeds from squash centers. Bake, cut side down, at 350 F. for 35 to 40 minutes, or until tender.

2. Sauté onion in butter until it is creamy white. Add mushrooms and parsley. Season with salt and pepper. Fill squash.
3. Bake for 15 to 20 minutes longer. Then sprinkle with bread crumbs and cheese and place under broiler until cheese melts and bubbles. Serves 6.

Pork-Stuffed Butternut

2 butternut squash, halved
melted butter
¼ C. cooked ground pork
1 small onion, chopped
¼ C. sliced mushrooms
2 shallots, chopped
¼ tsp. nutmeg
salt and pepper to taste

1. Remove seeds from squash centers and brush well with melted butter.
2. Sauté onion, mushrooms, shallots, nutmeg, salt and pepper in a little butter. Combine with cooked pork. Stuff squash and place on a cookie sheet.
3. Bake at 350 F. for 1 hour. Serves 4.

ELEGANT EGGPLANT

The regal purple eggplant is one of the most versatile members of the vegetable family. Its subtle taste goes well with a variety of sauces and seasonings, and also combines well with other foods. Here is a profusion of ideas for preparing eggplant–many of them are Mediterranean inspired, but some come from other corners of the world.

Lamb-Stuffed Eggplant

2 1-lb. eggplants
2 tbsp. butter
1 onion, chopped
1 lb. ground lamb
½ C. dry white wine

1 1-lb. can tomatoes, drained and chopped
1 tbsp. chopped fresh parsley
½ tsp. oregano
salt and pepper to taste
2 eggs
4 tbsp. grated Parmesan cheese
2 tbsp. bread crumbs

1. Remove stems from eggplants and cut in half lengthwise. Place in boiling salted water for 10 minutes. Drain and cool. Scoop out pulp and chop.
2. Sauté onion and meat in butter until they are quite dry. Add wine, tomatoes, parsley, oregano, salt, pepper and eggplant pulp. Cook until all liquid is absorbed.
3. Beat eggs and Parmesan together and add to mixture. Stuff eggplants and top with bread crumbs. Place in a baking dish.
4. Bake at 350 F. for 45 minutes. Serves 4.

Dolma

This is stuffed eggplant from Greece that can double as a main dish or be served as an appetizer if you use small eggplants.

3 medium eggplants
1 tbsp. olive oil
1 C. diced onion
1 lb. ground lean lamb
2 6-oz. cans tomato paste
½ C. water
3/4 C. raw rice
2 tbsp. chopped fresh parsley
½ tsp. dried mint
1 tsp. chopped dill
1 tsp. salt
¼ tsp. pepper
1 fresh tomato
buttered bread crumbs

1. Remove stems from eggplants and cut in half lengthwise. Using a sharp

knife and spoon, scoop out insides, leaving shells about 3/4" thick. Chop pulp coarsely and reserve.

2. Heat oil in a large skillet and sauté onion about 3 minutes. Add lamb and cook until meat is no longer pink. Drain off excess fat. Add eggplant pulp and stir in tomato paste and water. Cook 10 minutes, stirring occasionally.

3. Remove from heat and mix in rice, parsley, mint, dill, salt and pepper. Stuff eggplant shells and place in a buttered baking dish. Add water to about ¼".

4. Cover with aluminum foil and bake at 350 F. for 45 minutes, or until eggplant is tender.

5. Cut fresh tomato into 6 slices and place 1 on top of each eggplant. Top with buttered bread crumbs. Place under broiler just long enough to heat tomato, but not to cook it. Serves 6.

Note: The dolma can be prepared ahead of time and refrigerated. Simply make stuffing and put into eggplant shells. Then cook just before serving time.

New Orleans Stuffed Eggplant

2 1-lb. eggplants
2 tbsp. butter
½ lb. ground beef
1 garlic clove, chopped
¼ C. chopped onion
¼ C. chopped green pepper
¼ C. chopped celery
1 1-lb. can tomatoes, with liquid
¼ tsp. thyme
¼ tsp. oregano
½ tsp. Tabasco sauce
½ C. pine nuts
salt to taste
½ C. bread crumbs
¼ C. melted butter

1. Remove stems from eggplants and cut in half lengthwise. Place in boiling salted water for 10 minutes. Drain and cool. Scoop out pulp and chop.

2. Melt 2 tbsp. butter and sauté beef and garlic until done. Add onion, green pepper and celery. Simmer 5 minutes. Add tomatoes with liquid, herbs, Tabasco, nuts, salt and chopped pulp. Stuff eggplants.

3. Combine bread crumbs and melted butter and spread over eggplants. Place in a baking dish.

4. Bake at 350 F. for 45 minutes. Serves 4.

Imam Baaldi

This is a famous Turkish recipe whose title can be translated as "The Imam Fainted." The Imam in question supposedly swooned with delight when this eggplant creation was served to him the first time.

2 1-lb. eggplants
oil
2 onions, chopped
4 tomatoes, peeled, seeded and chopped
1 C. currants, soaked in boiling water
salt and pepper to taste
2 C. water

1. Remove stems from eggplants and cut in half lengthwise. Place in boiling salted water for 10 minutes. Drain and cool. Scoop out pulp and chop.
2. Sauté onion and chopped pulp in a little oil until tender. Add tomatoes and drained currants, salt and pepper. Cook slowly for 10 minutes.
3. Stuff eggplants and place in a baking dish. Add water and ½ C. oil to the dish.
4. Bake at 350 F. for 1 hour. Serves 4.

Eggplant Catalan

2 1-lb. eggplants
2 medium onions, chopped
½ C. chopped fresh parsley
2 garlic cloves, chopped
4 hard-cooked eggs, chopped
salt and pepper to taste
4 tbsp. bread crumbs
butter

1. Remove stems from eggplants and cut in half lengthwise. Place in boiling salted water for 10 minutes. Drain and cool. Scoop out pulp and chop.
2. Sauté chopped pulp, onion, parsley and garlic until tender. Add eggs, salt and pepper. Stuff eggplants and place on a cookie sheet.

3. Top with bread crumbs and brush with butter. Bake at 350 F. for 40 minutes, or until eggplant is tender. Serves 4.

Italian Eggplant

2 1-lb. eggplants
2 C. rice, cooked in bouillon
½ C. chopped fresh parsley
½ tsp. garlic powder
½ tsp. oregano
salt and pepper to taste
grated Parmesan cheese
melted butter

1. Remove stems from eggplants and cut in half lengthwise. Place in boiling salted water for 10 minutes. Scoop out pulp and chop.
2. Combine rice with the pulp, parsley, garlic powder, oregano, salt and pepper. Stuff eggplants and place on a cookie sheet.
3. Top with Parmesan and brush with butter. Bake at 350 F. for 40 minutes, or until eggplant is tender. Serves 4.

Variation

Substitute 2 C. cooked ground sausage for the rice.

Ham-and-Chicken-Stuffed Eggplant

3 medium eggplants
¼ C. butter
1 C. diced cooked chicken
½ C. diced boiled ham
1 small onion, chopped and sautéed
¼ C. chopped celery
salt and pepper to taste
bread crumbs

1. Remove stems from eggplants and cut in half lengthwise. Scoop out pulp, leaving about ¼" in the shell. Melt the butter and sauté the shells until they are tender. Chop pulp and sauté it.
2. Combine pulp, chicken, ham, onion, celery, salt and pepper. Stuff the shells. Top with bread crumbs.
3. Bake at 350 F. for 35 minutes.

The Sauce

1 tbsp. butter
1 tbsp. instant blending flour
1 C. milk
½ C. grated cheddar cheese

1. Melt the butter and add flour. Blend well and add the milk. Stir until mixture thickens. Add cheese and cook sauce until the cheese melts. Pour hot sauce over the eggplants and serve. Serves 6.

Stuffed Eggplant with Tuna

2 medium eggplants
1 small onion, chopped and sautéed
2 garlic cloves, chopped and sautéed
1 7-oz. can tuna, drained and flaked
2 eggs, beaten
1 C. soft bread crumbs
½ tsp. oregano
salt and pepper to taste
Parmesan cheese

1. Remove stems from eggplants and cut in half lengthwise. Place in boiling salted water for 10 minutes. Drain and cool. Scoop out pulp and chop.
2. Combine pulp with remaining ingredients, except Parmesan, and stuff eggplants. Place in a baking dish.
3. Top with Parmesan and bake at 350 F. for 35 minutes. Serves 4.

STUFFED PEPPERS SWEET AND GREEN

Stuffed Peppers with Corn

6 medium green peppers
2 large cans creamed corn
dash of cayenne

1. Slice off tops of peppers and remove all seeds. Place in boiling salted

water for 5 minutes. Drain well.
2. Season corn with cayenne and stuff peppers. Place in a baking dish.
3. Bake at 400 F. for 10 to 15 minutes. Serves 6.

Russian Stuffed Sweet Peppers

6 sweet red peppers, halved
butter
1 onion, chopped
½ green pepper, finely diced
¼ C. chopped fresh parsley
3 tomatoes, peeled, seeded and chopped
¼ tsp. crushed fennel
2½ C. cooked rice
salt and pepper to taste
3/4 C. chicken bouillon
juice of 1 lemon
3 tbsp. tomato paste
¼ C. oil

1. Seed the peppers and place in boiling salted water for 5 minutes. Drain.
2. Melt some butter and sauté onion, green pepper and parsley until tender. Add tomatoes and fennel. Cook for 5 minutes. Drain off any excess liquid. Combine with rice and salt and pepper. Stuff peppers. Place in a large skillet.
3. Combine bouillon, lemon juice, tomato paste and oil. Pour over peppers and cook slowly until tender. Serves 6.

Cheese-Stuffed Peppers

4 green peppers
1½ C. grated American cheese
1½ C. flavored bread crumbs
¼ C. chopped celery
2 tbsp. butter, melted
¼ tsp. garlic powder
salt and pepper to taste

1. Slice off tops of peppers and remove all seeds. Place in boiling salted water for 3 minutes. Drain well.

2. Combine remaining ingredients and stuff peppers. Place in an oiled baking dish.
3. Bake at 350 F. for 20 minutes. Serves 4.

Crab Meat-Stuffed Peppers

4 large green peppers	*1 tbsp. onion powder*
1 can crab meat, flaked	*½ tsp. curry powder*
2 eggs, beaten	*salt and pepper to taste*
1 C. cooked rice	*3 tbsp. melted butter*
2 tbsp. lemon juice	*1 C. bread crumbs*

1. Slice peppers in half lengthwise. Core and parboil for 5 minutes.
2. Combine remaining ingredients, except butter and bread crumbs, and stuff peppers. Place in a greased baking dish.
3. Combine butter and bread crumbs and pat over crab meat mixture. Bake at 400 F. for 15 minutes. Serves 8.

Meat-Stuffed Peppers

6 large green peppers	*3 tbsp. tomato paste*
¼ lb. bulk sausage meat (no casing)	*3 C. beef bouillon*
¼ lb. ground beef	*salt and pepper to taste*
1 garlic clove, minced	*4 tbsp. grated Parmesan cheese*
1 onion, finely chopped	*3 slices mozzarella cheese, diced*
1 C. raw rice	*3 tbsp. melted butter*

1. Slice tops off peppers and remove all seeds. Place in boiling salted water for 5 minutes. Drain well.
2. Place sausage, ground beef, garlic and onion in a skillet and cook well. Pour off any liquid that remains. Add rice, tomato paste and bouillon. Season with salt and pepper and simmer until all liquid is absorbed.
3. Combine meat mixture with Parmesan and stuff peppers. Place in an oven-proof dish.
4. Top peppers with cubed mozzarella and brush with melted butter. Bake at 350 F. for 30 minutes. Serves 6.

ARTFULLY STUFFED ARTICHOKES

Traditionally, artichokes have been relegated to the lofty realms of haute cuisine. They are not difficult to prepare, however, and they make an attractive addition to any meal. Furthermore, in season they are not expensive. In fact, the artichoke is such an interesting vegetable it can be used very nicely as a highlighted separate course—either as an appetizer or first course.

To prepare the artichokes, remove the very coarse outer leaves and the stem. Then cut out the prickly choke from the bottom. Place them in boiling water that has been flavored with lemon juice. Cover the pot and simmer for 30 minutes. Drain the artichokes in an inverted position. Then they are ready to be stuffed.

Beef-Stuffed Artichokes

8 large artichokes, prepared for stuffing
3 tbsp. butter
2 onions, chopped
3/4 lb. ground beef
½ C. red wine
½ C. water
1 tbsp. tomato paste
¼ tsp. dried dill
1 tbsp. chopped fresh parsley
salt and pepper to taste
1 tbsp. grated Parmesan cheese
2 tbsp. bread crumbs
1 C. Béchamel Sauce

1. Melt the butter in a skillet and sauté onion and ground beef. Add wine, water, tomato paste, dill, parsley, salt and pepper. Cook until all the liquid is absorbed and add the Parmesan.
2. Combine with bread crumbs and stuff artichokes. Place in a baking dish.
3. Top with Béchamel Sauce and bake at 350 F. for 30 minutes. Serves 8.

Ham-Stuffed Artichokes

4 artichokes, prepared for stuffing
2 tbsp. butter
1 garlic clove, chopped
8 mushrooms, chopped
½ C. chopped cooked ham
1 C. dry bread crumbs
¼ C. chopped fresh parsley
½ tsp. salt
½ tsp. pepper
4 tbsp. grated Parmesan cheese
melted butter
1 C. dry white wine

1. Melt butter and sauté garlic, mushrooms and ham until tender. Add bread crumbs, parsley, salt, pepper and Parmesan. Remove from heat and blend well. Stuff artichokes and place in a baking dish.
2. Brush with melted butter and add wine. Baste frequently during cooking.
3. Bake at 350 F. for 30 minutes. Serves 4.

Variations

1. Substitute ½ C. shrimp, crab or lobster for the ham.
2. Top cooked stuffed artichokes with mayonnaise before serving.

Anchovy Artichokes

4 large artichokes, prepared for stuffing
1 C. bread crumbs
4 tbsp. grated Romano cheese
4 anchovy fillets, chopped
2 garlic cloves, chopped
2 tbsp. chopped fresh parsley
salt and pepper to taste
6 tbsp. olive oil
1 C. water

1. Combine all stuffing ingredients except the oil and water. Stuff

artichokes and place in a skillet.
2. Pour 1 tbsp. oil over each artichoke and pour remaining oil in the skillet. Add water and simmer covered for 30 minutes. Serves 4.

Variation

Substitute 1 can tuna packed in oil for ½ the bread crumbs. (Drain oil.)

STUFFED ONIONS

The lowly onion is one of our best friends in the kitchen. In fact, cooking without it is virtually impossible, as food would be quite tasteless. Onions are versatile and come in many varieties, such as the leek, the shallot and garlic. While the onion family is normally used as flavoring for other dishes, here are some really zesty dishes with the spotlight focussed on the onion itself.

For these recipes, use large onions such as the Spanish or Bermuda onions, which can accommodate generous amounts of stuffing. Peel the onions and parboil them for 10 minutes in boiling salted water. Remove the centers and invert to drain.

Chicken-and-Mushroom-Stuffed Onions

4 onions, prepared for stuffing
½ C. finely chopped cooked chicken
½ C. finely chopped mushrooms
½ C. flavored bread crumbs
4 tbsp. melted butter
grated Parmesan cheese

1. Combine all filling ingredients except the Parmesan. Stuff onions and place in a baking dish with a small amount of water.
2. Sprinkle the tops with Parmesan. Cover dish and bake at 350 F. for 20 to 30 minutes. Serves 4.

Alternate Fillings

1. Substitute ½ C. chopped ham for the chicken.
2. Substitute ½ C. cooked ground beef for the chicken.
3. Use grated cheese combined with sautéed onion centers for sprinkling tops.
4. Sauté 2 C. finely chopped mushrooms and 1 C. chopped onions in butter. Add dash of Tabasco and some chopped fresh parsley. Substitute ½ C. dry white wine for the water.

Risotto Onions

6 onions, prepared for stuffing
2 C. rice, cooked in chicken bouillon
few shreds of saffron
salt and pepper to taste
olive oil
1 large tomato, seeded and chopped
1 garlic clove, chopped
1 pimiento, chopped
¼ tsp. oregano

1. When preparing onions for stuffing, reserve cored centers and chop.
2. Add saffron to rice while it is cooking. Also add salt and pepper.
3. Sauté chopped onion centers, tomato, garlic, pimiento and oregano in oil until tender. Combine with rice and stuff onions. Place in a lightly-greased baking dish.
4. Bake at 350 F. for 20 to 30 minutes. Serve cold. Serves 6.

Onions Catalan

6 onions, prepared for stuffing
2 C. rice, cooked in bouillon
1 pimiento, chopped
2 hard-cooked eggs, chopped
dash of cayenne
salt and pepper to taste
bread crumbs
bouillon

1. When preparing onions for stuffing, reserve the cored centers and chop them.

2. Combine chopped onion centers with pimiento, eggs, cayenne, salt, pepper and rice. Stuff onions and place in a baking dish.
3. Top onions with bread crumbs. Add bouillon until it comes to the half-way point in the dish. Bake at 350 F. for 20 to 30 minutes. Serves 6.

STUFFED MUSHROOMS

12 large mushrooms
2 tbsp. melted butter
1 tbsp. chopped scallions
1 tbsp. bread crumbs

1. Remove stems from mushrooms and reserve. Brush caps with butter and place in a baking dish. Chop the stems.
2. Sauté stems in additional butter with scallions, until tender. Add bread crumbs and mix well. Stuff mushroom caps.

The Sauce

2 tbsp. butter
1 tbsp. instant blending flour
½ C. heavy cream
2 tbsp. chopped fresh parsley
dash of nutmeg
salt and pepper to taste
¼ C. grated Swiss cheese
melted butter

1. Melt the butter and add the flour and cream. Cook slowly until the sauce is creamy. Add parsley, nutmeg, salt and pepper. Spoon sauce over each cap to moisten the filling.
2. Sprinkle grated cheese on top of the sauce and brush with melted butter. Bake at 375 F. for 15 minutes. Serves 4.

STUFFED LETTUCE

Try stuffing lettuce leaves instead of cabbage. You will find the flavor is much more delicate.

Lamb-Stuffed Lettuce

8 large iceberg lettuce leaves
2 tbsp. butter
½ lb. ground lamb, or beef
1 onion, finely chopped
¼ C. milk
1¼ C. bread crumbs
1 egg, beaten
½ tsp. rosemary
salt and pepper to taste

1. Parboil leaves in boiling salted water for 3 minutes. Drain.
2. Sauté meat and onion in butter until tender.
3. Combine milk and bread crumbs and add to the meat. Add egg, rosemary, salt and pepper.
4. Divide mixture and place in the center of the leaves. Fold sides inward and roll. Place rolls in a baking dish.

The Brown Béchamel Sauce

3 tbsp. butter
2 tbsp. instant blending flour
1 C. beef bouillon

1. Melt the butter and add the flour. Blend well. Add bouillon and cook until sauce thickens. Pour sauce over lettuce rolls. Bake at 375 F. for 15 minutes. Serves 4.

Lettuce Bundles

This recipe is inspired by Chinese cuisine. These stuffed lettuce bundles are nothing less than sublime.

1 head iceberg lettuce, washed, drained and leaves separated
1/3 C. oil
3/4 C. ground pork
1 egg, beaten
cornstarch

2 tbsp. soy sauce
½ C. diced bamboo shoots
1 C. sliced water chestnuts
3 mushrooms, shredded
2 tbsp. dry sherry
1½ tsp. sugar
2 tsp. salt
½ C. chicken bouillon
1 C. finely chopped celery

1. Heat oil in a skillet (or wok if you have one) and add pork, egg, 1 tbsp. cornstarch and soy sauce. Stir constantly until mixture is well-cooked.
2. Add bamboo shoots, water chestnuts and mushrooms. Stir and fry for 1 minute.
3. Add sherry, sugar, salt, bouillon, 1 tsp. cornstarch and celery. Stir and fry for 3 minutes.
4. Remove from heat and serve immediately, with lettuce leaves on a separate dish. The leaves should be filled and rolled at the table. Serves 2 to 5 as a main course.

Stuffed Escarole

Escarole is an interesting member of the lettuce family. This recipe could also serve as a main course if made in larger quantities.

2 medium heads escarole, washed, drained and leaves separated
5 tbsp. olive oil
½ C. ground beef
5 olives, chopped
4 anchovy fillets, chopped
1 tbsp. pine nuts
1 tbsp. seedless white raisins
½ C. bread crumbs
1 tbsp. chopped fresh parsley
salt and pepper to taste

1. Fry ground beef in 2 tbsp. olive oil for 10 minutes. Remove from heat. Add remaining ingredients, except the oil. If mixture is too dry, add a little water.

2. Place some filling in the center of each leaf. Roll, folding sides in, and tie with string. Place rolls in a pan.
3. Pour remaining 3 tbsp. oil over rolls. Cover and cook over low heat about 20 minutes. Turn rolls occasionally to avoid burning. Serves 4.

PIMIENTOS STUFFED WITH CHEESE

1 can pimientos, well-drained
Swiss cheese slices, cut into thirds
salt
cayenne
flour
butter
buttered toast

1. Sprinkle cheese strips with salt and cayenne. Place 1 slice in each pimiento. Dredge pimientos in flour and sauté in butter until cheese melts.
2. Serve on buttered toast.

POTATOES WITH PIZZAZZ

The potato had rather modest beginnings and was at one time considered to have a baneful effect. Once used simply as an ornamental plant, it has become of course a staple in many diets. And it certainly has a place in rolled and stuffed cookery.

Stuffed Potatoes with Poached Eggs

2 large potatoes
4 slices boiled ham, chopped
2 tsp. chopped chives

6 tbsp. sour cream
salt and pepper to taste
4 poached eggs
tomato sauce
4 slices of American cheese

1. Bake potatoes and cut in half lengthwise. Scoop out insides and mash.
2. Add ham, chives, sour cream, salt and pepper. Replace in potato shells.
3. Place 1 poached egg on top of each stuffed potato. Place in a baking dish and pour a little tomato sauce around the potatoes. Top each with a slice of cheese.
4. Bake at 400 F. for 10 minutes. Serves 4.

Varied Stuffed Baked Potatoes

4 large potatoes
1 tbsp. milk
1 tbsp. butter
salt and pepper to taste

1. Bake potatoes and cut in half lengthwise. Scoop out inside and mash. Add milk, butter, salt and pepper, and any filling you choose. Stuff potato shells.
2. Return to oven and bake at 450 F. for 5 to 8 minutes. Serves 8.

Filling Variations

1. ½ C. grated cheese.
2. 1 tbsp. chopped onion and 1 tbsp. chopped green pepper sautéed in a little butter.
3. 6 minced anchovies. Top potatoes with grated cheese.
4. 1 tbsp. tomato paste instead of the milk. Add oregano and basil to taste.
5. 6 strips of cooked bacon, crumbled.
6. ½ C. chopped boiled ham.
7. 6 tbsp. sour cream and 6 tbsp. chopped chives.

Stuffed Potatoes with Eggs and Sour Cream

6 large potatoes
½ C. sour cream
¼ C. light cream, at room temperature
2 hard-cooked eggs, chopped
1 garlic clove, minced
½ tsp. cumin
salt and pepper to taste
6 tbsp. butter

1. Bake potatoes. Cut a thin slice from top of each potato. Carefully scoop out insides and mash.
2. Add remaining ingredients, except the butter, and stuff the potato shells. Top each with 1 tbsp. of butter. Stand potatoes so that butter will not run out.
3. Bake at 375 F. for 10 to 15 minutes. Serves 6.

Californian Potatoes

5 large potatoes
1 C. sour cream
½ C. diced avocado
salt and pepper to taste
butter

1. Bake potatoes and cut in half lengthwise. Scoop out insides and mash.
2. Combine with sour cream, avocado, salt and pepper. Stuff potato shells and brush with butter.
3. Bake at 375 F. for 10 minutes. Serves 10.

Potato Rollatini

2½ lbs. potatoes, peeled and diced
2 eggs, beaten
½ C. grated Parmesan cheese
1½ tbsp. chopped fresh parsley
salt and pepper to taste
bread crumbs
oil for frying

1. Boil potatoes until tender. Drain well and mash.
2. Add remaining ingredients, except bread crumbs and oil. When

potatoes are cool enough to handle, fashion them into sausage shapes about 3" long.
3. Roll in bread crumbs and fry in oil. Serves 6 to 8.

VEGETABLE MOLDS

Here is a medley of refreshingly cool vegetable molds particularly nice for summertime, buffet-time, lunchtime—or any time. All serve from 6 to 8 people. The basic recipes are given for the molds, and the salad stuffings are left to your imagination, although we have suggested a few.

Tomato Mold

2 cans vegetable or tomato juice (1 pt. 2 oz. each)
2 packages lemon gelatin
3 tbsp. lemon juice
1 tsp. salt
dash of pepper
6-C. ring mold

1. Heat 1 C. of juice to the boiling point and add the gelatin, stirring until it is dissolved. Combine with remaining ingredients and pour into mold.
2. Chill until firm and unmold.
3. Stuff center hole with German vegetable salad.

The German Vegetable Salad

1 medium tomato, cut in wedges
1 4-oz. can cut string beans
1 4-oz. can green peas
1 4-oz. can wax beans
1 4-oz. can asparagus spears, cut in pieces
3 tbsp. sour cream
3 tbsp. mayonnaise
dash of lemon juice
garlic powder to taste
salt to taste

1. Mix all ingredients together and stuff center hole of salad mold.

Green Vegetable Mold

1 C. boiling water
1 package lime gelatin
½ C. cold water
3 tbsp. vinegar
½ tsp. salt
1½ C. cooked peas, string beans, lima beans or chopped spinach
2 tsp. chopped chives
4-C. ring mold

1. Dissolve gelatin in boiling water. Add cold water, vinegar and salt. Chill until thick and add remaining ingredients.
2. Pour into mold. Chill until firm and unmold.
3. Stuff center hole with chicken, shrimp or tuna salad.

Fresh Vegetable Mold

1 C. boiling water
1 package lemon, lime or orange gelatin
3/4 C. cold water
2 tbsp. vinegar
2 tsp. chopped chives
½ tsp. salt
dash of pepper
2 C. chopped fresh vegetables (tomato, cauliflower, pepper, radish, carrot, cabbage, celery)
4-C. ring mold

1. Dissolve gelatin in boiling water. Add cold water, vinegar, chives, salt and pepper. Chill until thick and add remaining ingredients.
2. Pour into mold. Chill until firm and unmold.
3. Stuff center hole with seafood salad.

Rainbow Vegetable Mold

2 C. boiling water
2 packages lemon gelatin
2 C. cold water
2 tbsp. tarragon vinegar
2 tsp. chopped chives
2 tsp. salt
1½ C. cooked peas
1½ C. chopped carrots
1½ C. chopped cabbage
6-C. ring mold

1. Dissolve gelatin in boiling water. Add cold water, vinegar, chives and salt. Stir well.
2. Divide mixture into 3 portions and combine each portion with 1 of the vegetables.
3. Pour the pea mixture into mold and chill until set.
4. Add cabbage mixture on top and chill again.
5. Finally, add carrot mixture and chill until firm. Unmold.
6. Stuff with cottage cheese or tuna salad.

STUFFED MELON SALAD

1 medium cantaloupe, or honeydew
1 C. boiling water
1 package fruit gelatin (any flavor)
3/4 C. cold water, or drained fruit syrup
1 C. drained canned fruit, or frozen
3 3-oz. packages cream cheese
2 tbsp. milk
chopped nuts (optional)
food coloring (optional)

1. Dissolve gelatin in boiling water. Add cold water and chill until thick, but not solid.
2. Peel melon, leaving it whole. Cut off 1 slice at end and scoop out seeds. Stand melon upright in a bowl.
3. Fold fruit into thick gelatin and spoon into melon. Replace cut slice and secure with toothpicks. Chill well.
4. Blend cream cheese and milk. Cut a very thin slice from side of melon so that it will stand without rolling on a plate. Just before serving, frost the melon with cream cheese mixture. If you wish, mix some food coloring into the cream cheese to tint it. Also, the outside of the frosted melon can be decorated with chopped nuts.
5. To serve, just slice through melon so that you have stuffed melon rings. Serves 4 to 6.

VIII. CHILD TEMPTERS

We believe very strongly that it is important to educate children in adventurous eating by giving them something a little out of the ordinary. Therefore most of our "child tempters" provide zesty, gastronomic experiences that should serve as an introduction to the development of broader and more sophisticated tastes.

We also highly recommend setting an attractive table. Nothing has to be elaborate or expensive, but good design and color should be kept in mind. Children can be lured into eating, and educated in good eating, by making the stage setting as appealing as possible–which is as true for children as it is for adults. Lavishness and expense are not necessary, but thought, a spark of originality, and intelligent planning are.

We offer here a collection of sure-fire child pleasers. Our children adore them all. (Actually, children of any age should enjoy almost any recipe in this book provided it is not too highly spiced.) If you experiment and have fun, your children will be tempted—even those with the most finicky appetites—for these are dependable, yet interesting, tried-and-true standbys. They are good for all age groups and all occasions—for every day and special days.

In addition, because many of these dishes are composed of such foods as ground beef or frankfurters, they can be used to feed large numbers of children economically—hence are perfect for party fare, before the cake and ice cream.

They are easy to make, take very little time and of course can be prepared in advance and frozen.

FUN WITH PIZZAS

What child doesn't love pizza in any way, shape or form? Here are some simple and intriguing variations on the pizza idea that are certain to brighten your children's appetites.

Pizza Roll

2 lbs. ground beef
¼ C. chopped onion
1 egg
1 C. flavored bread crumbs
1 10-oz. jar pizza sauce
1 4-oz. can mushrooms, chopped (optional)
salt and pepper to taste
1 6-oz. package mozzarella cheese, sliced

1. Combine all ingredients, except the cheese. Place on waxed paper and shape into a 14" x 10" rectangle.
2. Place sliced cheese on top and roll carefully. Place on greased cookie sheet.
3. Bake at 350 F. for 1 hour. Serves 6 to 8.

Pizza Franks

6 frankfurters
6 frankfurter buns
½ lb. ground beef
½ lb. bulk pepperoni sausage (no casing)
½ tsp. salt
pepper to taste
1 slice white bread, crumbled
1 egg, beaten
¼ C. milk
1 C. pizza sauce

1. Combine beef, sausage, salt, pepper, bread, egg and milk. Divide into 6 portions.
2. Roll each portion out and wrap it around a frankfurter, leaving the ends open. Chill well.
3. Grill or broil frankfurters, brushing with pizza sauce occasionally.
4. Place frankfurters in buns and top with remaining pizza sauce. Serves 6.

Pizza Meat Pie

1 lb. ground beef
¼ C. non-dairy coffee creamer
½ C. dry bread crumbs
1 tsp. salt
¼ tsp. pepper
1 garlic clove, crushed
1 C. water
½ C. shredded cheddar cheese
1 6-oz. can tomato paste
1 tsp. oregano
1 tsp. grated onion
1/3 C. grated Parmesan cheese
1 4-oz. can mushrooms, drained
cooked sausage, sliced (optional)
green pepper, sliced (optional)

1. Combine ground beef, coffee creamer, bread crumbs, salt, pepper,

garlic and water. Mix well. Pat into a 9" pie tin or a deep casserole.
2. Combine remaining ingredients, except the Parmesan and mushrooms, and spoon over the meat. Sprinkle with Parmesan. Garnish with mushrooms. (If desired, garnish also with sausage and green pepper slices.)
3. Bake at 350 F. for 30 to 40 minutes. Serves 4 to 6.

HAMBURGER FUN

Here are some economical and new ideas for tempting children afresh with their beloved ground beef.

Hamburger Cups

This recipe makes 9 cupcake-size hamburgers that children cannot resist because of their original presentation and delightful tastiness.

1 lb. lean ground beef
1 egg
1 tbsp. ketchup
1 tbsp. soy sauce
1 garlic clove
9 eggs (optional)
1 package frozen mixed vegetables, cooked (optional)

1. Combine egg, ketchup, soy sauce and garlic in a blender. Blend about 30 seconds, or until all garlic particles have disappeared. Pour this mixture over the meat and mix by hand.
2. Using a muffin tin, line bottoms and sides of muffin cups with the meat mixture.
3. Bake in a pre-heated oven at 400 F. for 20 minutes, or until done.
4. Scoop out the liquid that has formed in the center of the cups and fill with 1 egg, or cooked vegetables. If an egg is used, return meat cups to oven long enough to cook the egg. If pre-cooked vegetables are used, this is not necessary. Serve hot. Serves 6 to 9.

5. The size of the cups can vary according to your need. If you wish larger ones, simply bring meat up a little higher than the rim of the muffin cups. Or, you can use smaller cups if you wish to serve them unfilled. Small cups served with fancy picks add a touch of fun for children.

Beef Turnovers

1 lb. lean ground beef
1 10-oz. package pie crust mix
¼ C. cold water
1 to 2 tbsp. cooking oil
1 small onion, chopped
¼ tsp. salt
2 tbsp. ketchup
1 C. mashed potatoes, or cooked rice
1 egg yolk, beaten with 2 tbsp. milk

1. Make pastry according to package directions, using ¼ C. cold water to mix pastry. Form into a ball of dough and wrap in waxed paper, or plastic wrap, and refrigerate while making the filling.
2. Heat cooking oil. Add onion and sauté until soft. Add ground beef, sautéing it until all pink color disappears. Add salt, ketchup and potatoes and mix well. Let mixture simmer for 10 minutes. Then set aside while preparing crust.
3. Roll out dough to 1/8" thickness. Cut into ten 5" or twelve 4" circles. (An overturned saucer makes a good guide.) Spoon 3 to 4 tbsp. filling onto each circle. Fold in half and crimp edges with a fork.
4. Brush each turnover with egg yolk and milk mixture. Prick tops with fork.
5. Bake in a pre-heated oven at 375 F. for 30 minutes, or until pastry is lightly browned. Allow turnovers to cool before serving. Serves 5 to 6.

Note: Pastries will freeze well if they are well-wrapped and sealed. If cooked they will last 6 months. If uncooked, they will last 3 months.

Burgers Filled with Cheese

2 lbs. ground beef
American or Swiss cheese
salt and pepper to taste

1. Shape 16 very thin patties. Top 8 of them with cheese. Place a second patty on top and press edges down to seal. Season to taste and broil. Serves 8.

Stuffed Meat Pies with Sour Cream Sauce

2 lbs. ground beef
1 medium onion, chopped
salt and pepper to taste
1 package prepared, uncooked jumbo biscuits

1. Brown meat and onion. Season to taste.
2. Roll biscuits out on a floured board, making large circles. Divide filling among them. Fold over and press edges down to seal. Prick tops with a fork.
3. Bake at temperature indicated on package.

The Sour Cream Sauce

1 can chicken broth
½ can water
1 tsp. soy sauce
1 tsp. cornstarch
2 tbsp. water
2/3 C. sour cream

1. Combine broth, water and soy sauce. Bring to a boil.
2. Combine cornstarch and 2 tbsp. water and add to boiling mixture. Simmer for 3 minutes.
3. Add sour cream, a little at a time, to prevent curdling. Pour over pies to serve. Serves 4 to 6.

Cheese and Beef Roll

1½ lbs. ground beef
1 C. flavored bread crumbs
2 tbsp. ketchup
1 egg
1 C. shredded cheddar or American cheese
¼ C. chopped green pepper
2 tbsp. water

1. Combine ground beef, ½ C. bread crumbs, ketchup and egg. Place on waxed paper and shape into an 8" x 14" rectangle.
2. Combine remaining ingredients and place on top of beef. Roll carefully and place on a greased cookie sheet.
3. Bake at 350 F. for 30 minutes. Slice to serve. Serves 4 to 6.

FUN WITH CHEESE

All of the recipes here use cheese in delightfully different ways that will be sure to please even the most reluctant eaters. They are all tasty and attractive, and one of them is a famous French classic–Croque Monsieur.

Hot Cheese Sandwiches

2 tbsp. butter
2 tbsp. instant blending flour
2 C. hot milk
salt and pepper to taste
3 eggs, beaten
8 slices toast
8 slices American, Swiss or mozzarella cheese

1. Melt butter in a saucepan and add flour. Blend and add the hot milk and salt and pepper. Simmer until sauce is thick. Cool slightly and add eggs.
2. Butter a baking dish large enough to hold 4 slices of toast on the bottom. Place 4 slices in the dish and top each with 1 slice of cheese. Pour the sauce over and top with a second slice of toast. Place remaining cheese slices on top.
3. Bake at 350 F. until egg mixture is firm. Serves 4.

Mozzarella and Salami Turnovers

4 C. biscuit mix
1 C. cold water
olive oil
1 C. cubed hard salami
3/4 lb. mozzarella cheese, sliced
1 egg, beaten

1. Combine biscuit mix and water. Mix well. Knead on a floured board until the dough is elastic. Divide into 8 portions and roll each one into an 8" circle. Brush with olive oil.
2. Divide salami and mozzarella among the circles. Fold and press edges down to seal. Brush with egg and olive oil.
3. Bake at 350 F. for 30 to 35 minutes. Makes 8 turnovers.

Croque Monsieur

6 to 8 slices white bread, crusts removed
6 to 8 slices Swiss cheese
6 to 8 slices boiled ham
3 eggs, beaten with ¼ C. milk
oil for deep frying

1. Make sandwiches with cheese and ham.
2. Dip sandwiches in egg and milk mixture and fry in oil. Serves 3 to 4.

HOT DOG FROLICS

Even the simple, down-to-earth hot dog can be dressed in attractive and delicious wrappings—a treat for children and adults alike.

Rolled-Up Hot Dogs

1 package prepared crescent roll dough
8 hot dogs
cheddar cheese strips

1. Unfurl crescents into 8 triangles.
2. Slit hot dogs to within ½" from the ends. Insert strips of cheddar cheese in each hot dog and place them on the triangles. Roll, making sure to wrap well so that the cheese will not drip out during cooking.
3. Place on a cookie sheet, cheese side up. Bake at 375 F. for 10 to 15 minutes, or until golden. Serves 8.

Cheese-Filled Hot Dogs

8 hot dogs
¼ C. grated cheddar cheese
1 tbsp. prepared mustard
8 strips of bacon

1. Slit hot dogs to within 1" from the ends.

2. Mash cheese with the mustard and fill the slits.
3. Wrap hot dogs with bacon strips and fasten with toothpicks.
4. Place on a rack in a pan and broil until bacon is crisp. Serves 8.

Hot Dogs and Fruit

hot dogs
apple, peach or orange pieces dipped in sugar and cinnamon; or banana; or canned pineapple chunks; or cooked pitted prunes

1. Slit hot dogs to within 1" from the ends.
2. Fill slits with the fruit of your choice.
3. Broil until hot dogs are done and the fruit is glazed.

Hot Dogs in Wraps

1 package prepared, uncooked refrigerator biscuits
hot dogs

1. Roll each refrigerator biscuit into a long rope. Wrap each in spiral form around a hot dog and skewer.
2. Grill hot dogs until done and the dough is golden, or about 10 minutes.

Hot Dogs and Potatoes

8 hot dogs
3 medium potatoes, boiled and mashed
¼ C. mayonnaise
2 hard-cooked eggs, chopped
¼ C. chopped celery
2 tbsp. chives
2 tbsp. chopped sweet pickle
salt and pepper to taste

1. Slit hot dogs about 3/4 of the way through.

2. Combine all filling ingredients and fill hot dogs.
3. Bake at 400 F. for 15 to 20 minutes. Serves 4 to 8.

FRUIT TURNOVERS

This is a simple, yet delightful treat for children for party snacks or dessert–or any time.

1 package prepared, uncooked biscuits
1 can pie filling
sugar and cinnamon mix
oil for frying

1. Roll each biscuit into about a 6" circle. Place 2 tbsp. of pie filling in each circle. Fold and press edges down to seal. Prick tops with a fork.
2. Fry in oil until golden. Sprinkle with sugar and cinnamon. Serves 8.

IX. THE GRAND FINALE:

Desserts

Desserts, even though they may seem to be somewhat rich fare in today's diet-conscious world, have a real purpose in a meal. Whether simple and low-calorie, or more voluptuous, desserts serve to restore a taste balance after the main dish. In planning your dessert, it is most important to keep the plot of your total performance in mind. If the main course was an elaborate production, serve a simpler dessert. If the center stage offering was unadorned, then go all out with a fascinating dessert finale. If you think ahead, prepare ahead and freeze ahead so that your staging moves smoothly, you will then have time to enjoy your company and their resounding praise for a memorable experience–from start to finish.

Desserts should be served with as much flourish as possible, and these splendid creations deserve such treatment. And surely, one cannot be wrong in this, as many people are dessert fanciers for whom the last course is often the most tempting. Accordingly, here is is glamorous collection of mouth-watering delights—flamboyant fruits, delectable rolled cakes, pastries with exotic fillings, creamy charlottes, bombes oozing with richness—that will absolutely guarantee lingering memories.

We have also added a special section giving you a variety of interesting crusts. And we've included an almost encyclopedic selection of rolled and filled cookies, stuffed horns and tarts, and a host of other refreshing dessert ideas.

And now, some serving tips. If you have dessert plates or an attractive set of odd cups and saucers, by all means use them. Fresh napkins are certainly in order, as is a deft brushing of the table before dessert is served. Decorative, inexpensive utensils can be purchased for this purpose.

Even the simplest dessert fare can be touched with a bit of elegance by adding a few crystallized violets, a fresh sprig of mint, an embellishment of fruit sauce, a puff of whipped cream or a splash of sherry, brandy or rum.

A word about wines . . . sweet dessert wines, or sweet sparkling wines, enhance any dessert creation and can only help to make the experience of your dinner more heady. We recommend the sweet sparkling wines because they are fun—and because dry champagnes may seem sour when paired with ultra-sweet desserts.

Further festive effects can be achieved with coffee—which can be served in the living room with assorted liqueurs for the ultimate dash of graciousness. If you have served a dessert wine, liqueur can be omitted. Instead of regular coffee, you can offer dark, aromatic café espresso for a special touch. Serve the espresso in tiny, fragile-looking demitasse cups. Both the cups and inexpensive espresso machines can be readily obtained in any good department store.

And now, what's for dessert?

CHARLOTTES GALORE!

Charlottes are glorious! They are mousse-like delights usually packed in layers, or other patterns, in molds lined with lady fingers or macaroons. They make wonderful, stellar attractions as desserts—when they are unmolded and sliced to show off all their variegated glory.

Manifold combinations can easily be achieved with different flavored fillings laced with frozen and glacéed fruits, whipped creams, liqueurs, bits of macaroons, shaved chocolate, slivered nuts—or what you will. Enjoy experimenting!

In addition to the grand, traditional charlottes, we also suggest delightful short-cut variations that can be made with packaged dessert mixes.

Note: To unmold all charlottes, run a sharp knife around the edge of the mold and turn the mold upside down onto a chilled serving plate. Occasionally, you may need to hold a towel that has been soaked in warm water against the bottom of the mold for a few minutes.

Charlotte Royale

An elegant, super-rich French classic.

1 qt. fresh strawberries, or raspberries
2-qt. cylindrical mold
1 package slightly stale lady fingers
½ lb. sweet butter, softened
1 C. sugar
½ C. orange liqueur, or kirschwasser
¼ tsp. almond extract
½ tsp. vanilla extract
1-1/3 C. ground blanched almonds
2 C. heavy cream, whipped

1. Hull strawberries. Wash quickly and dry on paper towels.
2. Line bottom of mold with a round of waxed paper. Oil sides lightly.
3. Line mold with lady fingers and reserve any remaining. (Orange liqueur may be drizzled over the lady fingers if you wish.)
4. In a very large mixing bowl, cream butter and sugar together for 3 to 4 minutes, or until pale and fluffy. Beat in the orange liqueur, almond and vanilla extracts. Continue beating for several minutes, until sugar is completely dissolved. Beat in the ground almonds. (These can be ground in a blender.)
5. Whip the cream in a chilled bowl until a beater drawn across the top of

the cream leaves light tracks. Fold cream into butter mixture.
6. Turn 1/3 of almond cream mixture into lined mold. Place a layer of fruit in it, heads down. Cover with any remaining lady fingers.
7. Repeat with another layer of almond cream and berries and almond cream. Cover with a round of buttered waxed paper. Place a saucer on top which will just fit the mold, and place a 1-lb. weight on it.
8. Refrigerate for 6 hours or overnight. Butter must be chilled firm so that dessert will not collapse when unmolded.
9. Just before serving, remove saucer and waxed paper and run a knife around inside of the mold. Turn mold upside down on a chilled serving platter. Peel waxed paper from top and return to refrigerator for a moment.
10. Decorate with berries and accompany with whipped cream or thawed frozen berries served as a sauce. Serves 8 to 10.

Charlotte Russe

1 3-oz. package fruit gelatin
1 C. boiling water
3/4 C. cold water
1 C. heavy cream
¼ C. sugar
¼ C. chopped walnuts
16 lady fingers, split

1. Dissolve gelatin in boiling water. Add cold water and chill until slightly thickened.
2. Whip cream and sugar and fold into gelatin. Fold in nuts.
3. Arrange lady fingers around individual serving dishes and divide mixture among them. Chill until firm. Serves 8.

Nutty Fruit Charlotte

3 eggs, separated
2 C. milk
¼ tsp. salt
1 3-oz. package fruit gelatin
½ C. boiling water
½ C. heavy cream
¼ C. sugar
½ tsp. vanilla extract
¼ C. glacéed fruits
¼ C. chopped nuts
16 lady fingers, split

1. Make a custard by cooking egg yolks, milk and salt in a double boiler

until mixture coats a spoon. Stir constantly.
2. Dissolve gelatin in boiling water and slowly stir into custard. Let cool.
3. Beat egg whites until they hold stiff peaks. Fold into cooled custard.
4. Whip cream with sugar and vanilla. Add glacéed fruits and nuts and fold into custard.
5. Line a loaf pan on bottom and sides with lady fingers. Pour in custard and chill until quite firm. Unmold and serve. Serves 8.

Raspberry Charlotte

1 3-oz. package raspberry gelatin, or peach gelatin
1 C. hot water
1 package unthawed frozen raspberries, or peaches
½ pint vanilla ice cream
lady fingers
kirschwasser (optional)
1½-qt. mold

1. Dissolve gelatin in hot water. Stir in frozen berries and add ice cream. Stir until melted.
2. Line mold with lady fingers. (Drizzle with kirschwasser if you wish.)
3. Pour berry mixture into mold. Refrigerate until set, or for at least 2 hours. Spoon into serving dishes. Serves 6.

Strawberry Charlotte

1 3-oz. package strawberry gelatin
1 C. hot water
1 C. cold water
1 pint strawberry ice cream
1 pint fresh strawberries, hulled, washed and dried
lady fingers
kirschwasser or brandy
2-qt. mold

1. Dissolve gelatin in hot water. Add cold water. Add ice cream. When ice

cream is melted add the fresh strawberries.
2. Line mold with lady fingers drizzled with kirschwasser.
3. Pour berry mixture into mold and refrigerate for at least 3 hours. Serves 8.

Zuppa Inglese

This is the Italian version of the English trifle. Although its name translates as English soup, it is hardly that. A tipsy concoction of cream, fruits and sherried cake, it can be a dramatic ending to almost any meal. Zuppa Inglese also fits into the charlotte department as it is a mold-like arrangement of pudding and cake. It is simply a layered ring of cake filled with a heart of cream. (As a short cut, you can buy the yellow cake layers.)

4 9" yellow cake layers
1 package vanilla pudding mix
1 tsp. grated lemon peel
1 C. heavy cream
¼ C. sugar
2 tsp. vanilla extract
½ C. dry sherry
1½ C. strawberry jelly
whole strawberries

1. Prepare pudding according to package directions and add lemon peel. Chill.
2. Whip cream with sugar and vanilla.
3. Brush top of 1 cake layer with sherry. Cut centers out of others, leaving 1" ring. Brush rings with remaining sherry.
4. Combine pudding with ½ the whipped cream, making certain they are well-blended.
5. Spread ½ the jelly on top of whole cake layer. Top with some pudding mixture. Place 1 ring on top. Spread a little jelly and some pudding mixture on the ring. Place a second ring on top and repeat process. Place third ring on top and repeat process.
6. Pour remaining pudding mixture into center of cake. It should come to the top. Spread remaining jelly over pudding mixture only and top with strawberries.
7. Frost sides and top of ring–but not center–with remaining whipped cream. Serves 8 to 10.

Variations

1. Use apricot jam instead of strawberry jelly and substitute chocolate pudding and crumbled macaroons for vanilla pudding and fresh strawberries.
2. Make cake out of chocolate layers and use rum instead of sherry. Substitute cherry jam and cherries for strawberry jelly and strawberries.

Frozen Sicilian Cassata

3-qt. mold
2 packages lady fingers
1 tbsp. orange liqueur
3 oz. unsweetened baking chocolate
2 tbsp. sweet butter
2 C. heavy cream
¼ C. sugar
½ tsp. vanilla extract

1. Moisten lady fingers with 1 tbsp. orange liqueur and line a 3-qt. mold.
2. Melt chocolate and butter together over low heat. Beat cream, sugar and vanilla together and combine with chocolate. Pour into bottom of mold. Smooth and freeze.

2 C. heavy cream
3 tbsp. sugar
1 tbsp. orange liqueur

1. Beat cream, sugar and orange liqueur together. Spread around sides and bottom of mold. Freeze again.

1 C. heavy cream
1 C. pitted sweet cherries
¼ C. sugar
¼ C. chopped glacéed fruits

1. Beat cream. Combine cherries, sugar and glacéed fruits and fold into cream. Place in center of the mold. Freeze again.
2. To unmold, place a warm, moist towel around mold. Loosen with a

knife if necessary, and invert on a serving platter.
3. If desired, cover entire mold with additional sweetened whipped cream.
Serves 12.

BOMBES AWAY!

The name "bombe" means bomb. The idea dates back to the days when bombs were round—as were most dessert molds. Today bombes come in tall, conical or melon shapes, among others. They are fun to make, delightful to look at, festive to serve and delicious to eat. Basically, making bombes is a matter of layering ice cream or mousse-like mixtures in a mold and freezing or chilling. By all means, serve bombes whole and take advantage of the delightful mixture of colors and textures.

Bombe Espagñol

2½-qt. mold
aluminum foil
1½ C. crushed chocolate wafers
3 tbsp. butter, melted
1 package vanilla frosting mix
3 pints heavy cream
3 tsp. dry instant coffee
3 tbsp. brandy flavoring

1. Grease mold. Place two 1"-wide strips of foil across bottom and up sides of mold.
2. Combine 1 C. wafer crumbs with butter and press onto bottom and up sides of mold.
3. Blend dry frosting mix into cream in a large mixing bowl. Beat until soft peaks begin to form. Reserve 1/3 of this mixture. To remaining mixture, add instant coffee, brandy flavoring and remaining ½ C. wafer crumbs. Blend well.
4. Spread coffee mixture on insides and bottom of mold, on top of

crumbs. Spoon vanilla mixture into center. Freeze until firm, or at least 4 hours.
5. Unmold by placing hot, moist cloth on bottom of mold and inverting it on a serving plate. Return to freezer until time to serve. Serves 8 to 10.

Ice Cream Raisin Bombe

1 large juice can, open at 1 end only
pistachio ice cream
raisins, nuts and glacéed fruits
vanilla ice cream
shaved chocolate

1. Line juice can with pistachio ice cream. Sprinkle with raisins, nuts and glacéed fruits. Pack center with vanilla ice cream and cover top with pistachio ice cream. Cover open end with foil. Freeze until firm.
2. To unmold, hold can briefly under warm water. Open closed end with can opener and push bombe out onto a serving plate. Sprinkle with shaved chocolate and serve with Melba Sauce. Serves 6 to 8.

The Melba Sauce

1 C. canned, frozen or fresh raspberries
3 tbsp. water
¼ C. sugar
2 tbsp. rum

1. Place raspberries, water and sugar in a saucepan and cook to form a heavy syrup.
2. Add rum and mix well. Pour over ice cream bombe and serve.

FLAMBOYANT FRUITS

Here is a panoply of featured fruits, with stuffing as an accent.

Peaches Mont Blanc

6 peach halves, fresh or canned
½ 8-oz. package cream cheese
2 tbsp. brandy, cognac or fruit liqueur
2 tbsp. confectioners' sugar
lemon juice
½ C. finely chopped pistachio nuts

1. Blend cream cheese, brandy and sugar together until fluffy. Sprinkle peach halves with lemon juice and fill hollow of each with cheese mixture. Chill until ready to serve. Serve with chopped nuts on top. Serves 6.

Variations

Substitute canned pear halves or baked apple halves for the peaches.

Stuffed Pears

6 large firm pears
3 oz. confectioners' sugar
4 maraschino cherries, chopped
½ C. ground toasted almonds
¼ tsp. almond extract
½ C. dry sherry

1. Wash pears and cut in half lengthwise. Scoop out cores.
2. Blend sugar, cherries, almonds and almond extract together. Stuff pears.
3. Place pears in a baking dish and pour sherry over them. Bake at 350 F. for 15 minutes. Serves 6.

Almond-Stuffed Peaches

6 large fresh peaches, or 12 canned halves
¼ C. toasted almonds, chopped
3 oz. confectioners' sugar
1 tbsp. chopped orange peel
½ C. dry sherry or rum

1. Peel, pit and halve the peaches.

2. Combine almonds, ½ the sugar and orange peel. Stuff peaches and sprinkle remaining sugar over them.
3. Place peaches in a baking dish and pour sherry over them. Bake at 350 F. for 15 minutes. Serves 6.

Tipsy Pineapple

1 large pineapple
¼ C. water
½ C. sugar
¼ C. rum

1. Remove top of the pineapple. Scoop out pulp and discard the core. Chop pulp and return to pineapple shell.
2. Combine water and sugar and boil for 5 minutes. Add rum and pour mixture over pulp in the pineapple. Replace top of pineapple and bring to the table. Spoon out pulp into dishes. Pulp can be served over ice cream or sherbet for an added touch.

Sorbet à l'Orange

There is nothing quite like the pungent, refreshing taste of European fresh fruit ices. They can be used in bombes, and the distinctive French version given here can be served in scooped-out pineapples, cantaloupes, grapefruits, lemons, limes, or oranges. Wafer-thin cookies filled with chocolate or whipped cream complement this sorbet perfectly.

4 C. fresh orange juice
3 C. less 2 tsp. sugar
2 C. water
2 tsp. grated orange rind
6 oranges

1. Combine all ingredients except the 6 oranges. Heat mixture until sugar is dissolved. Then boil for 5 minutes. Transfer to a bowl and chill for 2 hours. Transfer into an ice tray and freeze until mushy around the edges.
2. Place mixture in an electric blender and blend for 1 minute. Return to ice tray. Refreeze, stirring at 1-hour intervals until well-blended and firm.
3. Remove tops of oranges. Scoop out centers and fill shells with iced mixture. Scoop out caps and arrange as tops. Place in freezer until frozen. Serves 6.

TARTS AND PASTRIES

Here is a master collection of tarts and pastries from all over the world. There is a wide variation, the methods are simple and the results worth every effort. **Note:** When cooking tarts, do not allow fillings to boil or they will begin to crystallize.

Dutch Rolls

1 recipe "The Dough", or ready-made puff pastry
cinnamon-sugar, 3 parts cinnamon to 1 part sugar
canned sliced peaches
currant jelly

1. Roll out "The Dough" on a lightly-floured board into a large rectangle about 1/8" thick. Cut it into 6" x 2" pieces.
2. Sprinkle each piece with cinnamon-sugar and roll each side toward the center twice, leaving the middle exposed. Place on a greased cookie sheet.
3. Bake at 450 F. until golden. When done, spread centers with currant jelly and top with peach slices. Makes 15 to 18 pieces.

English Banbury Tarts

1½ recipes "The Dough"
1 C. currant jelly
juice and grated rind of 2 lemons
1 C. sugar
1 C. chopped seedless raisins
5 small soda crackers, crumbled
2 tbsp. cinnamon

1. Roll out "The Dough" on a lightly-floured board into a large rectangle. Cut it into 4" circles.
2. Combine remaining ingredients and divide among the circles. Fold over and seal well by pressing edges with a fork. Prick tops of tarts. Place on a greased cookie sheet.
3. Bake at 400 F. for 15 minutes. Makes 12 tarts.

Canadian Butter Tarts

1 recipe "The Dough"
½ C. raisins
¼ C. butter
½ C. lightly-packed brown sugar
½ C. light corn syrup
1 tsp. vanilla extract
few drops of lemon juice

1. Roll out "The Dough" on a lightly-floured board into a large rectangle. Cut into circles and line a greased muffin tin.
2. Pour a small amount of boiling water over raisins and allow them to soak for 15 minutes.
3. Cream butter and sugar together and combine with remaining ingredients. Drain and add the raisins.
4. Spoon filling into lined tins about 2/3 full. Bake at 375 F. for 20 to 25 minutes. Makes 12 tarts.

Neapolitan Pastry

1 recipe Murbeteig (See section on crusts at end of chapter.)
1½ lb. ricotta cheese
6 tbsp. sugar
2 egg yolks
¼ tsp. cinnamon
1 tsp. grated lemon peel
4 tbsp. raisins

1. Prepare pastry as directed and line greased muffin tins. Reserve a small amount for crisscross topping.
2. Combine remaining ingredients and divide among lined tins. Top with crisscrosses of pastry. Bake at 350 F. for 40 to 45 minutes. Makes 8 to 10 pieces.

Scotch Tea Tarts

½ recipe Cream Cheese Pastry (See Chapter 3.)
1 tbsp. butter
3/4 C. brown sugar
1 egg

1 tsp. vanilla extract
2/3 C. chopped nuts

1. Roll Cream Cheese Pastry on a lightly-floured board or between two sheets of waxed paper. Cut into 24 pieces and roll pieces into circles. Place in a greased 1¾" muffin tin.
2. Cream butter with sugar and then add the egg. Add vanilla and chopped nuts. Fill tarts and bake at 325 F. for 25 minutes. Makes 24 pastries.

Fried Banana Pastry

3 C. flour
½ C. vegetable oil
½ C. cold water
1 tsp. sugar
1 tsp. coffee liqueur

1. Combine all ingredients and blend well. Chill several hours before rolling. Roll on a lightly-floured board until it is about 1/8" thick. Cut into number of pieces to equal banana slices.

Filling

4 to 5 bananas
1/3 C. vegetable oil
confectioners' sugar

1. Slice bananas in 3 lengthwise slices. Roll each slice in a piece of dough and crimp edges to seal.
2. Fry rolls in hot oil until golden brown. Dust with confectioners' sugar. Makes 12 to 15 pieces.

Indian Fried Banana Pastry

1½ recipes "The Dough"
3 ripe medium bananas, mashed
1/3 C. flaked coconut
vegetable oil
confectioners' sugar

1. Roll out "The Dough" on a lightly-floured board into a rectangle about 1/8" thick. Cut into 3" circles.

2. Combine banana and coconut. Place 1 tsp. on each circle. Fold over and seal with fingers that have been dipped in water.
3. Drop in boiling oil and fry until golden. Dust with confectioners' sugar. Makes 18 pieces.

Mock Blintzes

1 loaf white bakery bread, unsliced
1 egg yolk
1 8-oz. package cream cheese
1/8 C. sugar
¼ lb. butter, melted
cinnamon-sugar

1. Slice bread lengthwise into ¼" slices. Trim off crusts. Using a rolling pin, roll slices as thinly as possible.
2. Combine egg, cheese and sugar and spread heavily on bread slices. Roll slices lengthwise, making long thin rolls. Saturate completely with melted butter. Dip in cinnamon-sugar. Place on a lightly-greased cookie sheet.
3. Bake at 350 F. for 20 minutes. Slice before serving. Makes 24 to 30 pieces. **Note:** Blintzes can be frozen after preparation and before baking.

Meringue Nut Horns

1 C. butter
1 C. sour cream
3 eggs, separated
dash of salt
3½ to 4 C. cake flour
½ lb. sifted confectioners' sugar
1 C. ground nuts

1. Combine butter, sour cream, egg yolks and a dash of salt. Beat well until blended. Use enough flour to make a stiff dough. You will need more if the weather is humid. Make 1½" balls of the dough and refrigerate for 3 hours.
2. Beat egg whites until foamy and gradually add sugar, beating until

mixture is stiff and glossy. Fold in the nuts.
3. Roll out balls on a lightly-floured board. Place 1 tsp. meringue in the center of each one and roll to form cone-shaped horns. Place on a greased cookie sheet.
4. Bake at 350 F. for 15 to 20 minutes. Makes about 20 pieces.

French Cream Horns

1½ C. sweet butter
3 C. sifted flour
1 C. sour cream
water
sugar
horn molds, or heavy-duty aluminum foil

1. Combine butter and flour using a pastry blender. Add sour cream and blend. Knead dough until it leaves sides of the bowl. Form into a ball. Chill thoroughly.
2. Work ½ the dough at a time. Roll out on a lightly-floured board into an 8″ x 10″ rectangle. Cut lengthwise into eight 1½″ strips. Moisten each strip with water and brush with sugar. Wrap around a horn mold, overlapping strip of dough.
3. Place on a lightly-greased cookie sheet. Bake at 400 F. for 20 minutes. Fill with desired filling and serve. Makes 16 horns.
4. If you do not have horn molds, make them out of aluminum foil. Cut 9″ squares into triangles. Roll each triangle into a cone, using the center of the longest side to make the tip. **Note:** The horns can be frozen unbaked.

The Custard Filling

½ C. sugar | *½ C. flour*
4 egg yolks | *1 C. milk*

1. Combine egg yolks and sugar and beat until lemon-colored. Then beat in flour.
2. Boil milk and gradually add egg mixture so custard will not curdle.
3. Cook over low heat and beat constantly until custard thickens. Cool and use for horn filling.

Filling Variations

1 pint of heavy cream
2 tbsp. sugar
½ tsp. vanilla extract

1. Whip cream with sugar and vanilla. Add any one of the following, depending upon your taste:

glacéed fruit flavored with ½ tsp. rum
chocolate syrup
nuts
cooked lemon, chocolate or fruit pudding
½ recipe Custard Filling

Cannoli

1-1/3 C. flour
pinch of salt
½ tsp. sugar
1 tbsp. grated orange or lemon rind
1 tbsp. butter
Marsala wine
1 egg white, beaten
oil for frying
cannoli tubes, or heavy-duty aluminum foil

1. Combine flour, salt, sugar, citrus rind and butter and blend well. Add Marsala by the teaspoonful until dough is stiff. Chill for 2 hours.
2. Roll dough on a lightly-floured board into a large rectangle. Cut into 4" squares. Wrap squares around cannoli tubes so that 2 corners fold over and 2 corners point outward. Brush the touching corners with egg white so that they will stick together.
3. Deep fry in hot oil until golden. Cool and remove from tubes. Fill. Makes 10 to 12 cannoli.
4. If you do not have cannoli tubes, make 2" diameter tubes out of heavy-duty aluminum foil and fold dough accordingly.

The Cannoli Filling

1 lb. ricotta cheese
2 tbsp. miniature chocolate bits, or shaved semi-sweet chocolate
1 tbsp. candied citron, or glacéed fruit, slivered
2 tbsp. sugar

1. Combine all ingredients and fill the cannoli.

Austrian Schnecken

2 C. milk
8 C. flour
1 package dry yeast
½ lb. plus 2 tbsp. melted butter
½ C. sugar
6 eggs, beaten

1. Heat milk to just below boiling point. Reserve ¼ C. milk. Mix 2 C. flour into remaining milk. Soften yeast in reserved ¼ C. milk and add to the mixture. Cover and set aside in a warm place until dough doubles in size.
2. Add butter, sugar, eggs and remaining flour and mix well. Refrigerate for at least 8 hours.
3. Roll dough on a lightly-floured board to 1" thick and fill.

The Schnecken Filling

1¼ C. brown sugar
3 tbsp. cinnamon
½ C. black raisins
½ C. white raisins
½ C. melted butter

1. Combine all ingredients and ½ the butter, reserving remainder.
2. Spread on dough and roll like a jellyroll. Cut diagonally into 1" slices. Cover slices and place in a warm spot for ½ hour to rise. Place on a lightly-greased cookie sheet.
3. Bake at 425 F. for 25 minutes. Brush with remaining butter and sprinkle with additional sugar. Serves 8 to 10.

COOKIE CAPERS

Praline Cookie Sandwiches

2/3 C. sweetened condensed milk
1/3 C. brown sugar
3 tbsp. melted butter
1 egg, beaten
¼ C. sifted flour
½ tsp. almond extract
1 C. chopped nuts
canned chocolate frosting

1. Blend milk and sugar in a double boiler. Stir constantly until thick. Remove from heat and add butter. Let cool.
2. Add egg and flour and blend well. Add almond extract and nuts.
3. Grease a cookie sheet and drop batter by teaspoonfuls on the sheet. Spread each to form a 2" circle. Bake at 350 F. for 15 minutes. Makes 24.
4. Spread frosting on half the cookies and top with other half. Makes 12.

Finikia

A honeyed sweetmeat from Greece that is truly a delicacy.

2 C. vegetable oil
½ C. sugar
2 tsp. cinnamon
½ tsp. nutmeg
½ C. orange juice
7 C. flour
2 C. chopped walnuts

1. Blend oil, sugar, cinnamon and nutmeg. Add orange juice. Add flour until a smooth dough is formed. Knead gently. Add nuts.
2. Pinch off small pieces of dough and form oblong rolls. Place on a greased cookie sheet. Bake at 375 F. for 35 minutes. When still warm, dip in warm syrup, but do not allow them to become soggy. Keep syrup warm while dipping. Makes 40 to 50.

The Finikia Syrup

2 C. honey
1 C. water

1. Combine honey and water and bring to a boil. Simmer for 5 minutes.

Franz Josef Cookies

A delight from a world-famous pastry shop in old Vienna.

3 C. sifted flour
1 tsp. baking soda
½ tsp. salt
½ C. shortening, softened
½ C. butter or margarine, softened
1 C. sugar
½ C. firmly-packed brown sugar
2 eggs, beaten
2 tbsp. water
1 tsp. vanilla extract
1 7-oz. package chocolate mint wafers
pecan nut halves (optional)

1. Sift flour, baking soda and salt together.
2. Cream shortening, butter and sugars together and beat until light. Blend in eggs, water and vanilla. Combine with dry ingredients and mix thoroughly. Cover and chill at least 2 hours. Overnight is better.
3. Roll out dough on a floured board. Cut 2" circles with a cookie cutter. Place 1 mint wafer on half the circles and top with remaining half. Press edges lightly together to seal. Top with pecan half.
4. Place on a lightly-greased and floured cookie sheet. Bake in a pre-heated oven at 375 F. for about 10 minutes, or until done. Makes 60 cookies.

Pinwheel Cookies

½ C. butter
½ C. sugar
1 egg
3 tbsp. milk
1½ C. sifted flour
1½ tsp. baking powder
½ tsp. vanilla extract
1 square unsweetened chocolate, melted

1. Combine butter, sugar, egg and milk and blend well.

2. Sift flour and baking powder and add to the butter mixture. Blend well and add vanilla.
3. Separate the dough into 2 parts. In 1 part, add the melted chocolate and blend well. Chill both sections of dough for 2 hours.
4. Roll chocolate dough on a lightly-floured board into a thin sheet. Repeat with the vanilla dough and place on top of chocolate dough. Roll together to form a roll 1½" in diameter. Chill until very firm.
5. Slice thinly. Place on a lightly-greased cookie sheet. Bake at 350 F. until done.
6. Additional flavoring and coloring can be added to the vanilla dough before rolling. Makes 48 cookies.

Ruggalach

These mouth-watering morsels have their origin in the Jewish kitchens of eastern Europe. They are rich in flavor and sure to please.

½ lb. butter
1 8-oz. package cream cheese
1 C. flour

1. Blend butter and cheese until smooth. Add flour and knead the dough into a ball. Refrigerate until firm.
2. Working about ¼ the dough at a time, roll out on a lightly-floured board and cut into triangles. Fill with one of the following: nuts, cinnamon-sugar, raisins, jelly or any sweetened fruit filling.
3. Roll each triangle in crescent fashion and seal point in the middle with fingers that have been dipped in water. Place on a lightly-greased cookie sheet.
4. Bake at 350 F. until golden. Makes 36 pieces.

Ukrainian Ruggalach

½ lb. butter
1 C. cottage cheese
2 C. flour
½ C. milk
½ C. sugar
½ C. chopped walnuts
½ C. chopped dates
2 tsp. grated orange peel

1. Combine butter, cottage cheese and flour. Mix until smooth. Refrigerate for 1 hour.
2. Combine remaining ingredients and cook over low heat until tender and thick. Cool.
3. Roll cottage cheese dough on a lightly-floured board and cut into 3" triangles. Place 1 tsp. of filling on each triangle and roll in crescent fashion. Seal point in the middle with fingers that have been dipped in water. Place on a greased cookie sheet.
4. Bake at 400 F. for 15 minutes. Makes 36 to 48 pieces.

Cookie Ropes

2 C. flour
2 tsp. baking powder
1/3 C. butter
3/4 C. milk
2 tbsp. melted butter
2 tsp. cinnamon
¼ tsp. nutmeg
¼ C. chopped nuts

1. Sift flour and baking powder. Blend butter with flour using a pastry blender. Add milk and blend well. Refrigerate for 1 hour.
2. Roll dough on a lightly-floured board. Brush with melted butter.
3. Mix remaining ingredients and sprinkle on dough. Cut dough into 6" x ½" strips. Fold each strip in half. Twist in rope fashion and place on a lightly-greased cookie sheet.
4. Bake at 450 F. for 20 minutes. Makes 24 ropes.

English Rolled Wafers

½ C. light molasses
½ C. butter
1 C. flour
½ tsp. ground ginger
2/3 C. sugar
1 C. chopped nuts
1 aerosol can ready-made whipped cream

1. Bring molasses to the boiling point and add butter. Stir constantly while adding flour, ginger and sugar. Blend well and add the nuts.
2. Drop by spoonfuls onto a greased cookie sheet. Spread with a knife to form 3" circles.
3. Bake at 300 F. for 15 minutes. When wafers are still warm, roll over a

wooden spoon handle and allow to cool. Fill with whipped cream. Makes about 40 wafers.

Variations

1. Substitute 1 C. instant oatmeal for the 1 C. chopped nuts.
2. Add ½ C. glacéed fruits to the basic recipe.

Swedish Rolled Wafers

½ C. butter
½ C. sugar
2 eggs, beaten
1¼ C. flour
½ tsp. vanilla extract
½ C. slivered blanched almonds

1. Cream the butter and gradually add sugar. Combine with eggs, flour and vanilla.
2. Drop by spoonfuls onto a greased cookie sheet and spread with a knife to form 3" circles.
3. Sprinkle with almonds and bake at 325 F. for 15 minutes. These wafers can be served flat and plain, or rolled and filled. To fill, roll wafers over a wooden spoon handle and allow to cool. Then fill. Makes about 40 wafers.

The Filling

1 package lemon pudding, made according to directions
heavy cream, whipped and added to pudding according to taste

1. Combine ingredients and use to fill rolled wafers.

Cornucopia Wafers

¼ C. butter
½ C. confectioners' sugar
½ C. milk
7 oz. flour

½ tsp. vanilla extract
sweetened whipped cream, flavored with liqueur, fruit extracts or shaved chocolate

1. Cream butter and sugar together. Gradually add milk. Then add flour and vanilla.
2. Drop by spoonfuls onto a greased cookie sheet and spread thinly with a knife to form 3" squares.
3. Bake at 325 F. for 15 minutes.
4. Cut each square into 2 triangular pieces. Return to oven to keep warm while working. Roll each triangle into a cornucopia shape. Let cool.
5. Fill with sweetened, flavored whipped cream. Makes 36.

COOKIE ROLLS TO SLICE

Date Marshmallow Roll

1 tbsp. orange juice
1 C. pitted and chopped dates
dash of salt
¼ C. chopped nuts
6 marshmallows, cut into pieces
½ C. cream, whipped
1½ C. graham cracker crumbs

1. Pour orange juice over dates and add salt.
2. Fold dates, nuts and marshmallows into whipped cream. Fold in crumbs, reserving 2 tbsp.
3. Sprinkle reserved crumbs on a sheet of waxed paper. Turn batter onto paper and shape into a roll about 3" in diameter. Refrigerate overnight.
4. Serve with more whipped cream. Slice to serve. Serves 6.

Raisin Roll

3/4 C. raisins, chopped
¼ C. chopped walnuts
dash of salt

1. Combine all ingredients. Shape into a small roll and slice. Serves 4.

Rock Rolls

3 eggs
1½ C. sugar
3 C. flour
½ C. hot water
1 tsp. baking soda
1 tsp. cinnamon
1 C. chopped walnuts
1 C. raisins
½ tsp. vanilla extract

1. Combine all ingredients. Form into several rolls and chill until firm.
2. Slice and place on a lightly-greased cookie sheet. Bake at 350 F. for 10 minutes. Makes 60 cookies.

No-Bake Chocolate Logs

2 6-oz. packages semi-sweet chocolate bits
2/3 C. evaporated milk
1 tsp. vanilla extract
¼ tsp. salt
4½ C. confectioners' sugar
finely chopped nuts or flaked coconut

1. Combine chocolate bits and milk in a saucepan. Stir over low heat until chocolate is melted and mixture is smooth.
2. Remove from heat. Stir in vanilla and salt. Beat in sugar. Chill until firm.
3. Place ½ the mixture on 1 end of a sheet of waxed paper. Pick up end of paper and slowly roll mixture into a "log" with your hand. Repeat with other half. Roll both in nuts or coconut. Chill until firm.
4. To serve, cut each roll with a sharp knife into 24 slices. Makes 48 cookies.

Refrigerator-Roll Cookies

1 C. butter
½ C. brown sugar
½ C. sugar
1 egg, beaten
2 C. flour
½ tsp. baking soda
½ tsp. vanilla extract
½ C. chopped nuts, raisins or coconut

1. Cream butter and sugars. Add egg, flour, baking soda, vanilla and nuts. Mix these ingredients together well.

2. Form into a roll about 1½" in diameter. Chill until firm.
3. Slice thinly and place on a greased cookie sheet. Bake at 400 F. until golden. Makes 40 to 50 cookies.
4. Additional flavorings can be added before chilling and baking. Try nutmeg, cinnamon or ground clove.

THE ART OF THE ROLLED CAKE

Long the stepchild of baking, the rolled cake is now gaining fresh acceptance. Its scrumptious variations can be achieved with a multitude of delectable fillings, and are limited only by your imagination. You will need a flat jellyroll pan for equipment. And the cakes can be prepared and frozen well in advance if you like to plan ahead. We have divided this section into two parts: basic cakes and basic fillings. Mix and match to meet your tastes and needs. Generally, most of these rolled cakes serve from 6 to 8.

The Basic Cakes

Basic Sponge Roll

4 eggs
1 tsp. salt
3/4 C. sugar
3/4 tsp. baking powder
½ tsp. vanilla extract
3/4 C. sifted cake flour

1. Beat eggs and salt until thick and lemon-colored. Add sugar and baking powder gradually. Add vanilla and fold in the flour.
2. Grease a 15½" x 10½" jellyroll pan and line it with greased waxed paper.
3. Spread batter in pan and bake at 400 F. for 15 minutes.
4. Turn cake out on a towel that has been dusted with confectioners' sugar. Cool and remove waxed paper. Roll cake and the towel together. Chill.
5. When ready to serve, unroll cake from towel. Fill and roll.

Chocolate Cake Roll

1 6-oz. package chocolate bits
5 eggs, separated
1½ C. sugar
3 tsp. coffee
1 tsp. vanilla extract

1. Melt chocolate in a double boiler.
2. Beat egg yolks with 3/4 C. sugar and add to the chocolate. Cook slowly. Add the coffee and vanilla and cool.
3. Beat egg whites with remaining 3/4 C. sugar until stiff and glossy. Fold into chocolate mixture.
4. Grease a jellyroll pan and line it with greased waxed paper.
5. Spread batter in pan and bake at 350 F. for 15 to 18 minutes.
6. Turn cake out on a towel that has been dusted with confectioners' sugar. Cool and remove waxed paper. Fill, roll and chill.

Mocha Cake Roll

6 eggs, separated
3/4 C. sugar
7 oz. sweet baking chocolate
3½ tbsp. strong coffee
cocoa powder

1. Beat egg yolks with sugar until thick and lemon-colored.
2. Melt chocolate with coffee in a double boiler and add to egg yolks. Cool.
3. Beat egg whites until stiff and fold into chocolate mixture.
4. Grease a jellyroll pan and line it with greased waxed paper.
5. Spread batter in pan and bake at 350 F. for 15 minutes.
6. Remove cake from oven and sprinkle with cocoa powder. Turn cake out on a towel, cocoa side down, and cool. Remove waxed paper. Fill, roll and chill.

Cocoa Cake Roll

5 eggs, separated
1 C. confectioners' sugar
3 tbsp. cocoa

1. Beat egg yolks with sugar until thick and lemon-colored. Add cocoa.
2. Beat egg whites until stiff and fold into egg yolks.
3. Grease a jellyroll pan and line it with greased waxed paper.
4. Spread batter in pan and bake at 350 F. for 10 to 15 minutes.
5. Turn cake out on a towel that has been dusted with additional confectioners' sugar. Cool and remove waxed paper. Fill and roll.

Walnut Cake Roll

6 eggs, separated
3/4 C. sugar
1 tsp. baking powder
1½ C. chopped walnuts

1. Beat egg yolks with sugar until thick and lemon-colored. Combine baking powder and nuts and add to egg yolks.
2. Beat egg whites until stiff and fold into egg yolks.
3. Grease a jellyroll pan and line it with greased waxed paper.
4. Spread batter in pan and bake at 350 F. for 20 minutes.
5. Turn cake out on a towel that has been dusted with confectioners' sugar. Cool and remove waxed paper. Fill and roll.

Spice Cake Roll

1¼ C. sifted flour
1/3 C. sugar
1¼ tsp. baking soda
1 tsp. cinnamon
1 tsp. nutmeg
¼ tsp. ground clove
1/3 C. melted butter
1/3 C. light molasses
½ C. warm water
1 egg, beaten

1. Sift flour, sugar, baking soda and spices. Add melted butter, molasses, water and egg. Mix until smooth.
2. Grease a jellyroll pan and line it with greased waxed paper.
3. Spread batter in pan and bake at 350 F. for 15 minutes.
4. Turn cake out on a towel that has been dusted with confectioners' sugar. Cool and remove waxed paper. Fill and roll.

The Basic Fillings

Jelly

1 jar of any suitable preserves, according to your tastes

Whipped Cream

1 C. heavy cream, sweetened, whipped and flavored with vanilla

(Flavoring with rum is advised for the chocolate and spice cakes. The whipped cream may also be combined with fresh or frozen fruit, and chocolate.)

Apricot

1-1/3 C. canned apricots, drained
¼ C. undiluted frozen orange juice
3 tbsp. cornstarch
½ C. sugar

1. Purée apricots in a blender.
2. Combine juice, cornstarch and sugar and mix well. Add the purée and bring to a boil. Stir constantly until mixture thickens. Cool.

Fresh Berry

1 qt. fresh berries, washed and sliced, if necessary
1 8-oz. package cream cheese, softened
3 tbsp. cognac or brandy

1. Cream the cheese with cognac until very fluffy. Spread on cake. Spread berries over cheese.

Frozen Berry

1 package frozen berries, thawed
½ package unflavored gelatin
2/3 C. heavy cream, sweetened and whipped

1. Drain the berries, reserving 3 tbsp. of the liquid. Use liquid to soften gelatin.
2. Purée berries in a blender.
3. Place softened gelatin in a saucepan over low heat and add the purée. Bring to a boil and simmer 2 minutes. Cool. Combine whipped cream with berries.

Citrus

2 egg yolks, beaten
½ C. sugar
2 tbsp. butter
1 tsp. grated citrus rind; orange, lemon or lime
2 tbsp. citrus juice
1½ tbsp. cornstarch
3 tbsp. water

1. Cook all ingredients, except cornstarch and water, over low heat. Stir constantly until mixture thickens.
2. Combine cornstarch and water and add to the cooking mixture. Stir until thick and clear.

Chocolate

4 eggs
¼ C. sugar
½ tsp. cornstarch
4 oz. sweet baking chocolate, melted
1 tsp. vanilla extract
½ C. butter, softened
½ C. ground nuts
1 tsp. rum

1. Combine eggs, sugar and cornstarch. Cook over very low heat. Stir

constantly until mixture thickens. Do not allow mixture to boil.
2. Add chocolate and vanilla and blend. Add butter and stir. Add nuts and rum. Keep stirring until mixture is of spreading consistency.

Pastry Cream

2½ C. milk
2/3 C. sugar
½ tsp. salt
3½ tbsp. cornstarch
3 egg yolks, beaten
1 tsp. vanilla or almond extract

1. Bring milk to a boil in a double boiler. Add sugar, salt and cornstarch and stir until lump free. Cook over low heat until mixture thickens. Cover and cook an additional 5 minutes.
2. Stir a little of the hot mixture into the egg yolks. Add yolks to pan and cook an additional 2 minutes until mixture thickens. Cool and add vanilla.

Cheese–This one is ideal for a chocolate cake roll.

1 lb. ricotta cheese
¼ C. sugar
2 tbsp. rum
1 tbsp. grated orange rind
½ tsp. vanilla

1. Combine all ingredients.

Date

1½ C. chopped dates
¼ C. sugar
½ C. water
1 tbsp. lemon juice

1. Cook dates, sugar and water together until mixture thickens. Cool and add lemon juice.

Fig

2 C. dried figs
1 C. drained crushed pineapple
3 C. water
¼ tsp. salt
2 C. sugar

1. Remove stems from figs and cut figs into strips. Combine with pineapple and water and simmer for 10 minutes.
2. Add salt and sugar and cook until mixture thickens and figs are tender, or about 15 minutes. Cool.

Lemon

3/4 C. sugar
2 tbsp. cornstarch
dash of salt
1 tbsp. grated lemon rind
1/3 C. lemon juice
½ C. water
1 egg, beaten
1 tbsp. butter

1. Combine sugar, cornstarch and salt. Add remaining ingredients and blend.
2. Cook in a double boiler until mixture thickens. Cool.

Lemon Butter

4 egg yolks
1 C. sugar
1 tsp. cornstarch
2 tbsp. butter
1 tsp. grated lemon rind
¼ C. lemon juice

1. Beat egg yolks and add sugar and cornstarch. Add remaining ingredients and blend well.
2. Cook in a double boiler until mixture thickens. Cool.

Orange

2 tbsp. butter
¼ C. sugar
2 eggs, beaten
1 tbsp. grated orange rind
1 tbsp. lemon juice
½ C. orange juice

1. Combine all ingredients and blend well. Cook over low heat, stirring constantly, until mixture thickens. Cool.

Sour Cream and Raisin

3 egg yolks
½ C. sugar
½ C. sour cream
1 tsp. vanilla extract
½ C. chopped nuts
¼ C. chopped raisins

1. Combine egg yolks, sugar and sour cream in a saucepan. Cook over low heat until mixture begins to bubble. Simmer for 2 minutes. Cool and add remaining ingredients.

Fruit and Gelatin

1 package fruit gelatin
1 package frozen berries, or cherries
1 C. sweetened flaked coconut
1 C. heavy cream, sweetened and whipped

1. Make gelatin according to package directions. Add fruit and stir in the coconut. Refrigerate until mixture thickens.
2. Spread on cake and roll. Frost with sweetened whipped cream.

RAVISHING CAKE ROLLS

The following cake rolls are complete, in that we have added specific filling ingredients, frostings and other toppings with which to accompany them.

Pineapple Upside Down Roll

2½ C. drained crushed pineapple
2/3 C. brown sugar
¼ C. chopped nuts
1 tbsp. butter
1 recipe Basic Sponge Roll
1 C. heavy cream, sweetened and whipped

1. Spread the pineapple on the bottom of a greased jellyroll pan. Sprinkle sugar and nuts over the pineapple and dot with butter.
2. Make the Sponge Roll according to directions and spread batter on top of mixture on the jellyroll pan.
3. Bake at 375 F. for 20 minutes.
4. Turn cake out on a towel that has been dusted with confectioners' sugar. Allow to cool 3 minutes. Roll the cake and keep it wrapped in the towel until it has completely cooled. Serve covered with whipped cream.

Buche de Noël

An unforgettable chocolate fantasy from France, it is often served at Christmas time.

6 tbsp. cake flour
6 tbsp. Dutch process cocoa
¼ tsp. salt
3/4 tsp. baking powder
4 eggs, separated
3/4 C. sugar
1 tsp. vanilla extract

1. Sift flour, cocoa, salt and baking powder together 3 times.
2. Beat egg whites until stiff but not dry. Gradually beat in ½ the sugar. Reserve.
3. Beat egg yolks until thick and lemon-colored. Add remaining sugar gradually and beat until creamy. Add vanilla. Gradually add dry ingredients until batter is smooth. Carefully fold in egg whites.
4. Grease a 10½" x 15½" jellyroll pan and line it with greased waxed paper. Dust inside of pan with flour and knock out excess.
5. Spread batter in pan evenly and bake in a pre-heated oven at 375 F. for

12 to 15 minutes, being careful not to overbake.
6. Turn cake out on a towel that has been dusted with confectioners' sugar. Cool and remove waxed paper. Trim off crisp edges.
7. Carefully roll cake lengthwise with the towel. Cool on a rack for 30 minutes. Make The Syrup.

The Syrup

¼ C. sugar
¼ C. water
¼ C. rum

1. Combine sugar and water in a saucepan. Boil together for about 4 minutes, or until syrupy. Add rum. Unroll cake and brush with ½ the syrup. Spread cake with Mocha Cream Frosting, reserving 1/3.

The Mocha Cream Frosting

3/4 C. Dutch process cocoa
1 C. sugar
2 tbsp. instant demitasse coffee
dash of salt
2 tbsp. butter, softened
1/3 C. hot water
½ tsp. vanilla extract
½ tsp. almond extract
3 C. heavy cream, whipped
¼ C. chopped pistachio nuts

1. Mix cocoa, sugar, coffee, salt and butter. Pour in hot water to make a paste. Add extracts.
2. Add mixture to whipped cream and blend well. Refrigerate.
3. Roll up cake that has been spread with syrup and frosted. Cut off ends of cake diagonally, to use as "branches" later.
4. Brush outside of cake with remaining syrup and spread remaining Mocha Cream on top and sides. Use a fork to give a barklike appearance to the frosting. Or, you can press the cream in ribbons with a pastry bag and notched tube.
5. Attach "branches" to the log and press into the frosting. Frost

with the Mocha Cream. Sprinkle with nuts. (May also be decorated with marzipan fruits.)

6. Refrigerate until ready to serve. May be frozen.

Spice Roll with Prune Filling

Make Prune Filling first.

2 C. pitted prunes	*2 tbsp. sugar*
1 C. water	*1 tsp. lemon juice*

1. Combine prunes and water and simmer until tender or about 30 minutes. Purée prunes in a blender, using some of the water in which they were cooked. When smooth, add sugar and lemon juice and reserve.

3/4 C. cake flour	*4 eggs*
1 tsp. baking powder	*3/4 C. sugar*
½ tsp. cinnamon	*1 tsp. vanilla extract*
¼ tsp. salt	

1. Sift flour, baking powder, cinnamon and salt together.
2. Beat eggs until thick. Add sugar and beat until eggs are lemon-colored.
3. Add vanilla to eggs and re-sift dry ingredients into eggs. Blend well.
4. Grease a jellyroll pan and line it with greased waxed paper.
5. Spread batter in pan and bake at 400 F. for 15 minutes.
6. Turn cake out on a towel that has been dusted with confectioners' sugar. Cool and remove waxed paper. Fill cake with Prune Filling and roll. Chill.

Danish Prune Roll

Make filling first.

1 C. dried apricots	*1 jar lekvar (prune jelly)*
½ C. water	*½ C. chopped nuts*

1. Combine apricots and water and bring to a boil. Simmer 10 minutes, or

until apricots are tender. Cool. Cut apricots in thirds and reserve.

2 C. flour
2 tbsp. sugar
1 tsp. salt
½ C. butter
1 egg, separated
1 tbsp. lemon juice
3 tbsp. milk
cinnamon-sugar

1. Sift flour, sugar and salt into a bowl. Add butter and cut into dry ingredients with a pastry blender.
2. Beat egg yolk and add lemon juice and milk. Add to mixture and refrigerate for 30 minutes.
3. Roll dough on a lightly-floured board into a large rectangle. Spread carefully with lekvar filling and sprinkle with apricots and chopped nuts.
4. Roll dough lengthwise and seal ends by pinching and tucking under. Slash top several times on the diagonal, evenly spacing the slashes. Brush with beaten egg white and sprinkle with cinnamon-sugar. Place on a lightly-greased cookie sheet.
5. Bake at 350 F. for 45 minutes.

Apple Roll

Make syrup first.

½ C. sugar
2 tbsp. butter
1 C. water
1 tsp. grated lemon rind
1 tbsp. lemon juice

1. Combine all syrup ingredients in a saucepan and bring to a boil. Boil for 5 minutes. Pour into a 10" x 6" baking dish.

1 C. sifted flour
1 tsp. baking powder
3 tbsp. butter
1/3 C. milk

1. To make dough, combine flour and baking powder. Add butter and cut

it into the flour until dough is crumbly. Add milk and mix to form a soft mass.
2. Place dough on a floured surface and knead about 10 times. Roll into a 10" x 6" rectangle.

1 C. peeled chopped apples
¼ C. sugar
cinnamon to taste

1. To make filling, combine apples and sugar and add cinnamon. Spread on dough rectangle and roll like a jellyroll.
2. Cut slices about 1½" thick and place cut side down in baking dish which contains syrup.
3. Bake at 450 F. for 35 minutes. Serve with ice cream or sweetened whipped cream.

FILO FOR DESSERT

We have dealt extensively with filo in Chapter 2, extolling its versatility for hors d'oeuvres and appetizers. It is also a marvelous pastry base for desserts and is used extensively in the cuisines of Austria and Germany—where it is called strudel—and in Greece and the Middle East.

Note: Filo tends to dry out very quickly, which makes it difficult to work with. When you work with 1 leaf, make certain the others are covered. And, make certain that the one you are working with is well-covered with melted butter. Any leftover filo may be wrapped in plastic wrap and frozen for later use.

Strudel

½ lb. filo leaves
melted butter (for brushing leaves)

1. For each roll, take 3 filo leaves and brush each with melted butter.

Place 1 on top of the other.

2. Spread filling down the center and roll. Place on a greased cookie sheet and brush with melted butter.

3. Bake at 350 F. for 25 to 30 minutes. Makes 2 rolls.

The Apple Filling

6 Rome apples, peeled, cored and sliced;
or 2 cans apple pie filling, drained
½ C. raisins
1 C. sugar
1 tsp. cinnamon
2 tsp. cornstarch
½ C. chopped walnuts

1. Combine all ingredients, except nuts, with a little water. Cook until mixture thickens, and apples are somewhat tender.
2. Add nuts and fill strudel.

The Cherry Filling

2 cans pitted sour cherries, drained of 3/4 the liquid
½ C. sugar
2 tsp. cornstarch
½ C. chopped walnuts, or almonds

1. Combine cherries, sugar and cornstarch and cook until mixture thickens.
2. Add nuts and fill strudel.

The Prune Filling

1 lb. pitted prunes
½ C. seedless raisins
1 lemon, with grated rind and juice
1 C. corn flakes, crumbled
½ C. chopped walnuts

1. Stew prunes in a little water until tender.
2. Combine with remaining ingredients and fill strudel.

Persian Baklava

1 lb. filo leaves
3/4 lb. melted sweet butter (for brushing filo leaves)
1 large can apricot halves, drained and reserved
1 C. ground almonds
1 C. apricot nectar
1 tbsp. lemon juice
½ C. sugar

1. Brush each filo leaf with butter. Place on top of an 8" x 8" pan and fold in sides to fit inside of pan. Sprinkle every third leaf with nuts until all nuts are used. (Freeze extra filo.)
2. Cut into 16 squares with a sharp knife. Bake at 350 F. for 1 hour.
3. Combine nectar, lemon juice and sugar. Boil for 15 minutes.
4. Top each square with 1 apricot half and pour the syrup over all. Let stand in refrigerator for 24 hours. Remove 1 hour before serving time.

Bourma

1 lb. filo leaves
1 lb. melted sweet butter (for brushing filo leaves)
1 C. chopped walnuts
2 tsp. cinnamon
4 C. sugar
wooden dowel ¼" in diameter and 18" long
1 C. water
2 tsp. lemon juice

1. Combine nuts, cinnamon and 2 C. sugar. Brush 1 filo leaf with butter and sprinkle with mixture. Fold ½" of leaf over dowel and roll filo up. Squeeze ends together in accordion fashion and slip off dowel. Brush with melted butter. Place on a greased cookie sheet and keep covered. Do the same for remaining leaves. until mixture is used up. You may have to do this in batches.
2. Bake at 350 F. for 20 minutes.
3. Combine remaining 2 C. sugar, water and lemon juice. Boil for 5 minutes. Pour over slightly-cooled bourmas. Cut bourmas into 2" pieces and serve.

Trigona

½ lb. filo leaves
½ lb. melted butter (for brushing filo leaves)
1 C. chopped pecans
1 C. chopped walnuts
1 C. chopped almonds
¼ C. sugar
½ tsp. ground clove
½ tsp. cinnamon
1 C. water
1 C. honey
1 tsp. lemon juice

1. Combine nuts, sugar, clove and cinnamon.
2. Brush 2 filo leaves with melted butter and place on top of each other. Sprinkle with 2 tbsp. nut mixture. Repeat process twice until you have 3 layers. Roll like a jellyroll. Use remaining filo and filling in like manner.
3. Cut rolls into 1" slices and place on a buttered cookie sheet. Bake at 350 F. for 20 minutes. Turn over and bake 15 minutes longer.
4. Combine water, honey and lemon juice and boil for 10 minutes. Cool.
5. Dip each slice of trigona in the syrup. Drain and serve. Makes about 35 to 40 trigonas.

A COLLECTION OF CRUSTS

Here is a collection of crusts and shells which will enable you to expand your pastry repertoire. Concoct unique fillings and you've created your own masterpiece!

Cream Cheese Crust

1 8-oz. package cream cheese
1 C. butter
2 C. flour

1. Beat cheese and butter together until soft. Add flour and blend well.
2. Chill 2 hours before rolling on a lightly-floured board.
3. Makes enough for a 2-crust, 9" pie.

Butter Crust Pastry

½ C. sweet butter
2 tbsp. sugar
1 C. flour

1. Cream butter and sugar together. Add flour and blend well.
2. Chill well before rolling on a lightly-floured board.
3. Makes one 9" pie shell.

Cookie Crust

½ C. butter
3 tbsp. sugar
1 C. flour
2 egg yolks
1 tsp. vanilla extract

1. Cream butter and sugar together. Add flour and blend well. Add egg yolks and vanilla and mix well.
2. Chill well before rolling on a lightly-floured board.
3. Makes one 9" pie shell.

Almond Crust

¼ C. butter
2 tbsp. sugar
3/4 C. sifted flour
¼ C. ground almonds
1 egg yolk

1. Cream butter and sugar together. Add flour and blend well. Add almonds and egg yolk and mix well.
2. Chill before rolling on a lightly-floured board.
3. Makes one 9" pie shell.

Murbeteig

This is the famous Viennese crust that is at the bottom of all those delicious tarts and cookies. It is a stiff crust that is especially suited for tarts with fruit or custard fillings. When made in a loose-bottomed, fluted pan, the results look quite professional.

3/4 C. butter
1/3 C. sugar
2 egg yolks
¼ tsp. salt
1 tbsp. milk
2 tsp. grated lemon peel
1 tbsp. brandy
2½ C. sifted flour

1. Cream butter and sugar together. Add egg yolks, salt, milk, lemon peel and brandy. Blend well. Combine with flour and knead until a ball of dough is formed.
2. Chill at least 2 hours before rolling on a lightly-floured board.
3. Makes enough for a 2-crust, 9" pie.

Meringue Shell

2 egg whites
dash of salt
pinch of cream of tartar
½ C. sugar
½ tsp. vanilla extract
½ C. chopped nuts, flaked coconut or chocolate bits

1. Beat egg whites with salt and cream of tartar until soft peaks form. Beat in sugar until mixture is thick and glossy. Fold in the vanilla and nuts.
2. Spread in a 9" lightly-buttered pie tin. Build up the sides to ½" height.
3. Bake at 300 F. for 50 to 55 minutes, or until browned. Cool before filling.
4. This shell must have a cold filling. It is ideal for ice cream or puddings. Chilled, canned pie fillings can also be used.
5. Makes one 9" pie shell.

Ice Cream Shell

¼ lb. butter
2 tsp. sugar
1 C. crumbled graham crackers
½ pint vanilla ice cream, softened

1. Combine butter, sugar and crumbs. Mix until mixture is crumbly. Fold in ice cream. Press mixture into pie tin as you would dough. Freeze.
2. Fill with fresh fruit steeped in brandy.
3. Makes one 9" pie shell.

INDEX

NOTES

NOTES

NOTES

NOTES

NOTES

NOTES